CASE STUDIE

CULTURAL ANTHR

GENERAL EDIT

George and Louise Spindler

STANFORD UNIVERSITY

THE TROBRIANDERS OF PAPUA NEW GUINEA

THE TROBRIANDERS OF PAPUA NEW GUINEA

ANNETTE B. WEINER
New York University

THOMSON
WADSWORTH

Australia • Canada • Mexico • Singapore • Spain • United Kingdom • United States

Cover photo: *About to leave the house for the first time after giving birth, a young Trobriand woman wears a long cape and covers her head.*

Library of Congress Cataloging-in-Publication Data

Weiner, Annette B., 1933–
The Trobrianders of Papua New Guinea / Annette B. Weiner.
p. cm.—(Case studies in cultural anthropology)
Bibliography: p.
Includes index.
ISBN 0-03-011919-7
1. Ethnology—Papua New Guinea—Trobriand Islands. 2. Trobriand Islands (Papua New Guinea)—Social life and customs. I. Title. II. Series.
GN671.N5W43 1987
306′.0995′3—dc19

87-18614
CIP

ISBN: 0-03-011919-7

Wadsworth Group/Thomson Learning
10 Davis Drive
Belmont CA 94002-3098
USA

For information about our products, contact us:
Thomson Learning Academic Resource Center
1-800-423-0563
http://www.wadsworth.com

For permission to use material from this text, contact us by
Web: http://www.thomsonrights.com
Fax: 1-800-730-2215
Phone: 1-800-730-2214

Printed in the United States of America
25 24 23 22 21 20

To the chiefs of Omarakana and the villagers of Kwaibwaga, who, from the beginning, took the work of this naive "dimdim" *seriously. To all of them,* agutoki kweverka besa gumugweguyau.

Foreword

ABOUT THE SERIES

These case studies in cultural anthropology are designed to bring to students, in beginning and intermediate courses in the social sciences, insights into the richness and complexity of human life as it is lived in different places. They are written by men and women who have lived in the societies they write about and who are professionally trained as observers and interpreters of human behavior. The authors are also teachers, and in writing their books they have kept the students who will read them foremost in their minds. We believe that when an understanding of ways of life very different from one's own is gained, abstractions and generalizations about social structure, cultural values, subsistence techniques, and the other universal categories of human social behavior become meaningful.

ABOUT THE AUTHOR

Annette B. Weiner, the eldest child and the only daughter of four children, was born on Valentine's Day, 1933, in Philadelphia, Pennsylvania. She graduated from the Philadelphia High School for Girls and became an X-ray technician. Married in 1951, she then studied art and wrote and published a series of childrens' foreign language learning books. In 1964, when she was 31, she entered the College for Women, University of Pennsylvania, as a freshman. She continued her art studies, but during her sophomore year she read *Stranger and Friend*, Hortense Powdermaker's autobiographical account of her anthropological fieldwork experiences. It was this book that redirected Weiner's interests to anthropology.

Upon graduation in 1968, she began graduate work in anthropology at Bryn Mawr College, where she studied with Frederica DeLaguna, Jane Goodale, and A. J. Hallowell. In 1971 and 1972 she undertook her predoctoral field work in the Trobriand Islands, Papua New Guinea. She received her Ph.D. in 1974. She taught at Franklin and Marshall College, the University of Texas at Austin, and, since 1981, has been chair of the Department of Anthropology at New York University, where she holds the David B. Kriser Professorship in Anthropology.

She made a total of five field trips to the Trobriand Islands. In 1979 she was awarded a John Simon Guggenheim Fellowship and in 1980 was a Member of the Institute for Advanced Study, Princeton. She is the author of *Women of Value, Men of Renown, New Perspectives in Trobriand Exchange* and many articles on Trobriand kinship, politics, and gender. In 1980, she did fieldwork in Western Samoa and recently has been writing on Polynesian societies. She is the coauthor (with Jane Schneider) of *Cloth and Human Experience* and has written various articles on comparative aspects of exchange, gender, and political hierarchy in Melanesia and Polynesia. She has two children—Jonathan Weiner, a lawyer, and Linda Matisse, an artist—and two grandchildren, Alexander and Nicholas Matisse.

ABOUT THIS CASE STUDY

There are a few cultures around the world that have served the anthropological community as classic cases to which one refers to illustrate, and sometimes to document, points or generalizations. These cases became classic because the way of life was interesting, because it was either the prototype of a significant phenotype or unique in the array of the world's cultures, and because the anthropologist-author made it interesting. Without these classic cases we would find our lectures and writings poor in living substance. The unity that anthropology had in its past and what little unity it has in the fragmented present is due more to the ethnographic examples we use than to our theories, which tend to factionalize rather than unify us.

Trobriand culture is one of the most classic of cases, and Trobriand society is one of the "holy places" in the anthropological cosmography. Bronislaw Malinowski put it on the anthropological map with a series of brilliant writings. He did his fieldwork a lifetime ago. Annette Weiner did hers only yesterday.

There are two attributes, among others, that particularly distinguish Professor Weiner's case study. One is that she found so much as Malinowski described it to be. The other is that she discovered some things that Malinowski did not and was able to correct some things that Malinowski misunderstood or overlooked. And, of course, she pays attention to those changes that have occurred over the sixty years between the time of her fieldwork and his.

The Trobrianders is not intended as a criticism of Malinowski's fieldwork or a rebuttal of his interpretive arguments. This case study stands on its own. Nevertheless, the expansion and emendation of Malinowski's findings give the study a special significance and add to the "classic case" status of Trobriand culture.

Professor Weiner provides us with a view of Trobriand behavior and cultural knowledge that is notable for both its depth and clarity. One is able to see further than even Malinowski can take us into what yam exchanges, matriliny, the famous *kula* ring, sexuality—particularly adolescent sexuality—and chiefly power mean to the Trobrianders and what meanings these matters have for us as interpretive ethnographers, theorists, students, and armchair tourists.

Annette Weiner takes us into the heart of one matter that Malinowski does not—the importance of women's work, influence, and wealth in determining male behavior and the nature of Trobriand society. We read very little about women's wealth or influence in Malinowski's works. It is difficult to see such relationships across sex-role boundaries. As a woman, Annette Weiner was led into, but also actively sought, knowledge of women's roles. We see the structure of a more balanced social system, and one where the mother's brother, on whose role Malinowski hung a challenge to orthodox Freudian interpretation of the Oedipal struggle, is not quite the person we thought he was.

The author balances her written expression, providing ancedotes and description of events to put the reader into the analytic context. The complexities of the exchange patterns and their relationship to the social organization become clear.

These are some of the attributes that make *The Trobrianders* an important case study and one that should prove useful in both introductory and more advanced courses. It is a contribution both to anthropology as a discipline and to instruction in anthropology.

GEORGE AND LOUISE SPINDLER
Series Editors
Calistoga, California

Acknowledgments

This book represents over fifteen years of study on a wide range of topics about Trobriand society and culture. I first went to the Trobriand Islands in 1971, and I returned in 1972, 1976, 1980, and 1981 for a total of twenty-two months of field work. In addition I did archival research in museums and libraries abroad and in the United States. My research, however, could not have been carried out without the cooperation and support of many people. I am especially indebted to Bryn Mawr College, the National Institute for Mental Health, the American Council of Learned Societies, the National Endowment for the Humanities, the University of Texas at Austin, the John Simon Guggenheim Foundation, and the Wenner-Gren Foundation for Anthropological Research.

Without the support of the Papua New Guinea government and the Milne Bay provincial government I would not have been able to continue my research after national independence. I also thank the Department of Anthropology and Sociology, University of Papua New Guinea, and the Institute of Papua New Guinea Studies for their cooperative assistance. The final draft of the manuscript was completed through the support of the National Endowment for the Humanities and New York University. Various versions of the manuscript were read by Fred Myers and T. O. Beidelman, whose comments, as always, were astute and penetrating.

Two people deserve special thanks. My daughter, Linda Weiner Matisse, stayed with me in the Trobriands in 1972 when she was fifteen years old. Her presence and the diary she kept provided me with stimulation and insights. William E. Mitchell was not only a sharply discerning and untiring reader of multiple revisions of this manuscript but also an unfailing source of encouragement and wisdom.

My greatest debt, however, will always be to those Trobrianders who gave so generously in an effort to make me understand a way of life that was for me confusing, exhilarating, depressing, maddening, and wonderful. The beauty of a moment could be totally reversed by someone's unexpected angry words, my own mistakes, or a villager's attempt to undermine what I needed to know. Fieldwork was never easy, but it was the most profound experience of my life. I treasure not only what Trobrianders taught me about their own lives, loves, fears, and desires but even more what I was forced to face about my own strengths and weaknesses.

One night at a large village meeting, Chief Waibadi spontaneously announced that the book I would write would be important long after everyone assembled had died. "Your children and your children's children," he said, "will read Anna's story and learn about the customs they may have lost. Nothing will be forgotten."

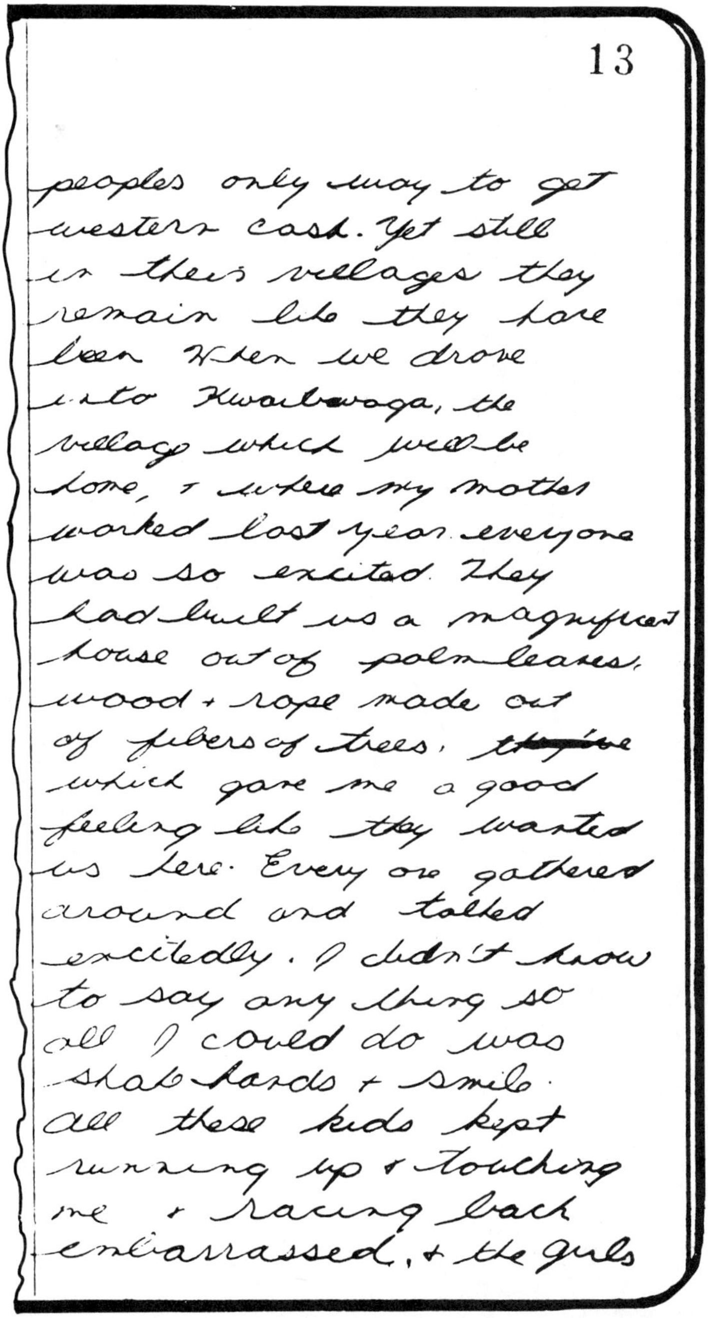

13

peoples only way to get
western cash. Yet still
in their villages they
remain like they have
been. When we drove
into Kwaibwaga, the
village which will be
home, + where my mother
worked last year everyone
was so excited. They
had built us a magnificent
house out of palm leaves,
wood + rope made out
of fibers of trees, ~~they've~~
which gave me a good
feeling like they wanted
us here. Every one gathered
around and talked
excitedly. I didn't know
to say any thing so
all I could do was
shake hands + smile.
All these kids kept
running up + touching
me + racing back
embarrassed, + the girls

Figure 1. A page from the diary of Linda Weiner, who was fifteen years old when she accompanied her mother to the Trobriand Islands in 1972.

Contents

List of Illustrations

CASE STUDIES IN
CULTURAL ANTHROPOLOGY

GENERAL EDITORS
George and Louise Spindler
STANFORD UNIVERSITY

THE TROBRIANDERS OF PAPUA NEW GUINEA

Introduction

A SACRED PLACE

Walking into a village at the beginning of fieldwork is entering a world without cultural guideposts. The task of learning the values that others live by is never easy. The rigors of fieldwork involve listening and watching, learning a new language of speech and actions, and most of all, letting go of one's own cultural assumptions in order to understand the meanings others give to work, power, death, family, and friends. As my fieldwork in the Trobriand Islands of Papua New Guinea was no exception, I wrestled doggedly with each of these problems. Doing research in the Trobriand Islands created one additional obstacle. I was working in the footsteps of a celebrated anthropological ancestor, Bronislaw Kasper Malinowski.

The Trobriand Islands are one of anthropology's most "sacred places," having attained scientific renown through Malinowski's seminal fieldwork. Anthropology was barely established as a formal discipline when, through unexpected circumstances, Malinowski first discovered its importance as a field of study. Malinowski was born in Kraców, Poland, in 1884, and he stayed in Kraców to pursue his undergraduate and graduate studies. At the university he did extensive work in the natural sciences, philosophy, and psychology and in 1908 received his doctorate with highest honors in philosophy of science. Ill health, however, forced him to postpone further research. During this respite he read Sir J. G. Frazer's *The Golden Bough* with mounting excitement. In Frazer's work Malinowski found not only "solace" for his sickness but also a lifelong passion for the problems of ethnograhic research.[1] So committed did he become that in 1910 he enrolled in the London School of Economics to begin postgraduate studies in anthropology. In 1914, he departed for Australia with plans to carry out ethnographic fieldwork in the southeast part of mainland New Guinea, then called Papua.

At the time, few ethnographic field studies in that part of the world had

[1] Malinowski began his essay "Myth in Primitive Psychology" (1926a) with a dedication to Sir James Frazer in which he described himself as "a student leaving the medieval college buildings, obviously in some distress of mind, hugging, however, under his arm, as the only solace of his troubles, three green volumes . . . of *The Golden Bough* (1954:92).

been done. Although the Russian anthropologist Nickolai N. Miklouchio-Maclay had spent almost three years on the north coast of New Guinea in the 1870s, his work was largely unknown because he died shortly after he left New Guinea.[2] Except for the Cambridge University expedition to the Torres Straits, led by Alfred Cort Haddon in 1898, and C. G. Seligman's 1903–1904 ethnographic survey of the Massim (the coastal area and ring of islands off the eastern tip of Papua, which includes the Trobriands), most anthropological knowledge of Papua New Guinea societies was based on reports and diaries from missionaries, government officers, and explorers. The few anthropologists who did fieldwork there rarely stayed with any one group longer than several months. The major research objectives were to survey as many unstudied Papuan peoples as possible and record their customs before colonization and missionary efforts created vast cultural changes in their traditions.

Malinowski's original fieldwork reflects this survey approach, but his plans were further complicated by the outbreak of World War I in 1914. Malinowski was in Australia at the time and was preparing to work among the Mailu who live along the Papuan south coast. As a Pole of Austrian nationality, Malinowski was technically an enemy alien, and although his status was continually in review by the Australian authorities, he was permitted to proceed with his research. He spent a little less than three months with the Mailu and then returned to Australia, where he wrote up a substantial report on many of their customs.[3] Malinowski then made plans to work with several other Papuan groups about which little was known. He booked passage on a trading ship from Samarai bound for some of these more northern coastal villages and offshore islands. When the ship made a brief stop in the Trobriands, Malinowski stayed on, altering the course of his work and the direction of social anthropology.[4] (See Map 1.)

Although twelve years earlier, his mentor, C. G. Seligman, had visited the Trobriands as part of his ethnographic survey of the Massim,[5] Malinowski decided additional Trobriand research would produce important results that would justify his decision not to continue his survey of other, unrecorded populations. He was intrigued by the local renown of Trobrianders, especially because Trobriand society, unlike most other New Guinea societies, was organized around high-ranking chiefs. Instead of leaving the Trobriands after a month or two to explore the northern coast as he originally planned, Malinowski spent a total of two years in residence between 1915 and 1918. In his field diaries he wrote with a burst of bravado that he was accomplishing in the Trobriands what none of his well-known colleagues had done. He had recorded vast amounts of information and his observations were detailed over

[2] Some of his material has been published in Russian, and more recently, his field diaries have been translated and published in English (Miklouchio-Maclay 1975).

[3] See Malinowski (1915).

[4] See Young (1984) for a discussion of why Malinowski stayed in the Trobriands instead of following his original plans.

[5] See Seligman (1910).

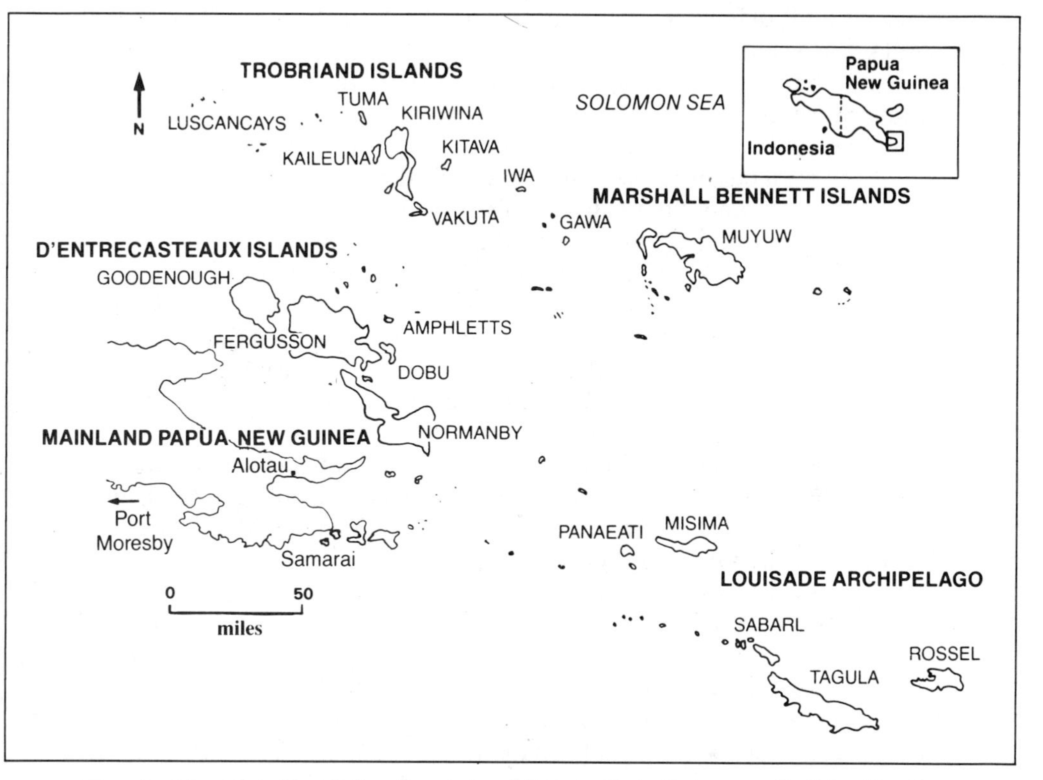

Map 1. The islands and tip of mainland Papua New Guinea, called the Massim by C. G. Seligman. Politically, the area is known as Milne Bay Province, one of the districts into which all of Papua New Guinea is divided.

a long time period. No one in England, he was well aware, had done this kind of fieldwork before.[6]

Following his return to England, he steadily poured out books and articles on various aspects of Trobriand life. In writing about the Trobriands, Malinowski argued against earlier conceptions of "primitive" societies made by "armchair" anthropologists. His intensive study marks a watershed in British social anthropology, making ethnology come of age as a scientific discipline. Malinowski not only brought to the fore new theoretical assumptions about the way individuals and institutions functioned in "primitive" society but also radically changed the way ethnographers approach fieldwork.

In the Introduction to *Argonauts of the Western Pacific*, his first monograph on the Trobriands, Malinowski wrote what became a classic treatise on doing ethnographic fieldwork. He argued for the importance of field studies that lasted for a year or more, cautioning the ethnographer to work in the local

[6] At this time, a few American anthropologists doing research among North American Indians had spent long periods in the field, for example, Franz Boas's (1888) year-long study, 1883–1884, among the Central Eskimo.

language and establish rapport with informants. The earlier methods of recording particular customs by questioning a few informants would no longer be acceptable. The ethnographer must understand the context of a people's behavior. An isolated outrigger canoe had no meaning without knowing who built it, who had the right to sail it, and who performed the necessary magical spells employed during its use. The cardinal field work rule, therefore, should be to see reality from "the natives' point of view."

A brilliant teacher, Malinowski conducted famed seminars at the London School of Economics, attracting students from many disciplines and training a generation of distinguished British social anthropologists in fieldwork methodology. His extensive writings on Trobriand society crossed the Atlantic to influence not only American anthropologists but psychologists and sociologists as well. Although he also studied and wrote on culture change in African societies and spent two summers doing fieldwork on peasant markets in Oaxaca, Mexico, Malinowski's lasting impact on anthropology came from his Trobriand ethnographic material.[7] In the late 1930s, he moved to the United States, where in 1942 he became professor of anthropology at Yale University. Tragically, in the same year, he suffered a fatal heart attack.

Malinowski's theoretical ideas about the functional relationship between basic human needs and social institutions have been displaced by other, more sophisticated theories.[8] Yet his reputation as an outstanding fieldworker prevailed, and his detailed Trobriand ethnographic corpus has a validity and timelessness that have not diminished. Malinowski used the Trobriand material to argue in general about economics, kinship, sexuality, religion, and myth, and in this way, the Trobriands became the classic example of a small-scale society. Long after his death, his Trobriand work stimulated new ideas as well as controversy.[9] Thus, the legacy of his Trobriand ethnography continues to play an unprecedented role in the history of anthropology.

ETHNOGRAPHIC COMPARISONS

In 1971, before my first trip to the Trobriands, I thought I understood many things about Trobriand customs and beliefs from having read Malinowski's exhaustive writings. Once there, however, I found that I had much more to discover about what I thought I already knew. For many months I worked with these discordant realities, always conscious of Malinowski's shadow, his words, his explanations. Although I found significant differences in areas of importance, I gradually came to understand how he reached certain conclu-

[7] Malinowski's (1945) essays on culture change in African societies were published posthumously, as were the preliminary results of his 1940 and 1941 summers of field work in Oaxaca, Mexico. See Malinowski and de la Fuente (1982).

[8] For more details about his approach see Malinowski (1944).

[9] See *Man and Culture*, edited by Raymond Firth (1957a), on Malinowski's most controversial and important contributions. The book was written by his students ten years after his death.

sions. The answers we both received from informants were not so dissimilar, and I could actually trace how Malinowski had analyzed what his informants told him in a way that made sense and was scientifically significant—given what anthropologists generally then recognized about such societies. Sixty years separate our fieldwork, and any comparison of our studies illustrates not so much Malinowski's mistaken interpretations but the developments in anthropological knowledge and inquiry from his time to mine.

This important point has been forgotten by those anthropologists who today argue that ethnographic writing can never be more than a kind of fictional account of an author's experiences.[10] Although Malinowski and I were in the Trobriands at vastly different historical moments and there also are many areas in which our analyses differ, a large part of what we learned in the field was similar. From the vantage point that time gives to me, I can illustrate how our differences, even those that are major, came to be. Taken together, our two studies profoundly exemplify the scientific basis that underlies the collection of ethnographic data. Like all such data, however, whether researched in a laboratory or a village, the more we learn about a subject, the more we can refine and revise earlier assumptions. This is the way all sciences create their own historical developments. Therefore, the lack of agreement between Malinowski's ethnography and mine must not be taken as an adversarial attack against an opponent. Nor should it be read as an example of the writing of ethnography as "fiction" or "partial truths." Each of our differences can be traced historically within the discipline of anthropology.

My most significant point of departure from Malinowski's analyses was the attention I gave to women's productive work. In my original research plans, women were not the central focus of study, but on the first day I took up residence in a village I was taken by them to watch a distribution of their own wealth—bundles of banana leaves and banana fiber skirts—which they exchanged with other women in commemoration of someone who had recently died. Watching that event forced me to take women's economic roles more seriously than I would have from reading Malinowski's studies. Although Malinowski noted the high status of Trobriand women, he attributed their importance to the fact that Trobrianders reckon descent through women, thereby giving them genealogical significance in a matrilineal society. Yet he never considered that this significance was underwritten by women's own wealth because he did not systematically investigate the women's productive activities. Although in his field notes he mentions Trobriand women making these seemingly useless banana bundles to be exchanged at a death, his published work only deals with men's wealth.

My taking seriously the importance of women's wealth not only brought women as the neglected half of society clearly into the ethnographic picture but also forced me to revise many of Malinowski's assumptions about Trobriand men. For example, Trobriand kinship as described by Malinowski has

[10] See, for example, Clifford and Marcus (1986).

always been a subject of debate among anthropologists. For Malinowski, the basic relationships within a Trobriand family were guided by the matrilineal principle of "mother-right" and "father-love." A father was called "stranger" and had little authority over his own children. A woman's brother was the commanding figure and exercised control over his sister's sons because they were members of his matrilineage rather than their father's matrilineage.

According to Malinowski, this matrilineal drama was played out biologically by Trobrianders' belief that a man has no role as genitor. A man's wife is thought to become pregnant when an ancestral spirit enters her body and causes conception. Even after a child is born, Malinowski reported, it is the mother's brother rather than the father who presents a harvest of yams to his sister so that her child will be fed with food from its own matrilineage, rather than its father's matrilineage. In this way, Malinowski conceptualized matrilineality as an institution in which the father of a child, as a member of a *different* matrilineage, was excluded not only from participating in procreation but also from giving any objects of lasting value to his children, thus provisioning them only with love.[11]

In my study of Trobriand women and men, a different configuration of matrilineal descent emerged. A Trobriand father is not a "stranger" in Malinowski's definition, nor is he a powerless figure as the third party to the relationship between a woman and her brother. The father is one of the most important persons in his child's life, and remains so even after his child grows up and marries. Even a father's procreative importance is incorporated into his child's growth and development. A Trobriand man gives his child many opportunities to gain things from his matrilineage, thereby adding to the available resources that he or she can draw upon. At the same time, this giving creates obligations on the part of a man's children toward him that last even beyond his death. Therefore, the roles that men and their children play in each other's lives are worked out through extensive cycles of exchanges, which define the strength of their relationships to each other and eventually benefit the other members of both their matrilineages. Central to these exchanges are women and their wealth.

To understand Trobriand kinship from this perspective has broader implications because kinship relations form the basis of chiefly power. Malinowski's studies never made clear whether Trobriand chiefs had supreme autonomy that made them "paramount" chiefs, as he called them, or whether, like most other societies in New Guinea, Trobrianders were more egalitarian in their relationships with each other and chiefs were merely first among equals. From my own and other recent research, we now know that of all the Trobriand Islands, only on Kiriwina are chiefs granted extensive authority and power; on Vakuta Island, to the south of Kiriwina, a chief has little advantage over anyone else; similarly, on Kaileuna Island, to the west, a chief is much less powerful than Kiriwina chiefs; and on Kitava Island, to the east, inherited

[11] Malinowski's analysis of Trobriand kinship sparked many long-standing controversies. See, for example, Fortes (1957); Homans and Schneider (1955); E. R. Leach (1958); Lounsbury (1965); Needham (1962); Weiner (1978b).

positions of chieftaincy are absent.[12] Malinowski did most of his fieldwork on Kiriwina, and therefore, he could not have known about these variations. But he also never recognized the profound extent to which Kiriwina women enter into the public world of politics. Only on the island of Kiriwina do exchanges of women's wealth reach such large proportions and involve men in such critical ways. For these reasons, exchanges of women's wealth establish stability in the exchange relationships between men, and the necessity for women's wealth each time someone dies requires the expenditure of certain kinds of men's resources. At the same time, the presence of women's wealth means that men are not totally dependent on their own shell and stone valuables at a death. These aspects of women's wealth, that is, stabilizing relationships and leveling some kinds of men's resources while keeping other kinds free, determine the level of hierarchy that chiefs are able to maintain, while alternatively showing the limitations chiefs face in gaining additional powers that would bring them greater autonomy.

That Malinowski never gave equal time to the women's side of things, given the deep significance of their role in social and political life, is not surprising. Only recently have anthropologists begun to understand the importance of taking women's work seriously. In some cultures, such as the Middle East or among Australian aborigines, it is extremely difficult for ethnographers to cross the culturally bounded ritual worlds that separate women from men. In the past, however, both women and men ethnographers generally analyzed the societies they studied from a male perspective. The "women's point of view" was largely ignored in the study of gender roles, since anthropologists generally perceived women as living in the shadows of men—occupying the private rather than the public sectors of society, rearing children rather than engaging in economic or political pursuits.

If Malinowski failed to set a precedent for women's studies that was far beyond his time, his visionary ideas about the nature of human societies put him in the forefront of his day. At the turn of the century, many scholars sincerely believed that "primitive peoples" exhibited nonrational, prelogical mentalities, and thus they placed such "savages" on the lowest rung of an evolutionary scale that in unilineal progression ended with "civilization." Malinowski's strongest arguments were leveled against those who drew a picture of "primitives" as mechanical beings without individual personalities, who as a group, merely followed the same customs without change.

Throughout his Trobriand writing, Malinowski exposed the ethnocentrism and even the racism behind these views. Yet his claims that rational behavior could be documented by finding the pragmatic function for each custom or institution prevented him from appreciating the complexity of meanings expressed through symbolic actions that illuminated social and political interaction. As Edmund Leach, one of Malinowski's most eminent students, pointed out, Malinowski, although a highly original thinker, remained in many ways

[12] Campbell (1983b: 203) on Vakuta; Hutchins (1980), J. W. Leach (1978), Powell (1960), and Weiner (1976) on Kiriwina; Montague (1974) on Kaileuna; Scoditti with J. W. Leach (1983:252) on Kitava. See also Brunton (1975) and Watson (1956).

tied to the very nineteenth-century philosophical ideas against which he fought.[13]

For example, the discovery that "primitive" peoples held strong beliefs in the power of magical practices was proof for many nineteenth-century scholars that such "false science" precluded any necessity for learning technical skills. To prove that "primitive" peoples could distinguish between fact and fiction, between technology and magic, Malinowski explained how complex were the technical skills for activities such as gardening, sailing, and fishing that Trobrianders controlled.[14] He then illustrated how carefully they discriminated between their reliance on magic spells and their use of technology. Malinowski's most quoted example involved the differences between fishing in the lagoon and on the open seas. According to Malinowski, when Trobrianders fish in the lagoon, the men never resort to fishing magic because the waters there are relatively calm. But when they take their canoes into the open seas, they turn to magic as protection from the hazards of strong winds and rainstorms. It is only when confronted by situations they cannot control, because their pragmatic skills are inoperable, that Trobrianders, out of psychological stress, turn from technology to magic.

My record of these events, and even those Malinowski reported in his early work, differ from this example.[15] There are times when men do use magic to fish in the lagoon, just as they may resort to magic spells when they fish without canoes along the reefs. They "turn" to magic, not out of psychological distress over a physical environment out of control, but when it is essential that they produce a large catch that must be used for an important exchange that has social and political consequences. To control the actions of the wind and the fish is ultimately proof of one's ability to control an exchange, thereby providing a measure of control over others. In this way, Trobriand magic is addressed to issues concerned with dominance and autonomy. To influence another person through successful giving is to establish proof of one's own potency. Trobriand magic *speaks* to the complexities inherent in social interaction. To influence and finally to dominate another person's thoughts and actions is a goal that most strive to attain. Since most Trobrianders feel they are impervious to the desires of others, such control is effected through magic. Even for chiefs, dominance depends on the power of magic.

Malinowski's functionalist theories obscured the subtleties and the significance of symbolic action. His interest was in the cause and effect of certain actions and activities rather than in the cultural meanings that Trobrianders give to the things and people around them. Although Malinowski in one respect showed that Trobrianders perceived their world through rational thought, such logic had definite limits. In all societies, including our own, logical

[13] E. R. Leach (1957:113–158).

[14] Malinowski's views on magic also influenced sociologists, especially Homans (1941). See also Nadel (1957) on Malinowski's problems and contributions to an understanding of magic and Tambiah (1968) and Weiner (1983a) on the power of Trobriand magic spells.

[15] Malinowski (1918:87–92); see also Malinowski (1922:368–371).

understanding of events and circumstances in the natural and social environment has limitations. Although Malinowski sometimes recognized the limits and dimensions of rational thought, he often ignored these ideas. At times, his explanations were as narrow as those he attacked. The problem is evident in his discussion of the function of magic, but it is most revealing in his views on Trobriand exchange.

For example, in *Argonauts of the Western Pacific*, Malinowski devoted over five hundred pages to a description of *kula*, an overseas network of exchange relationships that link Trobrianders with people living on other islands in the Massim region.[16] Men, and in some Massim societies, women, travel by canoe to obtain highly valued armshells and shell necklaces from their exchange partners who live on other islands. The armshells always circulate in a counterclockwise direction, whereas the necklaces pass clockwise from island to island. Malinowski's description of *kula* transactions, with all the attendant ritual and magic that accompany each *kula* voyage, was the first full-scale account of "primitive" economics in action, and his examples still are cited in anthropology textbooks. But despite his detailed observations, Malinowski analyzed *kula* activities as if Trobrianders were driven only by custom to carry out their arduous sea voyages. *Argonauts* ends with his claim that Trobrianders exchange *kula* shells merely because they "give for the sake of giving."

From my research and the work of anthropologists who recently have worked on other Massim islands, we know that *kula* transactions are far more intricate and more beset with difficulties than Malinowski recognized. Trobrianders do not simply give up one shell for another because of the dictates of custom, nor does their psychological need to exchange underlie the meaning of *kula*. Rather, in *kula* transactions, Trobriand men create their own individual fame by circulating objects that accumulate the histories of their travels and the names of those who have possessed them. These histories give value to the shells by symbolizing success in influencing and even dominating others. Behind the search for fame and the reciprocal exchanges of one armshell for a necklace, there are other motives at work. Malinowski never noticed that some shells are individually owned, so that a man can use them for his personal economic needs. In following the circulation of these *kitomu* shells, as they are called, we find that some few men can make a "profit" in *kula* by exchanging their own *kitomu* shells with their partners through very long, complex sets of exchanges. Although not the economics of a Western market system, this is not giving for the sake of giving. Thus, looking at Trobriand ethnography today, we have a broader vision for exploring the history, beliefs, and values of Trobrianders. Going deeper into the things that Malinowski first observed, we find the opportunity to view ourselves and the history of anthropology as part of the process of studying others.

[16] See Firth (1957b) for an assessment of Malinowski's contributions and Uberoi (1962) for a reanalysis of Malinowski's findings; see also the essays in J. W. Leach and E. R. Leach (1983) based on recent field research on islands in the Massim region where *kula* takes place.

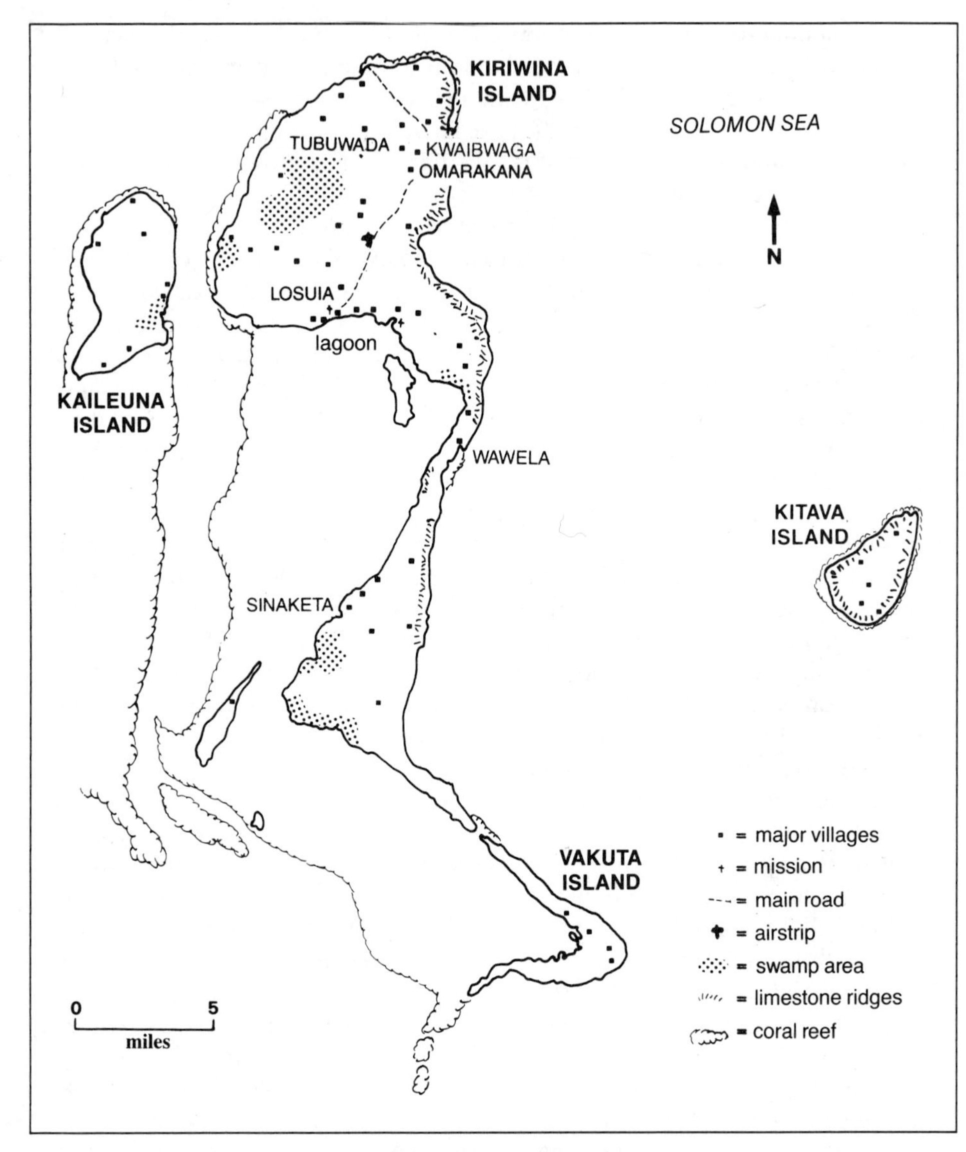

Map 2. The four major islands of the Trobriand group.

TROBRIAND HISTORY, GEOGRAPHY, AND LANGUAGE

Long before Malinowski first arrived in the Trobriands, many ships' captains made Kiriwina Island a port of call. As early as 1793, the area was sighted by the French explorer D'Entrecasteaux, who named the entire group after his first lieutenant, Denis de Trobriand. The group, as Map 2 indicates, includes the large, kite-shaped island of Kiriwina, flanked by the smaller islands of Kitava, Vakuta, and Kaileuna as well as over one hundred small uninhabited islands and islets. Kiriwina, socially and politically the most prominent, is 25 miles long and from 2 to 8 miles wide. It has a current population of 12,000 people who live in sixty villages. On the other three islands, the population is in the low hundreds, with less than eight villages on any one island. In the nineteenth century, foreign traders, whalers, and other entrepreneurs occasionally anchored offshore and explored the islands, purchasing food and artifacts from the local population. No Europeans settled in the area until 1894 when the first Methodist missionary arrived in Kiriwina. The Methodists were followed in ten years by Australian colonial officers, who set up a government station at the Losuia wharf nearby the Mission. A few traders purchased land in Losuia, opened stores, and engaged in pearling activities. In the 1930s, the Sacred Heart Catholic Mission built a settlement about 6 miles from the government station, where the missionary teachers opened a primary school.

With colonization, the name "Trobriand" became the political designation for these islands, although important cultural differences give each island population its own distinctive character. Despite the many variations in dialect even within one island population, everyone speaks some version of Kilivila. This language is one of approximately five hundred Austronesian languages common to Polynesia, Micronesia, Indonesia, and much of the coastal and island areas of Melanesia.[17] One of the distinguishing features of Kilivila is that unlike many other Austronesian languages, it has an elaborate system of noun classification.[18] Five dialects are spoken on Kiriwina Island, which correspond to the major geographical divisions. Although English is taught in the mission and government schools, during the time of my fieldwork very few villagers spoke English. Melanesian pidgin, a language that is the general *lingua franca* throughout Papua New Guinea, is also rarely spoken in the villages. In this book the Trobriand words are from the Kilivila dialect spoken in northern Kiriwina and are italicized.[19]

Except for Kitava, which has a slight elevation, the islands are flat coral atolls. Because of their location just below the equator, they remain hot and humid throughout the year, with frequent rainfall. On Kiriwina, the eastern and northern shores have beautiful sandy beaches bordered by rough coral cliffs rising 8 to 10 feet high. Toward the south, the land area diminishes and mangrove swamps replace the cliffs. The majority of the population lives in the northern half of the island, and the largest land area is made up of swampy terrain surrounded by rich garden lands. There are no rivers or streams, and only tidal creeks drain the swamps. Caves along the coral outcroppings and springs at the edge of the swamps and along the shoreline provide fresh water.

[17] The phonetics of Kilivila are relatively simple. The vowel sounds are represented by *a*, *e*, *i*, *o*, *u*, and the consonants are *b*, *d*, *g*, *h*, *l*, *m*, *n*, *p*, *r*, *s*, *t*, *v*, *w*, *y*.

[18] Until the 1980s, however, little formal linguistic analysis had been done except for Hutchins (1980) and Lawton (1980). Recently, Senft (1986) compiled a dictionary and grammar based on the Kilivila dialect as spoken on Kaileuna Island.

[19] Many villagers receive English names given to them by the missionaries, schoolteachers, and government officers, but they are seldom used among themselves. In the text, I have occasionally used an English first name when it was appropriate to disguise a person's identity.

Reefs extend up to 6 miles offshore, offering excellent fishing both in the open seas and in the lagoon. During the two main seasons when the northwesterlies and the southeastern tradewinds blow, high waves often make long-distance canoe travel dangerous, but small planes and motor launches make access to the Trobriands easier than it once was.

Trobriand society, however, reaches beyond these tiny islands. Since 1975, the Trobriands have been part of the nation-state of Papua New Guinea, one of the largest countries in size and population of the South Pacific developing countries. In the last century, the country was divided into two territories: the southern part that included the Trobriand Islands was called the Territory of Papua and the northern half, the Territory of New Guinea.[20] Papua was first colonized by Great Britain and then ceded to Australia in 1904; earlier Germany had claimed possession of the northern half. With Germany's defeat in World War I, this territory, too, came under Australian governance under a League of Nations mandate. Following the end of World War II, the United Nations was instrumental in having Australia grant both territories independence as a united country. In 1964, the first national elections for seats in the House of Assembly were held, and in 1971, a national flag was adopted and the official name of the country was changed to Papua New Guinea. Two years later, self-government was established, with Australia still maintaining economic controls over defense and foreign policy. In 1975, full independence was proclaimed.

Today, Trobriand history is being written from three sources: (1) the national affairs of Papua New Guinea as a strong leader among Pacific developing nations; (2) the regional connections between Trobrianders and other Massim islanders; and (3) the internal affairs of Trobrianders played out with and against the pressures of change promulgated by the government, missionaries, or world events. Rather than give up traditional customs, Trobrianders are masters at transforming new ideas into ways that remain distinctively Trobriand. The view of villagers in control of their own interaction with other individuals and with the outside world may at times be an illusion, but it is a notion that Trobrianders believe in and live by. The abilities of Trobrianders to reshape external experiences into internal goals and histories form the core rhythms of Trobriand life. To understand the activities of *kula* exchanges, the use of magic, and the rituals that mark the important transitional moments in each person's life, including the rituals surrounding death, helps us discern the way individuals try to control others as a way to build their own support and power. It then becomes imperative to understand the intimate relation between people and the things they most value—such as *kula* shells, women's wealth, and even magic spells—as the markers of success in such achievements. In this way we are able to analyze the loci of power that create a hierarchy of relations between young and old, women and men, chiefs and commoners, and the living and the dead.

[20] The western half of the main island of New Guinea, now called Irian Jaya, was originally colonized by the Dutch, and in 1969 sovereignty was transferred to Indonesia.

TROBRIANDERS TODAY

A concern with dominance and hierarchy is of central importance because we are investigating a society with ranked chiefs, who by birthright are accorded special privileges and powers. These powers are not, however, unlimited, nor is their attainment absolute. A fragility exists in all social relationships, and even though chiefs have an omnipotent presence, their power, too, may collapse. There exists an intimate interdependence between the procurement of power and its limitations. The possibility of tragedy is a constant part of every encounter as individuals face the loss of wealth through their own miscalculations or the strategies of others, through illness and death caused by sorcery, and through the demands made on them at a death. Against these exigencies, the ability of someone to control the destiny of others is measured and feared.

From the time of birth, each person's social identity is enhanced by others who give their own names, knowledge, magic spells, and wealth to "build up" culturally the potential power of a child. As an adult, the major exchanges of yams, women's valuables, and men's valuables demonstrate a person's status and worth and are also devices to secure the effects of that status and worth for the future. Although things of value add to one's external growth, death undermines all that individuals strive for in the work of creating and expanding the social and political dimensions of their identity and authority. Therefore, when a person dies, the earlier work of building up and caring for him or her now must be attended to with equal diligence through the work of mourning. It is at death that we see how those things of value that created a person are too precious to be lost.

This book explores the relationship between power and death as men and women, each in their own way, with their own valuables, confront the eternal problem of sustaining hierarchical relations in the face of loss and decay. It is in the attempts made to resolve these problems—for all societal solutions to the existential problems of power and death are only partial—that we see the roots of Trobriand resiliency to change.

In the first chapter I discuss the vitality of Trobriand society as Trobrianders face the external changes of the 1980s. Drawing on my fieldwork, which I carried out from 1971 to 1982 on the island of Kiriwina, I introduce the basic principles instrumental in shaping these years; these were especially significant because Papua New Guinea was facing self-government and national independence. Therefore, this particular time period provided important insights into the past history of the islands while underscoring Trobrianders' impressive resistance to foreign intervention. A large measure of the determination to support traditional economic and political activities is linked to the wealth of the women and the role that wealth plays in the economic and political life of the men.

In Chapter 2, the deepest roots of Trobriand resistance to change are exposed at each death. The rituals surrounding death act as a conservative force ameliorating the disjuncture between change and tradition as the things of most value—for example, material wealth, land, and social and political relationships—are reconstituted for the living. Chapter 3 returns to the beginning and examines the different but complementary roles that men and women play in the birth process. These roles, even in relation to an infant, have political consequences.

Chapter 4 illustrates how the beauty of young people is culturally enhanced so that beauty itself becomes a powerful means of persuasion and seduction. Experimentation with this kind of power ends in marriage, but the ability to control others by influencing their minds remains a fundamental challenge to adults. As Chapter 5 discloses, after marriage the power of one's beauty is transformed from the surface of the skin to one's talents for producing and controlling objects of wealth. These objects then are used to enhance one's influence with others; and through the circulation of such wealth, cognatic kin (relatives by blood) and affinal relations (relatives by marriage) between men and women are tied to each other in such a way that affines become like cognates, securing networks of social and political relationships that have potential for generational continuity.

For chiefs, as Chapter 6 illustrates, these networks are multiplied through their polygynous marriages, but such marriages only occur when villagers themselves decide that a chief is influential enough to be supported by them. Wealth and the power of persuasion take on even greater importance as chiefs attempt to win fame and consolidate their resources. Here, too, as Chapter 7 describes, to spread one's fame among others necessitates enormous productive work and the expenditure of huge resources. A death of someone transforms a harvest of youthful energy and excitement into a productive effort of a different order in which men's resources are needed to procure women's wealth.

In Chapter 8 we explore the attention given to women's wealth as we see why this wealth remains such a conservative force in Trobriand society. In the vast exchanges of women's wealth that mark the end of the major mourning period, we see how men, including chiefs, remain dependent on women and their valuables. In these two chapters, the issues of dominance and hierarchy are raised, and we examine the potential and limitation for women and men, chiefs and commoners, to achieve fame and autonomy in the face of jealousy, sorcery, and death.

Chapter 9 makes explicit these concerns as we follow men in their interisland *kula* exchanges. When men, especially chiefs, are away from the demands made on them by the need for women's wealth, they have the opportunity to write the history of their own immortality in the shells they exchange with others. *Kula* is not a mechanical give and take of one armshell for another; rather it involves a complex set of exchanges that build toward achieving strong partners and the highest-ranking valuables. *Kula* players individually search for gains in the face of the unrelenting forecasts of losses, so that even the very best players are limited in what they can achieve.

In the concluding chapter, I return to the subject of how objects inform the most important stages in a person's life. The power and pathos embedded in the most valued objects make us understand how fragile are the social and political relations that define who people are and where they belong. Death destroys not only individual lives but also whole complexes of relationships. Against this never-ending, awesome finality, men strive in exchanges for the freedom of power, whereas women in their exchanges strive to transform death into a hope for the future. Ultimately, men's valuables make no inroads on women's valuables, and men's searches for fame cannot replace their matrilineal roots, which remain tied to women and death. The eternal sociological conflict between individual will and societal demands is exposed as Trobrianders, like people everywhere, ultimately fail to conquer time. Yet even with the limitations inherent in the objects at hand, Trobrianders use them in the most dynamic way possible to define who they are in relation to their kinship identities, to their own individual fame and dominance, and to the foreign influences that other people bring to their islands. Their success, although always in danger of being undermined, is an important and by no means small achievement.

1/The Trobrianders: Past and present

A TRAGIC RETURN

Even on a clear day, the flight in a small twin-engine plane from Port Moresby, the capital of Papua New Guinea, to the Trobriand Islands can be turbulent. Immediately after takeoff, the plane flies just above the rugged Owen Stanley Mountains, where vigorous updrafts toss the aircraft about. Once the sea emerges on the horizon, the flight begins to even out and the plane races over the blue-green waters to Kiriwina, the main Trobriand island.

Each time I make this flight, I watch intently for the long, narrow coral reef running for miles off the southern tip of Kiriwina. Because the island is flat, the reef is the only distance marker available. The plane flies directly over the reef, following the narrow tail end of the island. As we circle for the final approach, I search below for familiar villages. Thin lines of smoke from open cooking fires rise high above the coconut palms, signaling that women are busy stirring yams and sweet potatoes in their large cooking pots. I know the moment the plane is sighted from the ground, children will pause to watch its descent and, pointing to the sky, call excitedly, *"kaiyoyowa!"*— "Airplane!" "Airplane!"

Today, however, some children will look at the sky in silence. It is April 1982, and Vanoi, the highest ranking Trobriand chief, is dead. His village, Omarakana, in northern Kiriwina Island, has been the seat of the Tabalu chiefly lineage for several hundred years. Now the village is filled with mourners, and it is taboo for anyone, even children, to shout.

My few fellow passengers are tourists, and leaving the plane, we are greeted by islanders hoping to sell their carvings and other trinkets. "Ah, Anna, you are back!" one of the carvers calls out and jokingly teases me to buy something. A landing is always a social event, and among the crowd I catch sight of Bunemiga, Bulapapa, and Bomapota, old friends from Kwaibwaga, the village where I always live. Our greetings are warm as we firmly clasp each others' hands, and I kiss each of them on the cheek. We load my gear onto a pickup truck for the drive to Losuia, the island's administrative and commercial center. After I finish shopping at the main trade store for supplies, we wait several hours until I find another truck to drive us 13 miles north to Omarakana and then the few miles further to Kwaibwaga.

Perched on my gear in the back of the rented pickup, we bounce precar-

Photo 1. "Buy this carving!" Trobrianders call out as they vie with each other to interest tourists in their art.

iously along the packed coral road as the driver continually veers from one side to the other, avoiding the cavernous potholes. Bunemiga begins to tell me the story of Chief Vanoi's death. I already knew that Vanoi had been sick for four years. In my last meeting with him two years before, he complained that, although he had stopped smoking and was taking prescribed European medicines, his persistent cough and chest pains had not gone away. He appeared sickly, thin, and frail, although when I had first met him nine years earlier I had been awed by his prowess. Tall and handsome, he had worn a thick lei of tiny, fragrant yellow flowers around his neck, narrow white shell bands pulled up tightly on his muscular upper arms, and a colorful sarong knotted at his slim waist.

Livini, the goverment interpreter, who accompanied me on my first trip to Omarakana, warned me never to let my head rise higher than Vanoi's. It is only one of the many taboos surrounding Trobriand chiefs. To show disrespect to a chief may also be dangerous because some are renowned for their sorcery. When Vanoi visited me in Kwaibwaga before his illness began, my neighbor whispered, "Anna, be careful! That man is good, but he also is very bad. Remember, he knows sorcery." But now in death, Vanoi is the victim. He did not die of chest pains, I am told, but was killed by sorcery. A rival chief is blamed.

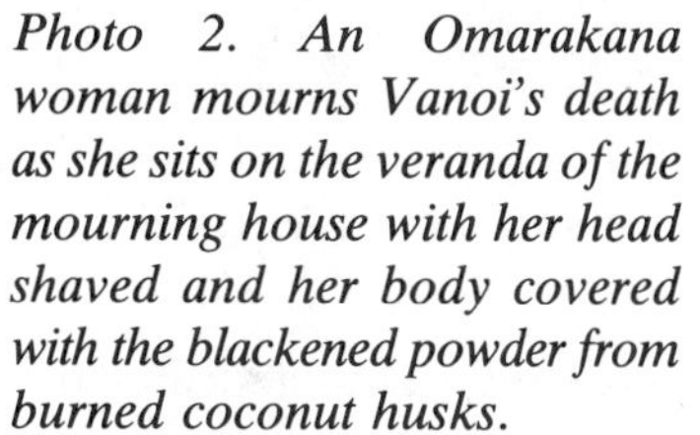

Photo 2. An Omarakana woman mourns Vanoi's death as she sits on the veranda of the mourning house with her head shaved and her body covered with the blackened powder from burned coconut husks.

Our truck cannot enter Omarakana because all the paths leading into the village are blocked with tree branches, marking Vanoi's death. We walk the short distance, but the village does not look like a chief's place. The grass is uncut, and no one is wearing flowers or vividly colored clothing. In the house of Vanoi's senior wife I find other women I know; I sit with them on the floor while they cry and chant the traditional mourning sounds that convey their sadness and longing. I cry with them for awhile and then walk across the open plaza to his grave. Red hibiscus flowers intermingled with long white cockatoo feathers and a few other decorations used for dancing adorn the burial place. Poignantly, Vanoi's grave is the only resplendent, animated spot in the village.

EARLIER TIMES

Vanoi's death marks the end of a stormy decade in the Trobriands, especially on Kiriwina Island. In the early 1970s, Trobrianders, like Papua New Guineans from all parts of the country, looked forward with great enthusiasm to the country's forthcoming independence after seventy years of Australian colonial rule. When in 1975 National Independence Day was declared, Tro-

Photo 3. The freshly decorated grave of a chief is surrounded with flowers, feathers, and other regalia.

brianders celebrated; but their own local political situation was in turmoil, and Vanoi's power as Tabalu chief was rapidly diminishing.

My Trobriand fieldwork spans the years before and after national independence. On my first trip to Kiriwina in 1971, I found the island in the midst of a tourist boom. Weekly charter flights from Port Moresby, filled mostly with Australians on holiday from government work elsewhere in the country, gave impetus to the local wood-carving industry. Villagers not only jammed the airstrip but also camped out around the small hotel, waiting anxiously to make a sale. This was the phenomenon I had come to study, the art and economics of wood carving. Since carving for the tourists was the villagers' major source of Western cash, I planned to examine both how cash affected the traditional exchanges of men's valuables and how much change had occurred in the traditional carving designs and techniques.

Most of the ten resident Europeans on the island, including the Catholic and the United Church missionaries, were heavily engaged in buying and selling Trobriand bowls, tables, and walking sticks; the ever-popular fornicating pigs; and the few superbly wrought sculptures of figures from myths and folktales, made by the most talented carvers. The charters were arranged by the Chinese merchant who owned the small hotel, and the fifty-odd visitors a week provided carvers with a competitive market for their work. If a carver was not pressed for cash, he waited for a tourist sale rather than accept the low prices paid by the traders and missionaries.

Saturday, when the charter plane arrived, was the busiest day of the week.

Photo 4. The sounds of chipping wood resound in the village when men work on their carvings before the weekend charter flights arrive.

By six o'clock in the morning, men with their carvings carefully wrapped in pieces of old cloth hurried along the "main road," the lone vehicular thoroughfare that traverses the island. They all walked in the same direction: first to the airstrip in the hope of an early sale, then on to Losuia, where they congregated outside the hotel.

For the lucky ones who sold a carving, some of the profit was spent in either of the two European-owned trade stores for tinned meat, rice, tobacco, or clothes. Some money was saved to buy fish. Although Kiriwina is surrounded on three sides by reefs rich with fish, only villagers who live along the coasts own fishing canoes. The village of Kwaibwaga is located inland, so I rarely ate fish more than once a week. Even then I had to be lucky. On Saturday afternoons, dozens of outrigger canoes head for Losuia with their day's catch. As the canoes approach, the waiting men crowded together at the end of the wharf jump into the water, racing to the incoming boats to throw their money into a canoe and claim some fish. If a man stays too long at the hotel or is busy in the trade store when the boats arrive, he misses his chance.

Sometimes large sea-faring outriggers from other islands, piled high with bales of betel nuts (*buwa*), dock at the wharf. Within minutes a crowd forms to buy betel, for no one, except chiefs, ever has enough. Trobrianders chew betel the way many Americans drink coffee. Upon waking in the morning, a villager reaches for a betel nut and a lime pot. Chewed alone, the nut is extremely bitter, but when mixed with a piece of pepper plant and some slaked lime, it becomes palatable. These ingredients turn the mixture bright

Photo 5. A young man on his way to Losuia adds a touch of Johnson's Baby Powder to make himself more attractive.

red. Whenever I visited other villages, someone usually would ask to see my teeth, approving of their red color, the sign that I chewed. Betel acts as a stimulant, but it is not hallucinogenic. Throughout the day, villagers pause in their work to chew betel, and although there are strict rules about not eating food in front of others, betel chewing is the most sociable of all activities.

During the tourist boom, young people flocked to Losuia on Saturday, as if they were attending a special village event to which they would wear their brightest, most attractive clothes. Most young men now wear cotton shorts, over which they tie vivid patterned cloth sarongs, although traditional men's dress—a white pandanus penis covering—still is worn by some. Few women have taken up Western clothes, and young girls continue to wear the very short, red miniskirts woven of dried banana leaves.

Regardless of whether or not they wear traditional or Western dress, young men and women adorn their bodies with care and style. They tease their dark, thick hair with delicately carved wooden combs and set it off with red hibiscus flowers. Some use black and white vegetable dyes to paint lovely designs on their faces. For others, Johnson's Baby Powder, sold in the trade store, provides a quick touch of white, decorative makeup. Pungent grasses and aromatic flowers are tucked into woven or shell armbands, with the exotic mixture of fragrances adding to the allure. The skin glistens from coconut oil, carefully made by boiling the oil with special herbs, over which the spells for love magic are recited.

Dabweyowa, a friend from Kwaibwaga, once gave me a small bottle of oil that he made, but I was warned not to use it while I lived on the island. Because of its strength, he said, I might provoke an adulterous relationship and get into a lot of trouble. In the Trobriands, adultery is a crime, but premarital love affairs are not. For unmarried young people, each decorative element is carefully chosen to catch the eye of a possible lover, as each use of magic is calculated to "make someone want to sleep with you." Attraction and seduction are adolescent pursuits, and the presence of young people walking through Losuia, laughing, singing, and teasing, made Saturdays almost as celebratory as traditional yam harvest feasts. Not everyone was optimistic about the growing tourist industry. Some complained about the travel posters that advertised the Trobriands as "The Isles of Love." Others warned that men spent too much time carving, resulting in smaller yam harvests. Most felt positive about the future, however. With more cash available and national independence a certainty, these villagers expressed hopes that European prosperity would be theirs; as with other Papua New Guineans, they would control their own economic destiny.

EXPECTATION AND DISAPPOINTMENT

But expectations for the future are subject to unforeseen events. In the Trobriands, the economic boom came to an abrupt impasse, initiated in part by a young Trobriander, John Kasaipwalova, who had attended the University of Queensland and the University of Papua New Guinea. Having learned something of African nationalist movements, John K, as he is called, quit his university studies and returned to Kiriwina with plans to organize a Trobriand association for economic development. His plans included a Trobriand-style luxury hotel, an interisland shipping company, a chain of village-operated trade stores, and an art center and museum. These schemes took on greater economic dimensions when, in 1972, just as regular midweek tourist charters added to the growing carving market, a fire from a faulty kerosene freezer destroyed the hotel.

Suddenly, the tourists and their cash were gone, and to many villagers, the Kabisawali Economic Association organized by John K seemed like a positive alternative.[1] But John K's success did not proceed without strong opposition, resulting in huge intervillage meetings where tempers ran high as men spoke forcefully about whether or not "to follow John." In the beginning his most formidable opponents were Chief Vanoi and his heir apparent and sometimes rival, Waibadi, only a few years younger than Vanoi and already powerful. Among John K's most loyal supporters, however, were two chiefs, one of whom was his mother's brother and the other a member of a matrilineage in

[1] The Kiriwina word *kabisawali* means "to search for food in the ground during times of famine." See J. W. Leach (1982) for details on the Kabisawali Movement.

which former chiefs historically had competed with previous Tabalu chiefs for power. Although the conflict between John K and the Tabalu chiefs was expressed in terms of economic development, the controversy became a political confrontation tied to old antagonisms.

Despite the opposition, John K initially amassed wide village support, significantly threatening the power of Chiefs Vanoi and Waibadi. To stem John K's success, Chief Waibadi and Lepani Watson, a former member of the House of Assembly, organized an opposition movement, the Tonenei Kamokwita Development Corporation, called the "TK Movement," which started a fishery, exporting frozen fish to Port Moresby.[2] In an unexpected maneuver, however, Vanoi switched sides and joined John K's association, leaving Waibadi, the "number two" Tabalu chief, as he was called, the leader of the TK opposition movement.

Even with Vanoi's support, John K's success was short-lived. He never built the promised hotel; his shipping venture was a failure. By 1976, his stores were closed, his association's headquarters were boarded up and overrun with weeds, and many villagers complained bitterly about their unpaid labor and the money they had lost by investing in his cooperative enterprise. For John K, the situation grew worse when he was convicted of embezzling the national government funds he received for a Kiriwina art school and cultural center that were never built. Although after serving nine months of his jail sentence, his conviction was appealed and overturned, it marked the end of his strong local and national support to bring development to Kiriwina.

Waibadi's TK Movement never became economically self-sufficient either, but with skillful political acumen, he gained back his supporters even before John K's financial defeat. During one of our conversations about his success, Waibadi said, "Anna, in the Trobriands, we go step by step." Waibadi "beat John K" and became the most powerful chief on the island. Then Vanoi became ill, never regaining his power.

The hotel remains a mass of charred debris, leaving only a small guest house to accommodate tourist charters. Since national independence, far fewer Australians work in the country and tourism has declined rapidly. Men still hawk their carvings at the airstrip when the occasional charter plane arrives. Now the island's fine ebony woods are depleted, and the foreign outlets for Trobriand carvings have largely disappeared. Only a handful of men manage a steady income from carving. Except for the usual race to buy fish from the fishing boats, and the occasional basketball or soccer match that attracts young people, Saturdays in Losuia are much quieter. Young people spend more time in traditional village events, and men tend to their yam gardens. For most villagers, the major source of cash income is now the remittances sent home by children working for wages elsewhere in Papua New Guinea.

[2] The name Tonenai Kamokwita means "the search for truth." See May (1982) for more details about this movement.

A HISTORY OF RESISTING CHANGE

Trobrianders' resistance to change does not reflect individual unwillingness to explore new possibilities and to support new forms of economic endeavor, as John K's early backing indicates. Yet tradition wins out despite people's willingness to try something new. Withstanding more than a century of Western influences, Trobriand society has proved far more resilient to change than even Bronislaw Malinowski believed possible.

Malinowski's influence on the history of anthropology, as already discussed, resulted largely from his Trobriand fieldwork, undertaken during a two-year period between 1915 and 1918. When Malinowski settled in Kiriwina, Methodist missionaries already had been working on the island since 1894; in 1906, the Australian colonial government set up its local administrative center at Losuia. Because both the mission and the government were trying to change many traditional values, Malinowski fought against their impositions. Unless they ceased, Malinowski warned, within a few years the power of Trobriand chiefs would completely dissolve and the complex cycle of yam exchanges on which social and political allegiances depend would be destroyed. Not only were missionaries trying to persuade villagers that magic and sorcery had no basis in rational thought, but also they attempted to outlaw polygyny and the traditional premarital sexual liaisons.

Although monogamy is the rule practiced by most Trobrianders, the chiefs who want to become powerful must take more than one wife. Because of these multiple marriages, which involve long-term affinal exchanges of yams,[3] chiefs are able to establish more extended political alliances. Administrators too, for more practical Western economic reasons, advocated the abolition of polygyny to weaken the power of chiefs. They wanted men to stop their yam garden work for chiefs and to produce cash crops such as copra. Malinowski's dire prophecies did not come to pass, for over the years both the missions and the government failed to accomplish their goals. Some chiefs promised government officials that they would not take any more wives, but their intentions only lasted until their next marriages were arranged.

The circumstances of World War II abruptly changed the direction of colonial efforts. Although the Japanese did not invade the Trobriands, they occupied all the islands to the north. Missionaries and government officials were evacuated at the beginning of the war and, in preparation for an Allied offensive, American and Australian troops set up extensive base operations on Kiriwina.[4] Suddenly the Trobrianders had to reckon with the presence of airplanes, artillery, troopships, and soldiers. In the northern part of the island,

[3] There are two major species of yams cultivated in the Trobriands: *Dioscorea esculenta* and *Dioscorea alata*. Unless otherwise noted, my reference to yams are to the former, called *taytu* in Kiriwina. These yams are about the size of Idaho potatoes, although some varieties grow much larger. Over one hundred varieties are known by Trobrianders, and Malinowski (1935, II:9–22) gives a brief description of some of them.

[4] See, for example, Krueger (1953) and Miller (1959) for details on the Allied occupation of Kiriwina.

Photo 6. Blowing the conch shell announces to all villagers that Chief Waibadi's affines are about to fill his yam house.

the main road and two airstrips were built, and wounded from the fighting elsewhere were flown daily to the Kiriwina field hospital.

During the first months I lived in Kwaibwaga, almost every day an islander would come to my house to ask if I knew "Bill" or "Joe," American soldiers who were his "friends." Little except these memories remains from the war years. Even shortly after the war's end, few substantive cultural changes had occurred.[5] During his field research in 1950–1951, the anthropologist Harry Powell made a film, *The Trobriand Islanders* (1951), in which most of the action centers on Omarakana and Chief Mitakata, Vanoi's predecessor and the high-ranking Tabalu chief throughout the war years. In the film, Mitakata and his villagers are intensely involved in the celebrations attendant on yam harvests. In preparation for a forthcoming *kula* expedition to exchange shell valuables with partners on other islands, men are hard at work outfitting outrigger canoes with pandanus sails. The army camps are gone and, from the film, it is hard to believe that fewer than ten years earlier a war of such magnitude had dominated the lives of Kiriwinans.

Why did the presence of American & Australian troops not alter Trobriander's lives?

[5] In 1945, Hogbin (1946) briefly visited Kiriwina and noted how little effect the war years had had on village life. See Austen (1945) for a survey of Kiriwina during the 1930s.

Photo 7. Huge baskets filled with bundles of banana leaves surround each woman as she arranges them for the mortuary distribution.

AN EXTRAORDINARY DISCOVERY

Faced with almost a hundred years of new ideas and changes instituted by a colonial government, missionaries, traders, and even Allied soldiers, Trobrianders generally held firm to many of their most important beliefs. This resurgence of traditional cultural values reflects a worldview that is not easily threatened or profoundly disturbed. Such cultural resiliency raises the question of why these fundamental Trobriand beliefs and values remain so firmly anchored in tradition. To search out any answers demands careful examination of a part of Trobriand society that outsiders, including Malinowski, completely ignored.

Throughout all the years of public disputes, fighting, competition between chiefs, and changes brought about by colonial laws and traders' enterprises, women have gone about their business undisturbed by government officers and missionaries, who like Malinowski, never thought that they played any economic role. Men are the carvers, the gardeners, the fishing experts, the orators, and the chiefs. No one recognized the activity that is central to women's position and power in Trobriand society. Yet it is an activity that deeply interpenetrates the economics and the politics of men. The political presence of Kiriwina women necessitates studying Trobriand society from a perspective sensitive to the complementary productive efforts of women and men.

In Kiriwina, women manufacture and control their own wealth: red skirts (*doba*) made from banana-leaf fibers and bundles of banana leaves (*nununiga*). Skirts and bundles have economic value, and their major use as payment to mourners after a death directly incorporates the wealth of men. How could Malinowski, with all his attention to Trobriand exchange, have missed women's wealth? Undoubtedly, to an outsider's eye, even those of a trained anthropologist, the decorated *kula* shells and great mounds of yams are far more dramatic than skirts and flimsy-looking bundles of dried banana leaves. A European trader, resident in Kiriwina for ten years, told me that when he saw women on the road with large baskets on their heads, he just assumed that they were going to a village to cry for someone who had died. He never knew, until I told him, about the effect that the contents of those baskets, filled with bundles of banana leaves, had on his own store receipts.

Perhaps I, too, might have ignored women's wealth if the women themselves had not pushed me in the direction of their work. I had come to study male carvers, not women, and I wanted to live in one of the famed carving villages where expert carvers resided. I sought out the advice of Vanoi because he was the highest-ranking Tabalu chief. I wanted to explain my research to him and ask his advice about where I should live. Malinowski had done much of his fieldwork in Omarakana, where Vanoi now lived, although he also spent some months in Sinaketa, a village in the southern part of Kiriwina.[6] Since I wanted to work in a different village from his, I was delighted when Vanoi told me that a number of expert carvers lived in Kwaibwaga. I left Omarakana and went directly to Kwaibwaga to ask Bunemiga, a master carver and one of the village leaders, about living in the village. He agreed to build me a house and I agreed to pay everyone who helped with the construction. A week later, my small house stood ready.

Kwaibwaga, with a population of three hundred, is one of the largest villages in the northern part of the island. I planned to begin my first day by making a census of the residents and a map of the village. But early in the morning, two village women came to tell me that it was important that I go with them to another village. They were insistent, and other villagers called out to me to come along. I dutifully followed, but I had no idea where we were going or why.

Along the main road, other women from nearby villages joined the procession. Most of the older women had shaved their heads, and some had completely blackened their bodies and faces. As they walked quickly over the rough road, their long skirts of natural fibers shimmered in the sun, and even though they were in mourning, they possessed an authority that at that moment made them more dominant than the men who came along with them. Each woman carried a foot long woven basket on her head and occasionally

[6] Since only part of Malinowski's (1967) diaries have been published, it is difficult to know exactly how long he stayed in either place. Touluwa, who died in 1930, was the Tabalu chief in Omarakana when Malinowski lived there. Touluwa's successor, Mitakata, was chief when the anthropologist Harry Powell (1956; 1960; 1969a; 1969b) lived in Omarakana during his fieldwork from 1950 to 1951.

Photo 8. Men cook taro pudding in large clay pots that they will give to their sisters to thank them for bringing so many bundles of banana leaves and skirts to the mortuary distribution.

two young men would rush past us, straining under the heavy weight of a huge round basket suspended from a pole carried on their shoulders. I could not see what the baskets contained.

Finally, we turned off the main road and continued on a footpath. We entered a small village, and I immediately noticed that men at each house either were busy preparing earth ovens for roasting pigs or were cooking taro pudding. Trobriand houses are made of woven coconut-leaf walls with thatched roofs, placed back from a cleared center area—a public plaza of sorts—where all major events and meetings take place. At the edge of the plaza stand the yam houses, the storage places where yams, the major food, are carefully stacked after each harvest. As we entered the village, no one paid attention to yams or even to the men who were cooking. All the excitement was being generated by the activities coming from the central plaza, where hundreds of women sat or stood surrounded by as many baskets; I saw that the baskets were filled with something I had never read or heard about—banana-leaf bundles.

Women were completely involved in sorting out their bundles and arranging piles of red fiber skirts. One woman seemed to be in charge, and she continually took bundles into the center, threw them on the ground, and called out

Photo 9. The special long skirt marks this woman as the leader for the day's distribution of women's wealth.

someone's name. Other women rushed to the center, adding their bundles to the pile. Finally, another woman gathered them all up and carried them to her own basket. The same throwing and retrieving went on for hours. Sometimes the pile was small, with only about thirty bundles; at other times several hundred were given, with ten or so skirts thrown on top. Women laughed and shouted among themselves; occasionally, they argued over a particular distribution. A few women insisted that I throw down some bundles myself, and I was told, "Our bundles are just like your money."

Late that day, on my way home from the village, tired but exhilarated, I thought about what I had witnessed. I decided that any public activity precipitating so much energy and concentration must be important. If bundles really were like money, some women gave away or received an enormous amount. Although men did not participate in any of the action in the center of the village, they remained in the village throughout the day, sitting on the house verandas and casually watching the proceedings. When the distribution finally was over, however, they then entered the plaza to give yams to those women who now stood with empty baskets.

After that first day's experience my research interests shifted away from artists and their wood carvings—not simply because I recognized the importance of women's roles at death but also because women's wealth underscored the deep political significance of death to both Trobriand women and men. So it came as no surprise when the year after Vanoi's death a similar distribution of women's wealth was held. This one, however, did not take place only in Omarakana, as tradition would have it, but in Port Moresby. The Trobrianders who live in the capital, many of them with university educations, attended the exchange along with those who flew to Port Moresby from Kiriwina. The urbanites substituted lengths of cotton material purchased in the local stores, whereas the villagers transported bundles and yams. To hold a distribution at such great expense and so far geographically and culturally from Omarakana displayed the abiding commitment of urban Trobrianders to demonstrate publicly their relationship to Chief Vanoi and their allegiance to this deeply meaningful Trobriand tradition.

In the next chapter I explore the significance of this commitment as each death brings into public view what is most compelling about the deceased's social identity. The rituals and exchanges that follow a death not only measure the status of the person who died but also assess the involvement of cognatic and affinal kin throughout the dead person's life.

2/Death and the work of mourning

As we approached the village we heard a very loud sound of distressed people moaning and chanting. A man had died. I walked into the house and the man was laid out on twelve women's legs with one man at the head because the widow who usually does this was sick. Some other people were sitting around. A small lantern burned and everyone was chanting and crying. I was in shock and couldn't keep tears from flowing. I'd never seen a man die or knew anyone close who had. At breaks in the crying, laughter and joking came over. One by one the children came in and lay down on their father and wept. Talking to him, thanking him. . . . After a little while a woman led me out and said, "sleep."

Linda Weiner

UWELASI'S DEATH

There is no village sound more chilling than the shrill, poignant cries announcing a death. Even when a person is seriously ill and everyone knows that death is imminent, the lamenting wails still come as a shock. The house where the dead person lies fills quickly with close relatives who throw themselves across the body, sobbing, "my mother," "my sister," or "my father," "my brother." The message of death spreads rapidly to other villages where the dead person has relatives or friends. Each person now has a role to play that will change the direction of his or her work for at least half a year. Death halts all joyful activities as sharply as if a solar eclipse suddenly turned bright day into darkest night. Attention to death is swift and then drawn out over a long period of time; the deceased is far too valuable to disappear quickly from the minds and hearts of those who mourn.

Uwelasi—an old but powerful chief, second only to the Tabalu chief—who lived in Tubuwada, a village about 5 miles from Kwaibwaga, had been ill for several weeks when my neighbors, Bomapota and her mother, took me to see him. The rumors were that he was close to death, but to my amazement I found Uwelasi, although gravely ill, surrounded by villagers who were making him look young and beautiful. They washed his body and dressed him in the traditional white pandanus penis covering. As if in preparation to meet a lover, his skin was rubbed with coconut oil and aromatic grasses were tucked into his armbands. Only one thing was missing. No one held a pearl shell

Photo 10. Uwelasi is beautifully adorned with shell decorations that designate his chiefly rank.

over his face as women do when they perform beauty magic for young dancers.

Face painting was applied in decorative lines of black and white, and the traditional sliver of polished shell, now worn only at death, was inserted through the tiny holes in his nose made when he was a child. White cowrie-shell decorations, the mark of his chiefly rank, were tied around his legs, waist, and forehead, and the red shell necklace that all young people wear was placed around his neck. Internally Uwelasi's body was dying, but outwardly he was adorned with the cultural symbols of youth and chiefly rank, expressive of his past seductiveness and fame.

We remained with Uwelasi for several hours, chewing betel nuts with him and gossiping quietly among ourselves. I knew that one question, although never to be discussed openly, was uppermost in everyone's mind. Whose magic was killing Uwelasi? Almost every death that occurs is believed to be the result of sorcery (*bwagau*) effected by a specialist who chants magic spells into the victim's betel nut or tobacco. Villagers chew betel and smoke in addictive ways, and these objects, which they continually take from each other, are used as the agents of illness and death. Only when a person is very old and dies while asleep is death considered "natural." Then villagers simply say, "His time was up; he lived a full life without angering anyone."

Uwelasi was old, but he was chief and someone wanted him dead. For everyone connected to the afflicted person, illness signals danger: An enemy is showing his intent. Privately, Uwelasi had been questioned by his closest kin. Who gave you betel to chew? Who walked to Losuia with you? With whom did you talk when you went to the gardens? The suspect may be Uwelasi's ally, his successor, or even the very person who questioned him. Villagers are circumspect in their relations with everyone. Suspicion and danger are the underside of love and affection. Every death reaffirms this contradiction. The hostility projected by an enemy that results in death not only culminates in the loss of a person but also is viewed as an attack against the very vitality of a matrilineage.

When the deceased is a politically important person, the intent to reduce the chief's power is obvious; but even when a child dies, villagers see this death as an attack against the continued power of the matrilineage for the next generation. Trobrianders, like some societies found in other parts of the world, such as the Navaho or the Hopi among North American Indians, reckon descent matrilineally. All persons born are believed to be related by blood ties to their mother and their mother's mother and so on, tracing their descent through women back to the ancestors who first came to Kiriwina. The ancestors, usually a woman and her brother, of each matrilineage (*dala*) brought with them some or all of the following: special body and house decorations, ancestral names, magic spells, food taboos, and songs and dances.

Each ancestral pair also chose a place to build their houses and marked out areas for garden lands. According to the histories of specific matrilineages, some ancestors brought with them many of the things just described, whereas others came with much less. The more important these paraphernalia were, the higher were ranked the members of the matrilineage who owned them. Some ancestors were able to take over fertile lands, and others had trouble finding large tracts of land; therefore, even today, matrilineages remain unequal in their resources. All of a matrilineage's properties are controlled in each generation by a chief or other leader who inherits these rights and obligations. Because of deaths or offenses such as murder or adultery, some matrilineages lose parts of their ancestral land or the paraphernalia, making relations between matrilineages a source of possible distrust and competition.

In addition to membership in a matrilineage, a person belongs to one of four named matrilineal clans (*kumila*); unlike matrilineages, however, matriclans have no chiefs or leaders nor do they share any property, for example, land, decorations, or magic spells. The members of each clan have the same animal, bird, and plant totems, which serve to attach them in a general way to some communal past; but the important function of clans, as we will see later, is that they work to separate villagers into marriageable or nonmarriageable categories.

Trobrianders believe that if a matrilineage is weakened through the death of a man, someone is deliberately trying to weaken the autonomy of the

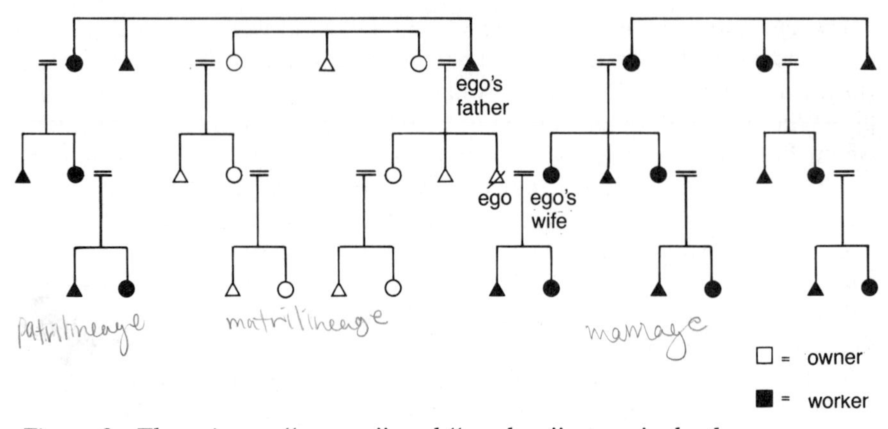

Figure 2. The primary "owners" and "workers" at ego's death.

matrilineage's leader or chief, taking away his supporters and potential heirs. Even greater fear is felt when girls or women of child-bearing age die, for then villagers believe that someone desires the destruction of the entire matrilineage itself. Without women to bear children, the matrilineage dies out and the property and even the rank of the lineage may be claimed by others. Each death brings these fears into sharp focus.

"OWNERS" AND "WORKERS"

Uwelasi lived for only two more days after my visit. Then the mourning cries resounded through the village, and the intense work of death began. Kinship is the key factor in defining the part in the ensuing drama that each person will play. The widening network of people who congregate around Uwelasi are differentiated by the labor they must perform and by the mourning taboos they must uphold. Each action designates the status of their relationship to Uwelasi.

The "owners of the dead person's things" (*toliuli*) are those who are members of Uwelasi's matrilineage, assisted by other villagers who belong to his clan. They organize the burial and the exchanges that follow. The "workers" (*toliyouwa*) are villagers from other clans who are related to Uwelasi through marriage or patrilaterally. Figure 2, in a simplified form, shows the relationship between workers and owners whenever someone dies. As the diagram illustrates, the major owners are the members of the dead person's matrilineage, whereas the major workers are the wife and father of the dead person and the other members of their respective matrilineages. In actuality, these categories incorporate many more people, each of whom is related to the major owners or workers, either through marriage, patrilateral ties, or friendship. In Uwelasi's case, primary workers include all his wives and the members of their matrilineages, the members of his father's matrilineage, his own or adopted children,[1] and in addition, his friends and political allies. These people are the public mourners. They sit with the body and prepare the grave. After the burial, they are the ones who shave off their hair, paint their bodies black with charred pieces of coconut husks, and wear mourning clothes.

The owners cannot touch the corpse, dig the grave, or carry the body to the grave site. Nor will they shave their heads, blacken their skin, or put on mourning clothes as the workers must do. The owners are not required to demonstrate their grief publicly in this way; but they have the onerous task of giving away their resources, such as yams, pigs, and stone axe-blades (*beku*), the traditional male valuables, as well as skirts and bundles of banana leaves, the valuables of women. The members of Uwelasi's matrilineage must repay all those members of other matrilineages who were close to him during his life, including his friends, allies, wives, and children.

As the news of Uwelasi's death quickly spread throughout the island, men in the worker category hastened to Tubuwada. While walking with the workers coming from Kwaibwaga, I saw people from many other nearby villages also going to Tubuwada. To demonstrate their affection for Uwelasi, they will help care for his body and mourn publicly. By early evening, several hundred men had congregated in the central plaza close to Uwelasi's resting place. The workers sat together in village groups, but in the dim light of the small fires I could see little except a sea of bodies. Traditionally, at a chief's death, villagers gathered for three days and nights to mourn. However, after colonization the Australian government demanded that burial, for sanitation reasons, occur more quickly, and now it takes place on the day following the first all-night vigil.

Part of the men's work is to mourn by singing their repertoire of ancestral songs. As with all public events, competition underlies the dirges, as each village group tries to prove they are the best. Even with this competitive element, singing unifies the entire gathering and dispels some of the tension produced by the belief in death by sorcery. No one sleeps throughout the night. To do so is to show disrespect to the owners, as I was discreetly told when my eyes involuntarily started to close about four o'clock in the morning. Later, I learned that more than disrespect is involved. Not to mourn appropriately is to imply that you caused the death. Some of the men's songs described Tuma, an island about 20 sea miles from Kiriwina, where Uwelasi's spirit (*baloma*) would join the other spirits of dead Trobrianders. Villagers believe that on reaching Tuma, the spirit is revitalized by returning to a state of youth and thus continues to live. In preparation for Tuma, Uwelasi's body was adorned with all his youthful, chiefly attire, except that his legs and arms were tied together so that his body remained straight and dignified.

[1] Adoption of young children occurs frequently. Usually when a couple has many children, an older matrilineal kin of either the husband or wife will ask for the child. In most cases, those who want to adopt a child are villagers whose own children are grown. Adopted children always stay in contact with their own parents, visiting them and sometimes returning to live with them when they are adolescents. If they are unhappy, they can return to their parents. There is no stigma attached to adoption, and sometimes it is an advantage since such children may learn many magic spells and other important things from their adopted parents.

Photo 11. Uwelasi's sons and daughters cry and dance solemnly outside his house until it is time for the burial.

While the singers maintained their vigil outside, other workers, mostly women, attended Uwelasi. They sat facing one another, their backs straight and legs extended under Uwelasi as they "carried the body." This responsibility for the dead person is called *kopoi*, the same term used for feeding and caring for a baby. Together they chanted the mourning cry, stopping occasionally to smoke or chew betel. Uwelasi's first wife sat behind his head, and overcome with sadness, from time to time she leaned down against his face, covering it with her tears. The crying reached a peak each time one of his children briefly entered the house. Sobbing, "my father, my father," he or she fell across the body, embracing it.

Each of his sons wore a pubic covering made from a green pandanus leaf and each of his daughters was dressed in an undyed banana-fiber skirt that hung below her knees. When the sons and daughters returned outside, they gathered together and danced, arms around each others' shoulders and tears openly streaming down their faces. They moved in a solemn, slow two-step, first separating from each other and then coming together, each holding some personal article of Uwelasi's, such as his lime pot or his cassowary feathers, an important part of a chief's dancing regalia at the joyful harvest celebrations.

Every death dramatizes the magical success of someone else's deadly desires and the danger inherent in that achievement. Each person's grief is demonstrated either by singing and dancing outside or crying inside, thereby removing that person from overt suspicions of sorcery. The culturally dictated emotions expressed in this first stage of mourning mask each person's inner feelings. For some, grief is deep; for others, it is more difficult to know how they feel.

THE THREAT OF SORCERY

Trobrianders are adept at disguising their feelings about each other. For me, nothing was more difficult than trying to learn this same behavior. Time and again, my closest friends warned me that I must not allow my face to express what I truly thought about someone. "Anna, the words we say are not the words we think. You must keep your face smiling, even when you are angry with someone." To express anger openly evinces fighting, and once these hostile feelings are exposed, they can never be recalled. In the minds of Trobrianders, such behavior ultimately leads to sorcery. No one forgets a past mistake.

Attention to these aspects of interpersonal relations permeates each person's daily life. Adults and children alike fear little in their daily activities except sorcery. Children, who seldom are under close parental supervision, are taught at an early age to refuse food from anyone while their parents are away working in the gardens, just as American children are warned about accepting candy from a stranger. On moonless nights a neighbor might rush into my house and ask to borrow my flashlight because he thought he heard someone—a sorcerer—walking in back of his house.

Yet sorcery is more complicated than any one person's anger or jealousy. A member of a matrilineage may be killed for the wrongdoings of other living or dead kin, and children may be sorcerized in an attempt to weaken their father's power. Villagers say that "big mistakes" such as sorcery, killing, and stealing land are remembered from one generation to another. No one says, "I'm sorry," hoping that a mistake will be forgotten. Past errors are always part of present circumstances.

The most powerful magic spells for sorcery are known by only a handful of men. Many, but by no means all of them, are chiefs. Others must seek out one of these men and ask him to perform his craft. The payment is heavy, for only a large stone axe-blade is acceptable. Not surprisingly, men who are wealthy enough to possess one or more stone axe-blades keep them buried under their houses. Some chiefs are reputed to have as many as ten, but because the axe-blades stay hidden, no one ever knows exactly how many a man has given away or received. A few women also learn the spells, but they are not suspected of sorcery because, as Ipukoya told me, "Women do not walk about at night." Some women and a few men, however, are thought to be "flying witches," individuals who are believed to have the ability to leave their bodies while asleep.[2] In an invisible state they attack someone by destroying a vital organ, and only another flying witch can recite spells that will counter the attack and cure the patient. Therefore, a flying witch can be good or evil, and villagers take great care when they associate with anyone believed to have these powers. I often saw young women or men give an old

[2] This power is believed to be inherited through women, and certain children of such women are trained, for example, to eat raw meat and drink salt water. See Malinowski (1922: 237–248) for further details; also Tambiah (1983: 171–200).

woman they met on the road their last betel nut because they thought she might have been a flying witch and did not want to anger her.

Flying witches may attack a person at any time, but dark nights are especially dangerous. Therefore, on moonless nights, most villagers pull their doors tightly shut and go to sleep early, whereas when the full moon ascends people move freely about until quite late and young people's laughter rings out into the early morning hours. Dark nights intensify villagers' fears, for they also believe that plans and payments for sorcery are made at these times, often at some specially arranged place in the bush so no one else is witness to the meetings. A specialist can refuse a person's request to perform the magic, and sometimes he even will warn the intended victim. Planning sorcery through someone else has its own dangers. Only those who know the magic spells have the power to act autonomously.

Even the strongest traditional sorcery works slowly; the deadly poisons believed to be in betel or tobacco can be countered if an afflicted person gains the help of a curing specialist. Recovery is a possibility until the spell has been transmitted three times. After the third betel nut has been chewed, there is no cure. Some villagers claim that poisons extracted from certain fish are used in conjunction with the most feared sorcery spells, making death come more rapidly. Western influences have tended to heighten rather than diminish these beliefs in the power of sorcery. With young men often working elsewhere in Papua New Guinea, now villagers believe that when some of them return, they bring back chemical poisons to kill their enemies. These Western poisons are believed to be impervious to traditional curing, and many deaths that occur after fewer than twenty-four hours of sickness are attributed to this new form of sorcery.

The tensions created by the beliefs about modern and traditional sorcery enter into every interaction. Judgments about people and expressions of power all are negotiated with great care. Stories circulate widely about the sorcery victims of certain chiefs. Unlike an ordinary specialist, if a chief has strong magic and is powerful enough, he himself will announce his responsibility for a death. Vanoi once told me about Leon, a villager who joined the church and, renouncing his belief in magic, openly mocked Vanoi's legendary knowledge of sorcery. One day the two met at a trade store where many villagers congregate to gossip. Leon brashly told Vanoi that he was unafraid of his magic. Vanoi offered Leon a cigarette and told him that if he doubted his, Vanoi's, magic powers he should smoke it. With everyone watching, Leon lit the cigarette and calmly inhaled it to the end. That night he became violently ill. A week later he died.

Everyone believed that Vanoi had prepared this poisoned cigarette in advance, carrying it with him until he was able to use it. For this reason, no one but a chief's closest ally can touch his carrying basket, and everyone is apprehensive when a chief offers only one person tobacco or a betel nut. So deep-seated are the beliefs in a person's ability to create a deadly object through poisons and magic spells that when someone is afflicted, her or his relatives seldom seek medical help from the small hospital in Losuia.

Each dead person is perceived as a victim of someone else's control. Once when I was collecting a genealogy I noticed that in the present generation, only one person out of ten children was still living. The others had all died in their twenties and thirties. When I questioned a friend about this unusual situation, he said, "Don't ever ask the family about this. It was sorcery because of a fight many years ago over land ownership and now there is only one person left in the matrilineage."

At a death, when the owners of the dead person stand together to repay the workers, they represent the strength of the matrilineage. Everyone reads the social message in numbers. How vital is this matrilineage? Power is never limitless; everyone recognizes sorcery as the ultimate threat. Even chiefs must reckon with such limits from within their own group. Succession to a chieftaincy is inherited within the matrilineage, so the right to become chief can only be taken at the death of the encumbent chief. In many cases, the chief's heir is suspect.

The new chief becomes the head of the owners. He makes all decisions about killing the chief's pigs to feed the workers and about the distributions of yams and men's valuables that follow the burial. Uwelasi's situation was more complicated than most because he had no successor. His matrilineage, once strong and of a rank almost as high as the Tabalu, now was finished. There were no women or children left who belonged to Uwelasi's matrilineage. Sorcery had victimized everyone, so that Uwelasi's death was more deeply disturbing than the loss of one person. Another chief who belonged to a lower-ranking matrilineage had been boasting for a long time that his lineage was of higher rank than Uwelasi's. With Uwelasi dead, through time the other chief's boasts would become more truthful. Even if others know these circumstances, the defense can come only from Uwelasi's kin; but in this case no one was left. Uwelasi's son took his father's place as the head of the matrilineage, but as he could not claim to be a member of the matrilineage, everyone knew he was not truly the chief.

"CARRYING" THE DEAD PERSON

Late in the morning, about ten workers began to dig Uwelasi's grave, while others attended to his body. First, they removed his shell decorations, for these symbols of rank are too valuable to bury. Uwelasi then was wrapped completely in large pandanus mats. Before the burial proceeds, one final operation takes place. Some effort is made to keep part of the body for the living. The women workers who "carried" Uwelasi's body during the night of mourning removed a few of his fingernails and cut off some of his hair. They carefully placed these physical mementos in small white cowrie shells, which were attached to a long red shell necklace. A few women workers who were the closest to Uwelasi, for example, his father's sister's daughters and his own daughters, each wear one of these necklaces. For several years, they will "carry" Uwelasi in this way as a sign of continual mourning.

When it was time to bury, ten or so men workers hoisted the body onto their shoulders and walked rapidly to the grave site at the edge of the plaza. Everyone else hurried with them. Many rushed at the body, grabbing hold of the mats in an attempt to halt the burial. With a crescendo of terrible moans and cries, the workers carefully lowered Uwelasi into the grave lined with woven mats. When most villagers die, nothing is buried with them, but when a chief dies, often some important object will be placed in the grave with the body. In Uwelasi's case, three 12-foot-long yams (*kuvi*) were brought to his grave and buried with him.[3] These yams, so difficult to grow, are presented to a chief by his affines and allies. Only he can display them as a symbol of his political power. Like the *baloma* spirit, the spirit of the yams will follow Uwelasi to Tuma to assure him that he will retain the same position of importance.

Because Uwelasi was known to have powerful magic, including sorcery, he was buried face down to prevent his dreaded malevolent spirit (*kosi*) from escaping from the grave. Unlike the *baloma* spirit, who travels to Tuma, this other spirit can bring illness and death to survivors. Trobrianders believe that the *kosi* spirit only lingers for several days, so during that time the grave must be guarded by someone who also possesses powerful magic. Once the grave is filled with soil, the display of frenzied emotions ceases abruptly. A few workers stay to attend the grave by hammering small fence posts around it, to which they string flowers and feathers. The rest depart for their own homes, tired after a long night and day with no sleep and with little food.

Burial is only the initial part of the obligations surrounding a death. The heaviest taboos involve strict seclusion and fall on the surviving spouse. Although the spouse took the greatest care of the deceased throughout their married life, suddenly with death, the attention that was given may be questioned. Even a spouse is not above suspicion, and the oppressive mourning prohibitions give testimony to the spouse's innocence and, by extension, to the innocence of his or her matrilineal kin. By observing such stringent seclusion, the surviving spouse publicly expresses the intense grief felt over the inability to prevent such sorcery attacks.

For months, the widow or widower must remain inside the mourning house behind a curtain of mats, the length of time determined by the importance of the dead person and the age of the surviving spouse. The widow or widower sits up on a high bed, the same kind of bed used for childbirth. At childbirth, a small fire is kept burning underneath, but now there is no fire and no "good food" such as yams, taro, pigs, or fish. During the first few days following the burial, the secluded spouse is not permitted to talk to anyone or even to smoke or chew betel nuts. All work of any kind is taboo, and the spouse must be hand-fed common food such as sweet potatoes or tapioca by someone else because it is also taboo to touch food. The present prohibitions are not

[3] These yams (*kuvi*) belong to the other major species, *Dioscorea alata*, that Trobrianders cultivate. The largest *kuvi* yams grow from 2 to 12 feet in length and as much as a foot thick. Another variety of the same species is round instead of long, many of them reaching a foot or more in diameter.

nearly as long and arduous as they were before the Australian government forced some changes. Earlier a spouse could not leave the house even to attend to excretory functions and workers had to remove the excreta. Today, the widow or widower is permitted to leave the house and hasten into the bush, but he or she must be covered completely with a large woven mat like the ones in which Uwelasi was wrapped.

As the months of mourning seclusion progress, a few of the more rigorous taboos are suspended each time the members of the spouse's matrilineage bring valuables, fish, and yams to the owners to solicit a lessening of the taboos. Yet for at least four months, and usually much longer, the spouse must stay within the village, rarely leaving the house and foregoing all "good food." The same prohibitions apply to the father of the dead person and to his sister or others from their matrilineage who "take their place." If the father of the deceased has already died, at the time of the major distributions his brother or some other member of his matrilineage will take his place. The spouse, father, and the father's sisters are the major public mourners. They must keep their heads shaved and their bodies blackened. Women wear long, undyed banana-fiber skirts that reach to their ankles. Today men usually wear black sarongs rather than the green pandanus coverings. The spouse and father also wear black necklaces. In the past, these necklaces were made from the hair of the dead person, but now they are woven from plant fibers. The necklaces stay in place until the final mourning is terminated when, in a special ceremony, the necklaces are cut off by members of the deceased's matrilineage. Only after these are cut are the spouse and father freed from all connections with the dead person.

Not only do mourners stay secluded or cover their bodies in black, but even their own names become taboo. The major mourners, including owners and workers, such as the dead person's parents, siblings, children, spouse, father, and father's siblings, are called by a special kin term that defines who he or she is in relation to the deceased. When Dabweyowa's father died, I forgot that his name had become Tomilabova (the son of a dead man). One day, shortly after his father was buried and while we were working together, I called him Dabweyowa. Immediately, without saying a word, he got up and left my house. I did not see Tomilabova for two days, and when he did reappear we never discussed the incident. I never made that mistake again.

KEEPING THE DEAD ALIVE

After a death, the tragic crying continues to resound month after month. The spouse is joined in the mourning house by her or his women kin and the dead person's father's sisters. These villagers stay in the house, and four times during the day they "cry." So regular are the moments of crying that they become the village clock announcing daybreak, midday, late afternoon, and twilight. The only break in the rhythm occurs when someone who has missed the funeral comes to the village. For example, when students or those working

Photo 12. A widow, having just put on her mourning necklaces, is overcome with grief.

away come home, they must hasten "to cry" immediately on their return if any relatives died while they were absent. For this reason, when I returned to Kiriwina after Vanoi's death, before I even went to Kwaibwaga I stopped at Omarakana to mourn.

The other workers, who may number from fifty to several hundred depending on the status of the person who died, each observe some of the mourning taboos. Most shave their heads. Those who are more closely related to the dead person also refrain from eating "good food," and those more distantly related may wear dark clothes or even tie a black cloth around their arms. Before taking on these taboos or symbols of mourning, each person first receives a payment from the owners for the part she or he played in the burial proceedings.

The first set of exchanges (*sigiliyawali*), involving yams, taro, and small amounts of money, takes place the day after the burial. Both the large yams (*kuvi*) and the regular-sized yams (*taytu*) are used for the necessary payments, but the sizes and the amounts given vary depending on the status of the person and upon her or his relationship to the deceased. After Uwelasi's burial, because I sat with the mourners all night, I received a *kuvi* yam (about 3 feet

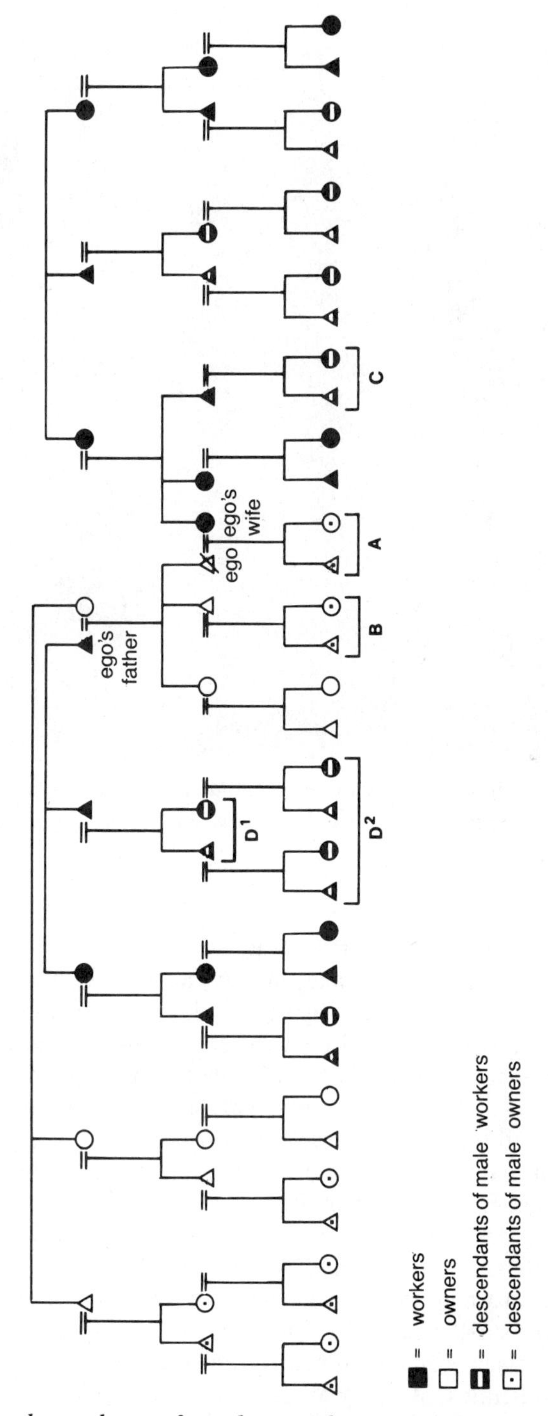

Figure 3. The descendents of workers and owners who participate in their father's or mother's father's mortuary obligations.

Photo 13. Kwaibwaga villagers who are related to the owners collect yams and betel nut to help their kin with the payments that must be made to the workers after the burial.

long) and fifty cents, which everyone said was a great honor. The distribution by the owners to the workers takes all day; name after name is called, with continual interruptions and lengthy discussions over what should be given to whom. The largest distribution goes to the spouse and spouse's matrilineal kin and to the dead person's father or father's representative and members of his matrilineage. As a chief, Uwelasi had three wives, so extensive payments also were needed for all his spouses and their kin.

So important is this distribution that the owners must call on their supporters for help in amassing the necessary numbers of yams. Here, for the first time, the owners demonstrate their strength and the vitality of their matrilineage. When a man dies, his children receive payments as workers, but if they are married, they also help the owners. Such help is especially important when a matrilineage is small in numbers. Visually, however, they cannot be confused with "true owners" because their heads are shaved and their bodies blackened. As Figure 3 illustrates, at any death, if a man is either a worker or an owner, his children help the members of his matrilineage as if they themselves were owners or workers. Therefore, the children labeled A, although workers, act

Photo 14. Livenai brings a clay pot and a stone axe blade—men's wealth—to the distribution.

like owners supporting their dead father's matrilineage. The children labeled B, also as owners, support their father, who is the brother of the dead man. The children labeled C act as workers because their father is the widow's brother. Often the descendants of men will continue such support. Those workers labeled D^1 are the dead person's father's brother's children, and D^2 the dead person's father's brother's children's children. At Uwelasi's death, because in a sense, the matrilineage died with him, all the owners were his children, making the distribution even more critical and more lamentable, at least for some.

One exchange that occurs during this distribution reverses the usual direction of giving. The matrilineal kin of each spouse present men's valuables, such as stone axe-blades, clay pots, large decorated shells, and sometimes money. These valuables are given as a "compensation payment" (*kulututu*) for their lack of care in allowing the death to occur. By paying compensation, such kin assume responsibility for the loss while simultaneously proclaiming their innocence of the crime itself. As they walk toward the owners, carrying their large clay pots and stone axe-blades, they still are filled with anxiety and fear. If the owners think that the payment is not large enough, they assume that truly the spouse's kin had a direct hand in the killing and may begin to plot their own retaliation. In this way, the valuables given play their own roles in calming or intensifying feelings of suspicion.

The following day, another distribution (*tadabali*) is held. Now women organize the exchanges as they give their wealth, bundles of banana leaves, to all the workers, who by their dress will continue publicly to express their grief. Skirts, the other valuables, are not given at this time. In addition to the spouse, father, and father's sister, the others who accept the bundles must either shave their heads, blacken their bodies, or wear dark clothes. This distribution is only a prelude to the much larger distribution held four to six months later, when all the workers will be handsomely repaid with large numbers of bundles and skirts that end the formal mourning period.

Until that time, the memory of the dead person and attendant mourning customs continue to color the life of the village. Uwelasi's village remains ritually closed, with branches of trees thrown across all the paths entering the village. No singing or dancing may take place, even if it is the harvest season when festivities of this sort usually occur. The village is oppressively quiet except for the periodic mourners' wailing. Behind these manifest signs of mourning, the owners are busy organizing their strategies to accumulate huge amounts of women's wealth for the distribution that will be held months ahead.

Throughout this time of intense preparation Uwelasi's presence continues to pervade the village in a material way. The other major mourner, in Uwelasi's case his father's sister's daughter, acknowledges the continued ties to her father's matrilineage by carrying the woven basket that served as his purse. Whenever she leaves the mourning house, she walks through the village with the basket hanging from a cloth strap around her neck. The basket is covered with betel nuts to which are attached some of Uwelasi's decorations —his armbands, aromatic leaves, and youthful red shell necklace. When a woman dies, her skirt is adorned and carried in much the same way.

The spouse and father of the deceased, the two key people in each person's life, remain secluded, and the dead person's father's sister "carries" the symbols of the dead person's social and political accomplishments. Until the mourning period is finished and the cord to which the basket is attached is cut by the women owners, Uwelasi's father's sister's daughter must "carry the dead man" wherever she goes. As the representative of Uwelasi's father, she is the constant reminder of the role that every man plays in the life of his child. Each person, built up and cared for by so many others, as the total congregation of workers makes clear, was nurtured from birth by her or his father. This man is a member of a different matrilineage, and in that capacity he is the first *outsider* to give his care and attention to his child. As his child grows up, he and the other members of his matrilineage contribute greatly to the child's continued well-being. When a person dies, a woman, usually the deceased's father's sister, represents the matrilineage that gave so much to the deceased during his or her lifetime. By carrying the symbols of beauty

Photo 15. Commemorating the death of her mother's brother's son, a worker carries the dead man's decorated basket wherever she goes.

and power that in youth and in adult life helped make that person strong and vital, she demonstrates all that was achieved through the years of giving.

In less overt ways, other major workers, such as Uwelasi's children and other members of his father's matrilineage, carry the physical parts of his body. Women "carry the dead person" by wearing the necklaces containing his fingernails and hair. Men also "carry the dead person" by caring for the grave. Before the government declared it illegal to practice secondary burial, the corpse's mandible, skull, and arm bones were removed and cleaned and then carried or stored in the house by these same women and men workers over a period of five or ten years, sometimes longer.

During the exchanges that followed Uwelasi's death, Becky, a Trobriander who lives in Losuia, privately complained, "It is not fair. One death and we have to work so hard." This hard work makes sense when we consider that because most deaths are perceived as the results of sorcery or the arbitrary nature of flying witches, deaths are felt to be direct attacks against the other members of their matrilineages. Death is seen as destroying and calling into question all the relationships that a dead person worked so hard to develop throughout his or her life. Through this work of mourning, the accomplishments of the deceased are measured by the numbers of workers who help with the burial and continue to mourn publicly for months afterward. In this way, the work of mourning echoes the success of the dead person's life just as it also defies the sorcerer's malevolent intent. A matrilineage strong in numbers and with the ability to pay workers indicates that the loss of a single person can be overcome. The work of mourning *is* arduous, as Becky said. It is not easy to regenerate for the living the most social part of the person who has died so that the previous work of "making" the person will not have been in vain.

By carefully examining the procedures following a death, we find how important it is to conceptualize the "social person" as someone who is created in part by others. The physical attributes and characteristics of each person only provide the beginning—the raw material—that is culturally shaped by other people and things, such as one's matrilineal identity; one's father, who is a member of another matrilineage; beauty magic; and even the productive efforts of one's affines.

Thus the attention to death, observed with stringent taboos and the expenditure of vast amounts of wealth, is a serious and time-consuming attempt to make some part of the dead person survive for the living. The exhaustive effort that surrounds mourning is an indication that the work of attending to the growth and development of the person has not been in vain. In the next chapter, we will begin with the birth of a child and start to examine the full range of what culturally making a person entails.

3/Fathers and matrilineality

The only thing I know for sure is death is a very special thing—more so than birth. When you die you go to another island, Tuma, and join your relatives. Babies also come from here. . . . There also is no big ceremony for birth. The woman must stay in her house for several weeks and the baby is placed high up in a wooden type crate above a fire which never dies. After this short period the child sleeps with his mother and the children a few years old sleep with their father.

Linda Weiner

INTERRUPTED SLEEP

I was awakened just before daybreak by an insistent scratching noise on the thin, coconut-frond wall of my house. I whispered, "Who?" in the usual Kiriwina way. Bomapota replied, "Get some tobacco and come to Naseluma's house." I knew what the message meant, for Naseluma was in the last days of her pregnancy. I hurried out into the darkness across the empty village plaza. The door of each house I passed was pulled shut. The village was dark and silent. The chilled dawn air fell on my shoulders and I walked faster. The house was just ahead. A patch of light shone dimly through the frayed edges of the woven mat door. I entered the small one-room house expecting to find Naseluma in labor, but I saw that I had come too late.

In the far corner stood a high bed like the ones mourners sit on when their spouses die. There Naseluma lay with her new baby wrapped in a blanket. Beneath the bed, a wood fire, barely smoking, gave off some warmth. Her mother and her mother's sister had assisted with the delivery and now sat relaxing in front of a small kerosene lantern on a pandanus mat near the door. They laughed at my surprise that Naseluma had already delivered. I knew then that they sent the message for me to come because they had no tobacco. Shrugging off my fieldworker's disappointment at not being notified earlier, I joined them while they broke off a tiny piece of the thick trade store twist, separated it into tiny pieces, and rolled them in newsprint, making a long funnel-shaped cigarette that, in the customary way, they passed between each other to smoke. How private the birth of a baby is, I thought, when

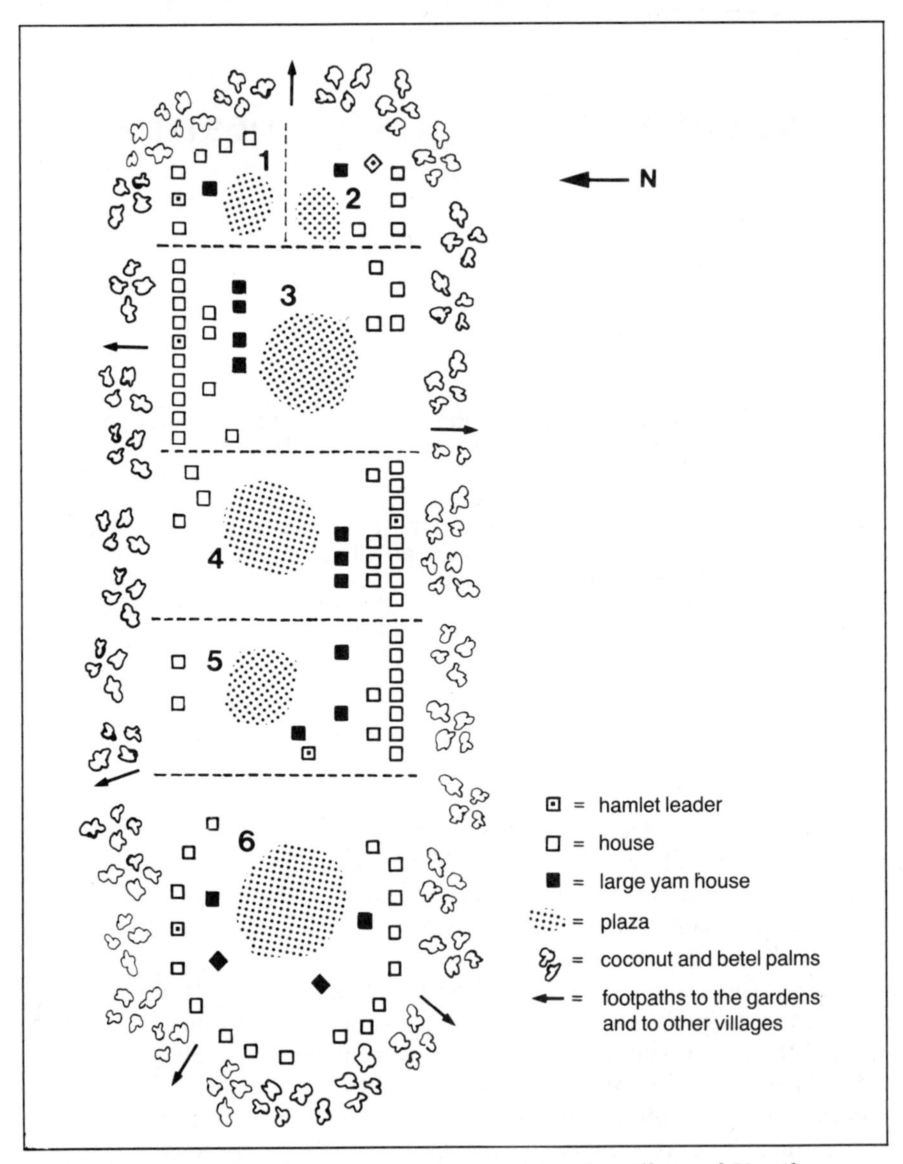

Map 3. The six hamlets that together comprise the village of Kwaibwaga.

most Trobriand events are so public. There was no village response to the infant's first cries. Naseluma's baby did not even draw attention from those in neighboring houses. What a contrast to the huge gatherings that the plaintive cries announcing a death precipitate. A birth never brings people together in the way that a death does; it only involves the closest matrilineal female kin and, occasionally, a visiting anthropologist.

At marriage, a woman goes to live with her husband; but shortly before she gives birth, she returns to her mother's house, where she remains throughout the rest of her pregnancy and for several months after the baby is born. Most marriages take place between young people who live near each other, usually within the same village or in neighboring villages. As Map 3 illustrates, each village (*valu*) is divided into sections called hamlets (*katuposula*). Each hamlet represents a matrilineage, although only a few members of the matrilineage may reside there, as discussed in Chapter 5.[1] Marriage is exogamous within a hamlet but not within the village. At marriage, even though a woman goes to live in her husband's place, she is rarely left without the support and continued companionship of her own kin. Naseluma grew up in Kwaibwaga, and when she married a Kwaibwaga man she had only to move her belongings to her husband's hamlet at the far end of the same village.

Now that Naseluma's son was born, she and her infant had to remain secluded for two months. Naseluma's husband and his kin were required to bring her food, but only her own matrilineal kin would cook for her and attend to her other needs. While she is nursing it is important that she observe stringent taboos on what she eats in order to protect the health of herself and her baby. During the first two months, the food taboos are even more inclusive. Her enforced seclusion also requires her to stay on the high bed, with a fire burning steadily, and to cover her body with a long, light-colored cape, made like a woman's skirt from dried banana-leaf fibers.

These restrictions for new mothers are similar to the prohibitions that a Trobriand widow or widower must observe. For example, separated from all but the most minimal social interaction, such women each sit on a high bed at the back of the room. Nursing mothers, like mourners, also must give up eating yams and pork, the two most favored foods. There are differences as well: For Naseluma a low fire burns under the bed, whereas for mourners there is no fire. Mourners blacken their bodies in an attempt to cover their own social identity. A woman who has given birth also covers her body, but with a light banana-leaf fiber cape that gives the effect of lightening the color of the body. The similarities of seclusion for birth and mourning, with their important oppositions between warmth and cold and light and dark, suggest that death and birth, although decidedly opposite states of being, nevertheless are linked together in a more deeply meaningful way.

BIRTH AND ANCESTORS

As described in the last chapter, Trobrianders believe that at death, the spirit (*baloma*) of the deceased becomes youthful again and continues its existence not far away on the island of Tuma. For a spirit, however, life on Tuma does not replicate itself without interruption. In time, it too ages and

[1] Neither Malinowski (for example, 1922; 1929; 1935, I) nor Powell (1969a; 1969b) recognized that villages were divided into hamlets. Therefore, they could not fully explain the variation in residence patterns within a village in relation to each matrilineage. But see Chapter 6 and also Weiner (1976: xvii–xviii, 38–43) for an extended discussion.

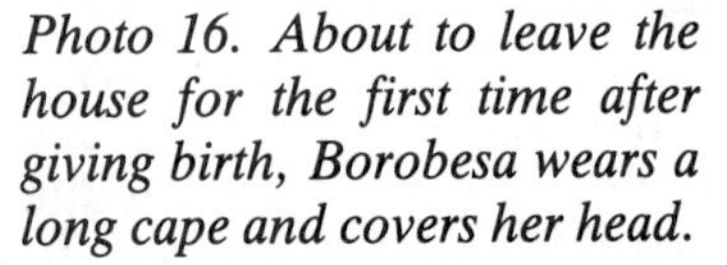

Photo 16. About to leave the house for the first time after giving birth, Borobesa wears a long cape and covers her head.

becomes feeble; but by bathing in sea water, its wrinkled skin is sloughed off and its life continues as before. When this occurs, however, a spirit child called *waiwaia*, a term that also means "infant" or "fetus," is created. Although such a spirit child is thought to belong to the matrilineage of its own birth, it is not recognizable by any personal name.

Unlike the *baloma*, which continues its presence on Tuma, the spirit child cannot stay on the island but must return to Kiriwina, where it enters a woman's body and causes her to become pregnant. It is believed to enter a woman who is a member of the same matrilineage to which its original *baloma* spirit also belonged during its life on Kiriwina. Because the fetus is formed by the combination of a woman's blood and an ancestral spirit (*sibububula*), it acquires its mother's matrilineal identity. At birth, an infant always receives a name from its mother that previously belonged to a deceased member of her matrilineage, making this ancestral connection even more apparent. Ancestral names and ancestral spirits, each in their own way, thus regenerate matrilineal identity through time.

My informants were not all in agreement on the details of how the *baloma* actually creates a spirit child. Nor did they all acknowledge an identical method by which the *waiwaia* impregnates a woman. Some of the women I knew said that they became pregnant only after a particular *baloma* came to them in a dream and told them that a *waiwaia* was being sent. Other women confided that their pregnancy was induced by magic spells. The words of the spell, known only by certain women, instruct the *baloma* to send a spirit child to the woman who wants a baby. To carry out the ritual, water is brought from a cave or from the springs along the beach and poured into a coconut-shell bowl. The owner of the magic spell chants the words into the bowl and the woman then drinks the liquid. Some of Malinowski's (1954: 216–218) informants told him that the *waiwaia* child was carried back to Kiriwina by a *baloma*, who placed the child in a woman's vagina while she was asleep. Women from coastal villages also reported to him that if a woman wanted to become pregnant she bathed in the sea, where *waiwaia* spirits often might be floating back to Kiriwina from Tuma.

These accounts are not necessarily contradictory, nor are they a reflection of the inability of informants to remember the "true" tradition. In any society, women sometimes have difficulty becoming pregnant and different facilitating techniques may be tried. Success produces increasing trust in the efficacy of certain methods and beliefs. Regardless of how different these versions may be, there is no disagreement among informants about the traditional idea that *waiwaia* cause conception. With the exposure that quite a few Trobrianders have had to primary and secondary education, many villagers now are well acquainted with the biological facts of procreation. Yet even among those who attend school, not all reject completely such traditional beliefs, which they often use to their advantage.

For example, great consternation erupted among some Kwaibwaga people when a woman received a letter from her husband, who had been working for a year in Port Moresby. He was returning home and she was six months' pregnant. When he returned and discovered the pregnancy, he angrily left his wife, shouting that he would report her to the government officers for adultery. The case was tried in the government court, but the woman's mother's mother testified that she had used magic to make her granddaughter pregnant. The local judge dismissed the case. In another example, a young unmarried woman found herself pregnant. Although most villagers gossiped about who her lover had been, there could be no claims made on any man and no stigma attached to the woman.

What is central to these beliefs is the notion that the matrilineal identity of each infant born is irrefutably linked to the past. Each dead person ultimately becomes the means for new life via the physical connection between women and the spirits of their matrilineal ancestors. In this way, each living generation is linked to matrilineal ancestors, who are perceived to play a continuing, active role directed toward future generations.

It is important to remember that not until the nineteenth century and the discovery of cell division did Western ideas about conception become biologically accurate. Until then, Western notions of how conception occurred varied widely; Trobriand beliefs on the subject are no more "primitive" or unusual than were those among early Western philosophers. In fact, Aristotle's theory of conception was very similar to the Trobriand view, except that he believed that all contributions came from the male; a woman served only as the receptacle for the growing fetus. What we find in the Trobriand case, however, is an attempt to define the cultural imperatives of matrilineal descent with absolute biological claims. I will now consider these complex matters in more detail.

THE OTHER MATRILINEAGE

Kopoi, the word used when villagers sit and care for a dead person before burial, also means "to feed" or "to nurse an infant." A woman nurses (*kopoi*) her baby for about a year and a half. But men as fathers also play roles of long-lasting importance in nurturing (*kopoi*) their babies. Similarly, when men take long *kuvi* yams to a chief, their presentation is also called *kopoi*, because they are helping to build the chief's power. Men contribute to the growth and development of their children in a way that complements rather than replicates what a woman bestows, and their contributions are directed toward enhancing the child's potential power.

The fundamental principle that shapes Trobrianders' ideas about matrilineal identity, as mentioned, revolves around the belief that conception occurs through women and their ancestral spirits. In this way, each infant born is both physically and socially identified with a particular matrilineage to which its mother and not its father belongs. As a right of birth, each child will have certain privileges and interests in the property of its matrilineage. The ancestral name that an infant is given marks the importance of claiming these rights and is the first public recognition of the infant's matrilineal identity.

What initially surprised me was that very few villagers, except chiefs, are called by their "true" ancestral names. If Trobrianders have such an elaborate biological and cultural explanation for securing matrilineal identity at conception, why then is a person's ancestral name so seldom used in daily social interaction? When a child is born, its father asks his sister to find an ancestral name from their matrilineage. In practice, a child is usually called by this name that it receives from its father. The bestowal of the name, however, is only a loan, and at no time can the child pass the name to her or his own child. Only women give ancestral names to their children, which their daughters in time may pass on to their children. The names women give to their brothers' children are regarded as their matrilineal property, which must be returned. The circulation of ancestral names illustrates the other side of matrilineality. A child has inalienable rights to an ancestral name and, as we will see later, other property from his or her matrilineage; but through his or her father, the child holds use rights in property from the father's matrilineage. So important is the circulation of a man's matrilineal property that a man's gifts to his children establish intimate bonds with them.

The significance of this paternal tie is directly incorporated into procreative beliefs. Trobriand kinship, for example, is based on two concepts that are exemplified by two stages in pregnancy. The first concept defines matrilineal descent as an identity that is unalterable through time; it is illustrated by the belief that in the first stage of pregnancy a woman conceives exclusively by an ancestral spirit from her own matrilineage. The second concept involves the necessity to use property from another matrilineage, thereby making connections with members of that matrilineage, which can have important potential for the future. In this way, a child's father's matrilineal kin add to what the child already gains from its own matrilineal identity, strengthening what the child is and will become. The second stage of pregnancy, that after conception, reveals the importance of patrilateral kin. Trobrianders believe that following conception, frequent sexual intercourse helps to develop the fetus. Whereas a woman is therefore responsible for the co-mingling of her blood (*buyai*) with a *waiwaia* spirit child, thus making the infant a "true" member of her matrilineage, her husband builds up and nurtures (*kopoi*) the fetus through intercourse without compromising its "true" (*mokita*) matrilineal identity.[2]

A man, then, supplies the fetus with something more than its own inherited matrilineal substance, but his contribution does not in any way alter the basic physiological connection between a woman's blood and a spirit child. A man is not a member of his child's matrilineage, and his help in the growth of the fetus implicates his matrilineage in his child's future rights and obligations. Therefore, a man's part in his child's procreation is publicly acknowledged when he gives his offspring a name from his own matrilineage, but this is done only if he and the pregnant woman are married. For example, when Sara, an unmarried young woman, became pregnant, the role that her lover played in her pregnancy was not given public acknowledgement. Their relationship could not be discussed openly because recognition of her lover's role would make it necessary for him to meet certain obligations to his child. Not only are these his own personal obligations of care and love, but they also involve the property of his matrilineage and mutual obligations on the part of other members of his matrilineage and of Sara's matrilineage.

Consequently, a socially unrecognized or unacceptable man's procreative role in the pregnancy of his lover must be ignored, so that after the birth the child or its kin cannot make any demands on the members of his matrilineage and vice versa. Sara's pregnancy was ignored by everyone. She and her baby continued to live with her parents, and no one spoke publicly about her being

[2] Since Malinowski (1916; see also 1929) first wrote about Trobrianders' beliefs that a man made no physical contribution to his child, the question of whether or not Trobrianders were truly ignorant of physical paternity has been the subject of extensive anthropological debate. Did Trobrianders think that spirits could cause a woman to conceive and that sexual intercourse played no role in pregnancy, as Malinowski reported (see also, for example, Spiro 1968; 1982), or were these ideas only abstract theories that no one actually believed, as Edmund Leach (1966; 1967) argued? Each position, however, misses the important distinction that Trobrianders make between conception and pregnancy, which illustrates the complementarity between the roles of women and men in procreation.

husbandless or about her child being "fatherless." Yet the situation was not without emotion. Sara told me that she and her kin felt "deeply shamed." The shame, however, was not for herself but for her daughter. A child without a father, even though it will be well taken care of by its mother and matrilineal kin, is socially disadvantaged. Not to have a father is to lose the social potential to be gained from the kinship ties he makes available. To be "fatherless" is to be denied a socially essential part of oneself.

When a married couple has a baby, the claim to the father's contribution is so important that it is not only expressed as necessary to the growth of the fetus but also represented at birth by noting the physical similarities between infant and father. After Naseluma's baby was almost two months old, she left the seclusion of her mother's house and returned to her husband. This was the first time that villagers had a chance to see the baby. When they did, they commented on how much the infant's features resembled its father's. No one mentioned that the baby looked like Naseluma.[3] In fact, to say such a thing is a dangerous insult that will never be forgiven or forgotten and could even lead to fighting. In the case of Sara's "fatherless" baby, there was no public discussion about whom it resembled, although in private I heard how much it looked like its mother's former lover.

A FATHER'S CARE

Trobriand babies receive an abundance of attention. Kissed, hugged, teased, and fondled, they are cradled constantly in their parents' and other villagers' arms. Women and men, young and old—even children—interchangeably become caretakers, lavishing continual affection on their small charges. Mothers nurse their infants on demand, never allowing them to cry if hungry. Men with young children walk around the village holding a baby or toddler straddled on their hips, often with another child in tow. Even very old men, who stay in the village while everyone else is working in the gardens, look after their grandchildren in this way.

In Trobriand eyes, however, public responsibility for the economic care of the child falls to its father. His capabilities and commitment to provide his children with food and wealth are observed by his wife and her kin and other villagers as well. No one can coerce a person into working hard, nor can anyone make demands of someone who elects to be lazy, but public recognition of a man's behavior in this regard is expressed in ways that have political consequences. It is therefore rare not to see men working hard for their small children, chopping firewood in the bush, buying fish in Losuia, catching small fish along the reef at night, growing yams and sweet potatoes in the garden, and occasionally butchering one of their few chickens or pigs.

[3] Because Malinowski (1929:173–177) believed that Trobrianders had no knowledge of physical paternity, he found their insistence that children looked like their fathers to be contradictory.

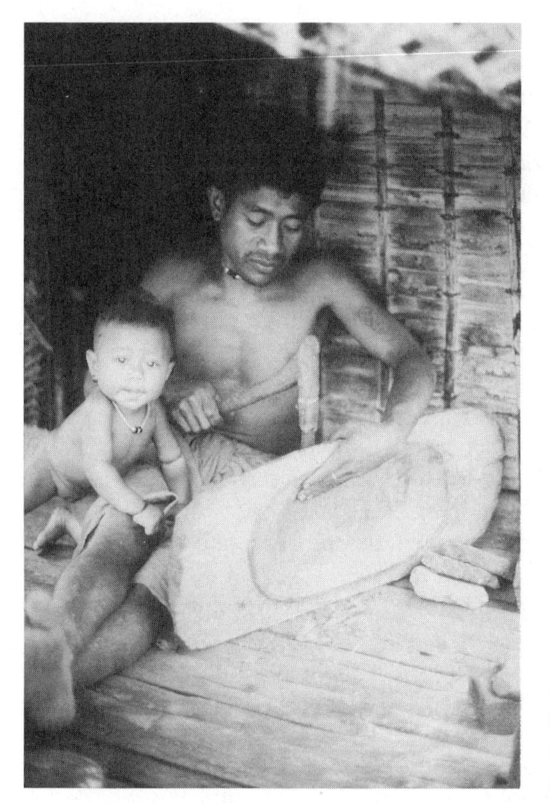

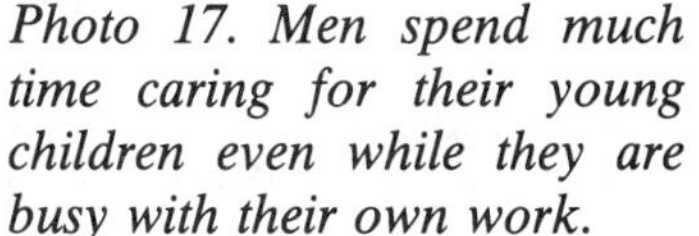

Photo 17. Men spend much time caring for their young children even while they are busy with their own work.

Long before Naseluma stopped nursing her baby, her husband was feeding his son yams and fish and, occasionally, even a taste of mashed betel nut. Weaning occurs abruptly when the mother simply leaves her baby in the care of others for a few days. This loss of physical closeness with the mother is immediately replaced by the father. Once a child is weaned, it sleeps with its father.

Men not only must provide food for their children but also are responsible for enhancing their children's beauty. When an infant is only a few months old, is still naked, and only beginning to eat a bit of yam, the baby is decorated with shells by its father to make it socially "beautiful." Of course, physical beauty is recognized, especially as children grow and begin their adolescent adventures of sexual liaisons and seductions. Light, unblemished skin is an important attribute, as is a round, smooth face; full but not bulging lips; and a nose that is not too broad or too long.[4] Beauty magic, discussed in the next chapter, is used extensively to enhance a person's facial features.

When an infant is born, however, shell decorations add new potential to the baby's social beauty. A few shell decorations may seem insignificant, yet

[4] See Malinowski (1929:288–303) for more details about physical beauty.

they symbolize the first important political step in a child's life. During a baby's first year its father tries to obtain a necklace of red *Chama* shells,[5] which, ornamented with a few black, dried banana seeds in the center, is fastened around the infant's neck. These necklaces (*kuwa*) are very valuable if the tiny shell discs are thin and uniformly polished. Color is also a distinguishing feature of a fine necklace since the shells that are a pale reddish-pink are more prized than dark red ones.[6] Access to these shells is difficult, for there are only a few islands in the southern Massim where men still grind and polish them. Today it is not uncommon to see children wearing necklaces that look like traditional *kuwa* but, on close examination, turn out to be imitation plastic.

The prestige attached to a particularly fine necklace comes from its relation to *kula* shells. The *Chama* discs tied around a baby's neck are the same shells used to make the long, elaborately decorated necklaces (*soulava* or *bagi*) that men from different islands exchange with each other through overseas *kula* voyages (see Introduction and Chapter 9). If a man is the owner of a few of these highly valued *kula* necklaces, he may take one apart and restring it into the shorter *kuwa* necklaces for his children.

To give his child a highly valued necklace, a man either must be powerful enough to own *kula* necklaces or, if he is unable to travel to where the shells are made, know other men who will find such shells for him. Because shells are ranked according to their value, the kind a man has indicates his wealth and his political connections with other men. When a child wears a necklace, its value is attached to the child as a representation of not only the child's father's political worth but the political potential of the child as well.

Before a necklace is given to an infant, however, its father must first present his child with tiny tortoise-shell earrings. This is an easier task than finding a *kuwa* necklace because the techniques for polishing the tortoise-shell rings are known by many villagers. For a girl, however, the earrings are elaborated by addition of flat red *kaloma*-shell discs fastened to the tortoise rings. These discs used to be made in the southern part of Kiriwina, but they are no longer produced there and they, too, must be found elsewhere in the Massim. Earrings are valued according to the number of shells inserted in the earlobes, and as children grow, more rings are added. Today, although many older boys have routinely stopped wearing earrings, they may put them on again when dressed in traditional style for the festivities during yam harvests.

For many years the mission teachers considered the wearing of earrings by children an unhealthy practice and tried to stop it because it tends to elongate the earlobes. Old people often have dangling split lobes, the result of pressure from too many shells. The missionaries probably never understood the deeper symbolic significance of earrings, for to Trobrianders they represent much

[5] Malinowski (1922) reported that these shell discs were made from *Spondylus* (thorny oysters), but recently Liep discovered that most of the shell discs probably are from the *Chama pacificus*, a different subclass than *Spondylus*, both from the class Bivalvia (see Liep 1983:85–86).

[6] For an excellent discussion of the principles of ranking *kula* shells see Campbell (1983a: 229–248).

more than ordinary ornaments. Like the necklaces, earrings are recognized as signs of a man's wealth and of his presence in the life of his child. If its ears are not pierced, a child is called *gudukubukwabuya*, an expression that means the child is "fatherless." The term is just as pejorative to a Trobriander as "bastard child" is to an American. If the child has pierced ears but no earrings, people think the child is "poor" (*namakava*).

Before I realized the significance of earrings, I noticed that although Sara's daughter was only six months old, she had more shells thrust into her earlobes than any other child in the village. Yet as mentioned previously, her mother was not married. Sara, with some embarrassment, quietly told me one day that her mother's brother gave the earrings to her baby so that she would not be shamed. Now, at least publicly, no one could point a finger at her daughter and say the painful and humiliating word that means you have no father.

Wearing earrings and necklaces emphasizes that a baby is indeed socially beautiful. Such attention to beauty is more than cosmetic. In writing about the Kaguru people of East Africa, T. O. Beidelman (1971: 30–31) sensitively noted the important association between the word *cosmetic*, meaning "attractive," and *cosmos*, meaning "the ordering of the world or universe." Both words derive from the same Greek root, and as Beidelman pointed out, the aesthetic element is an essential feature of the way social relations are ordered. Although individuals are constrained in their relations with others, these others provide a constant source of gratification that is both aesthetically and materially important.

For Trobriand children and young people to be made culturally more beautiful means that they have powerful and wealthy relatives. Even for an infant, the potential for social and political advantage is already established through the messages that decorations convey about the infant's father. Without a father, a child must depend on the support of the members of its matrilineage, who help to disguise the true situation. Once a child wears shell decorations, it has entered, if only minimally, into the world of politics.

"HARD WORDS"

The earrings that Sara's baby wore certainly did not fool other villagers into thinking the baby had a father, but the truth of such matters is not appropriate for open discussion. As long as the subject is not mentioned publicly, the situation is of no consequence. Yet no one forgets. If, for example, a man becomes angry at Sara, her daughter, or any of their matrilineal kin, he might scream out the truth in a public debate. The truth would not be that Sara got pregnant without being married but that her daughter has no father. By using these "hard words" (*biga mwau*) he would create a tense situation that would have to be resolved only by fighting, suicide, or sorcery.

Once the true story of a shameful incident is revealed publicly, the words go on record and become a threat that must be answered. At one level, villagers act as if they had great freedom in their behavior. If a woman says she is "tired and does not want to work hard," no one objects or tries to change her actions. Her neighbors simply remark, "We do not know what is in her mind." Yet at another level, this freedom may be sharply curtailed when someone's present practices without warning trigger the occasion for someone else to recall a past "mistake." The circumstances that involve land controversies, adultery, sorcery, or extensive fighting remain part of each person's history, and each shaming incident always encompasses the threatening potential for severe repercussions.

The danger in such confrontations became dramatically clear to me early one evening as I sat in my house chatting with a few neighbors. The situation developed not over Sara and her baby but around a similar use of hard words. On this particular night, Bunemiga, who was regaling us with the story of how he got his new *kula* shell, suddenly jumped up and rushed outside. He returned quickly, demanding that I hurry to the next hamlet. Bulapapa's relative Vincent had an axe and was threatening to kill Michael. Only five minutes before, Michael stood in front of Vincent's house and accused him of using a plot of garden land that belonged to Michael. When Vincent denied the charge, answering that the plot was his, Michael retorted with hard words, shouting, "Bwadala (Michael's mother's sister's daughter) has no father." At this point, Vincent bolted into his house and emerged with an axe. Everyone, including me, followed him as he pushed his way through the people who tried to stop him. In the meantime Michael had gone to the far hamlet to get a spear from his relative's house.

When the two men confronted each other, women and men screamed warnings to them not to fight, but no one got near Vincent. It was the most fearful scene I witnessed during my fieldwork. It seemed for a few minutes that Vincent could not be stopped, that he would smash Michael with the axe unless Michael speared him first. Suddenly, instead of moving in to attack, Vincent allowed himself to be pulled off to the edge of the plaza. Villagers still screamed warnings, and finally he heeded the exhortations yelled at him. Quickly he broke away and ran up the path away from Kwaibwaga to another village, where he stayed for a week. Later Bunemiga told me that if there had not been so much intermarriage among Michael's and Vincent's kin, making them closely related to each other, Vincent surely would have fought.

What the villagers feared most was that a killing would have escalated into more fighting, since Michael's relatives would have demanded retribution. This situation then would affect marriages between many people. From each person's individual perspective, the violent death of either Michael or Vincent would destroy the long-term relationships between their own matrilineal and affinal kin. The potential destruction of so many relationships concerned the children of these marriages even more than the adults. Because of the pivotal role that children play in linking the affinal relationships between the members of their mothers' and fathers' matrilineages, their own future is tied to the

Photo 18. A young girl shows off the decorations given by her father.

lasting strength of these relationships. Children intensify the political negotiations in which their parents are involved. As the example of Vincent and Michael illustrates, villagers know the danger they face when they ignore the claims of others.

A Trobriand child's decorations symbolize the social importance of the child's father's matrilineal kin, but the shells also underscore the fundmental dynamics of Trobriand social interaction. Each Trobriander attempts to seduce others into his or her orbit of social relations. Men engage their children, who later will work hard for them. As later chapters illustrate, chiefs entice followers, *kula* men negotiate for exchange partners, and women attract men who eventually as husbands must work hard for them. Attraction, however, is not easy or automatic. The ability to influence the mind of someone else when the minds of others are perceived to be inviolate must be worked at continually, and not everyone is successful. Physical beauty must be heightened and expanded by the work of others. With the proper magic, even "ugly" faces become handsome. In this way, the cultural construction of beauty depends on the strength of social relationships.

In the next chapter we will look closely at the transition from adolescence to marriage and how each person must learn to play out her or his own desires to attract someone against the often conflicting influences and plans of others. Among young people, their decorations and beauty are not only political statements about their parents' matrilineages but also symbols of their personal sexual powers in the seduction of others.

4/Youth and sexuality

> The system of boy-girl relationships is well defined and regulated here. Everyone knows everything about everyone. Girls, as I already said, start sleeping with boys when they are about thirteen, but the stipulation is she may only sleep with boys from her village and the same is true with boys. A boy from our village had a girlfriend in Diagila village, and he was continually harassed by two girls from our village. I don't even know if harassed is strong enough. The other day they beat him up and cut him with a knife in three places. But the real reason was jealousy.
>
> Linda Weiner

WAITING AND WATCHING

Bulapapa was the first person to tell me about his father. "When I was small," he said, "my father brought me food. He found fish for me and he collected firewood. Now I make a garden for him. I take care of him, because he always took care of me. That man is very good."

When villagers talk about giving, they are talking about caring and generosity. Giving also implies planning for the future; that is, giving expresses not only caring but also intention. Giving things communicates a person's desires and plans, but it also may be an attempt to control others by establishing a debt. A villager who brings yams to someone, in my informants' words, wants "to sweeten his thoughts" or "to turn her mind." Each act of giving is at once a pledge of caring and an act of obligating another person. A villager who presents someone with a basket of yams cannot ask for something in return. He must give and then wait. Perhaps later he gives something else and waits again, hoping that eventually he will receive more than he gave. Yet one villager's plans may not be what another villager desires. The recipient's mind may not be "sweetened" by the giving; he or she may not be persuaded to repay the debt. A degree of chance exists in even the closest kin relationships.

How one feels about someone else should not be expressed publicly with words. To maintain one's autonomy, a villager keeps her or his thoughts about others private, but in the form and style of one's giving are messages about the giver's intention. Ruth told me that if her brother gave her yams that were small and soft, she would know that he did not truly want her to have them. Therefore, her brother spends a great deal of time cleaning each yam and arranging them according to size so that the presentation looks impressive. Ruth then recognizes his intentions and not only tells her husband "what a good man" her brother is but also remembers his efforts for the future. If a villager is angry, annoyed, or distrusts another person, it is poor strategy to express such feelings aloud, for as we saw in the fight between Michael and Vincent in the last chapter, hard words lead to dangerous confrontations.

When a person receives a basket of yams, she or he may be thinking, "Perhaps that person is hiding something from me and did not bring me the best of what he had" or "That man gives me so much, I know he must want me for his friend" or "When that woman brought me food her face looked angry. Maybe she did not want to give me anything." These thoughts remain private, but they provide the basis for waiting and watching. To influence or even to try to control another person is difficult, yet such efforts are a major preoccupation throughout each Trobriander's life.

With young people, the strategies for influencing others are sharply developed during adolescence. For them, however, the means of persuasion are not with yams and other kinds of material wealth because these are controlled by adults. Instead, adolescents learn to deal with the wills and plans of others through their own sexuality. Their abilities to negotiate their sexual desires and seductive intentions are backed by their youthful physical and social beauty, made even more potent with love and beauty magic. Clothes, decorations, even the flowers and herbs thrust into armbands and hair heighten the aura of seduction. For young people, intention is written on their bodies, in their walk, and in their eyes. The shell decorations that are worn point to a young person's social status, and the flowers and the coconut oil enhanced with magic spells, as Bomapota and other women and men said, "make somebody want you."

ADOLESCENT SEXUALITY

By the time children are seven or eight years old, they begin playing erotic games with each other and imitating adult seductive attitudes. Four or five years later, they begin to pursue sexual partners in earnest. Young people change partners often, experimenting first with one person and then another. A rendezvous may be arranged at the beach or in a secluded place away from the gardens and the village, but these are usually brief meetings without any commitment to further encounters.[1] During this time, young people usually do not sleep in their parents' houses. They move to a small house next door or a few doors away, the young boys of the hamlet living in one house and young girls living in another. In this way, they have the freedom of their own sleeping quarters to which they can bring their lovers.

During adolescence, young people are watched by older villagers, who evaluate their potential as productive adults. Is a young woman capable of making fine skirts? Does a young man demonstrate his increasing knowledge of yam cultivation?[2] While older villagers watch and wait for young people to come of age, they also give them great scope for participating in their own activities. Little pressure is put on them to engage full time in adult productive pursuits. Although they help with household tasks, their responsibilities are limited and they have much freedom to pursue their own adventures. Young people are called "small boys" or "small girls" until they are in their thirties. Only when villagers are married, have children, and are fully committed to economic and political endeavors will they be considered adults.

Even while involved in the daily village routine, young people are preoccupied with their own plans and negotiations. Throughout the day, lovers send messages back and forth to arrange evening meeting places. Conversations between young people are filled with sexual metaphors that express a person's intention. Questions such as "Can I have a coconut to drink" or "Can I ride your bicycle?" are Trobriand ways to say, "Will you sleep with me?" Dabweyowa once told me, "Women's eyes are different than men's. When I talk to a girl I watch her eyes. If she looks straight at me, I know she wants me." Young women are just as assertive and dominant as men in their pursuit or refusal of a lover.

On Saturdays it is difficult to find a young person in the village because everyone is either watching a basketball game in Losuia or visiting other villages. The harvest season provides an arena for all-night village dancing, cricket matches, and large feasts, where young people gather and seek new lovers. Even at the distributions of food following a person's death, young people who are not related to the deceased congregate together, wearing their brightest clothes and flowers, joking and teasing each other. Their beauty and excitement stand in sharp relief to the blackened bodies and shaven heads of the mourners.

[1] Homosexual practices between men seem to have occurred only rarely in the Trobriands. Malinowski wrote that such a prohibition "is well entrenched," but he also noted that colonialism "creates a setting favorable to homosexuality" (1929:472–473). During World War II, some of the Allied soldiers stationed on Kiriwina paid young Trobrianders to perform homosexual acts. Even more recently, there have been several cases in which European men engaged young Kiriwina men in homosexual encounters for payments of money and European food. I could find little information about homosexual relations between women. Men never commented on it and women were very vague about specific cases. But young women may willingly engage in prostitution with white male visitors, as they have done for over a hundred years, usually without reproach or disgrace.

[2] Although this is the most common division of labor, there are no taboos on women engaging in yam cultivation. Sometimes a woman even makes a large yam garden for a man.

Both young women and men spend much time in adorning themselves in preparation for walking about. It is important to look attractive and to act in a manner that conveys independence and fearlessness. Often this attitude is carried to an extreme. Several times when I admired the beauty of a young woman from another village, Bomapota shook her head and told me that her beauty was marred because she acted "too proud." Disdain in one's walk and a look in one's eyes that conveys dominance carry the ideal of autonomy too far. Individual arrogance gives a message of overt competitive behavior. A person must learn to be strong without appearing to be competitive. Rather, a person's intentions are carried out covertly through magic spells that explicitly define the intensity of rivalry and the power of seduction, as in the following:

> My flashing decoration, my white skin.
> I will take the faces of my companions and rivals
> And I will win out over them.
> I will show my face, the face of Todarosi
> I will get a compliment tied around my arm
> For my beautiful shining, full-moon face.[3]

Even when a young woman (or a man) is complimented, for example, for her beauty, the compliment must be repaid so that the favored person does not become "too proud." At a dance, Weteli tied a string around Boiyagwa's arm, symbolizing her beauty and talent. Later, Boiyagwa had to give Weteli tobacco and betel nuts as payment for tying the string and publicly drawing attention to success. Even in village events that are obviously rival encounters, winners pretend that they lost. In cricket matches, regardless of the actual score, the host team must always win. In yam competitions, young men are given prizes of money or traditional stone wealth for growing the largest yams. Each winner usually makes a self-deprecatory comment such as "I did not really work hard in the garden" or "I am only a small boy and I do not know much about yams" when he receives his payment.

Even with such controlled attempts to submerge antagonistic and boastful behavior, yam exchanges exacerbate rivalry between villages. Sometimes during the harvest season fights break out because a few young men boasted too much about their big yam gardens. So on the one hand, an adolescent's days are free and much adult energy is invested in creating an easy milieu for sexual explorations; but on the other hand, the freedom accorded young people still has limits set by their peers, which sometimes are severe. Even at an individual level, to turn an initial attraction into a sexual liaison demands more than jokes and glances. Young men must give betel nuts and tobacco to the women they want, expressing their ability to continue to give presents as long as the relationship lasts. Yet a woman may tease a man, accepting these things and flirting but refusing to sleep with him. In seduction, giving is not enough; finally love magic must be used to overcome strong opposition.

[3] See Malinowski (1929:368) for a discussion of the same spell.

SEDUCTION WITH MAGIC

Just as young people cannot become "truly" beautiful without the help of older people, so too, their access to magic spells is limited. Although Kiriwinans believe that no one can make up a new magic spell, many traditional spells circulate widely. The most common way for young people to obtain magic spells is to learn them from their older kin by giving food, tobacco, and money. This giving must be generous and must last for many years if the younger person hopes to learn all his or her mentor's spells. Older people teach the spells by giving away only a few lines at a time. When they die, they may not have taught the full spell or all the magic they knew.[4] Therefore, spells are often lost in part or fully. Many villagers complained to me that a particular magic spell they had was weak because a mother, for example, only taught them part of it and when she died, the rest was lost.

A married woman sometimes may learn very important spells from a lover who is visiting from another island. The man gives the spells because he loves her very much and wants to give her more than betel nuts or tobacco. Magic spells may also be bought from others. When men travel to other islands, especially on *kula* voyages or to work in Port Moresby, they often return with magic spells they have purchased while away. Today, those villagers who are literate write their coveted magic spells in copy books, which they hide in the house's rafters or in a locked trunk.[5]

The words for beauty magic are chanted into coconut oil, which is then rubbed on the skin or into flowers and herbs that decorate armbands and hair. The spells are directed toward heightening the visual and olfactory effects of a person's body to create erotic feelings on the part of a lover. Certain spells are thought to make a person become so beautiful that even those recognized as physically ugly appear handsome in the eyes of the woman or man who wants them. This special beauty magic is recited while a pearl shell is passed over the person's face so that the face will take on the white, shiny qualities of the shell, making the person strikingly enticing. These spells, however, are not the property of young people but are practiced by women who use them only on their brothers' children. The performance of such magic links each young person to his or her father's sister in an important way: "Truly, Bogunuba is very good to me, because she made magic with a pearl shell for me when I was small."

[4] When a person who was known to have many magic spells dies, a ritual takes place after the burial. Each person who formerly received a spell from the dead person now publicly recites part of it, thereby showing which of the spells in the dead person's repertoire have been given to others (see Weiner 1976:70–72) for details).

[5] The rate of literacy varies within each village. The Methodist Mission, the Sacred Heart Catholic Mission (established in 1936), and the government each have small elementary schools on Kiriwina. Many young people have had at least a few years of primary schooling, although education is not compulsory; in 1981, only four Kwaibwaga children attended elementary school. Until a government high school was opened in 1982, all children wanting to go beyond sixth grade were sent to boarding schools in other areas.

Photo 19. No dancer would perform without first rubbing his body with sweet-smelling coconut oil prepared with magical chants to make his body glisten in a seductive way.

When young people reach their mid-teens, their lovers' meetings take up most of the night, and a new affair may last for several months or longer. About this time, some seriousness may enter into these meetings, for within a few years, marriage will be the next important step. To find someone for a long-term relationship is much more difficult than having a brief liaison at the beach. Small gifts and beauty magic will not be forceful enough to seduce the person one wants. As discussed earlier, Trobrianders believe that each person's mind is inviolate. No one professes to know what another person is thinking or why someone makes a decision in a particular way. Even politically, a person cannot demand that others follow one's desires or plans. To project one's own will over someone else necessitates exercising control over another person's feelings. For these reasons, young people may find it expedient to resort to the most powerful kinds of magic spells, known and practiced by only a few adults, who must be paid for their skills. So potent are these spells that villagers warn, "Be careful; it will destroy your mind." When the spell takes effect, the person will refuse to eat or listen to the advice of others and will do nothing but long for her or his lover.

The words of the strong love spells are chanted into betel or tobacco, the very things that continually are given back and forth among everyone.[6] In

[6] When a man decides that he wants a woman for his "good friend," he begins to send her small presents such as betel nuts and tobacco, using other young people as intermediaries. When my daughter Linda lived with me in Kwaibwaga, without my knowledge she acted as a messenger, relaying betel nuts and information between Ruth and Sylvester about their secret meeting plans.

order to "destroy someone's mind" this agent, that is, the betel or tobacco, must transmit the words to the person. Therefore, to take effect, the agent must be ingested or inhaled. The force of the words is thought to enter a person's body so that the spell controls his or her thoughts. In this way, a person's autonomous behavior is interfered with by the will of another.

Of course, the spell may fail. The words may not have been strong enough, and the lover may seek another expert who has access to spells thought to be even more powerful. In some cases, because the expert was not paid enough, he or she deliberately may not have chanted the words for the necessary length of time. Trobrianders believe that the agent carrying the magic only becomes effective when the words are chanted again and again throughout the night or for several days so that the betel nut or tobacco absorbs its power from the act of speech itself.[7] Therefore, additional payments finally may produce success. Yet counters to this magic exist: For example, when a woman (or a man) finds herself totally lost in her longings for the man who wants her, a relative who knows an equally powerful magic spell may be able to remove the debilitating effects of the original spell. Even under the best circumstances, however, a suspecting woman simply may refuse the betel nut and remain free to choose someone else. In the final analysis, even the most formidable love magic can be averted, making love relationships as full of chance as any other relationship.

Attracting lovers is not a frivolous, adolescent pastime. It is the first step toward entering the adult world of strategies, where the line between influencing others while not allowing others to gain control of oneself must be carefully learned. The procurement of magic spells "that destroy someone's mind" leads to dangerous actions because effective spells collapse a person's autonomy and establish control over the other person's thoughts. Sexual liaisons give adolescents the time and occasion to experiment with all the possibilities and problems that adults face in creating relationships with those who are not relatives. Individual wills may clash, and the achievement of one's desires takes patience, hard work, and determination. The adolescent world of lovemaking has its own dangers and disillusionments. Young people, to the degree they are capable, must learn to be both careful and fearless.

CHOOSING ONE LOVER

When a young woman begins to meet the same lover again and again and rejects the advances of others, the affair takes on a measure of seriousness and everyone believes that strong love magic has been used. She spends the night with her "good friend" in his house. She must enter the house after dark and leave before other villagers awake and begin to congregate on their verandas. The first cock's crow, just before daybreak, is a signal to all lovers

[7] For a more extended discussion of magic spells and their power see Weiner (1983a); see also Malinowski (1922; 1929; 1931; 1954) and Tambiah's analysis (1968; 1973).

that they must part. It is imperative that no one see lovers entering or leaving each others' houses. Several times I noticed that Mary was missing in the morning. She told me later how she slept too late in her lover's house and then had to wait until midday, when everyone was working in the gardens, before she could slip out of the house unnoticed and return to Kwaibwaga. Yet most Kwaibwaga villagers knew where Mary was spending the night.

A sensuous part of lovemaking is to bite off a lover's eyelashes or put scratches on each others' backs. Villagers watch for these signs, and then the news that Mary or her lover "lost their eyelashes" spreads rapidly. News such as this is gossip; no public statements about Mary's "good friend" can be made until they decide to marry. If Mary and her friend happened to be at the same village feast, they cannot share their food. Although there are no taboos on chewing betel or smoking together, lovers must never eat food in the company of one another. When Mary was trapped in her lover's house because she overslept, she had nothing to eat until late that day. Although lovers must hide the fact of their lovemaking and follow certain prohibitions, their liaison is being discussed discreetly by many interested parties. Peer constraints, however, may upset the privacy of the relationship. Jealousy is the most common problem. A confrontation suddenly may flare up because two young girls want to sleep with the same young man or vice versa.

On one occasion, Esther began sleeping with the young man that Ruth had been meeting each night. The problem was exacerbated because Ruth and Esther called each other "sister."[8] One late afternoon, the controversy escalated into a public dispute when Ruth's anger got out of control: She screamed abuse at Esther and hit her for sleeping with her friend. That night a hamlet meeting took place, bringing great shame to Ruth's and Esther's matrilineal kin. Esther was accused by her mother's brother of acting like "a dog," an animal who cannot tell the difference between good food and rubbish because she sleeps with anyone, regardless of her kin relations. The meeting went on for about an hour, with many relatives making speeches about how the two should work hard learning to make women's wealth like their mothers instead of fighting over boys.

On another occasion, Claire's lover began sleeping with a young woman from another village. Early one morning, Claire and a few of her girlfriends hid along the bush path before sunrise and attacked him as he hurried back to Kwaibwaga. They cut him with their knives in several places on his arm and shoulder. Because the woman he slept with had no relatives in Kwaibwaga, the incident passed without public notice. He, however, stopped seeing his distant friend and continued his relationship with Claire. In another case, Lily, a young Kwaibwaga woman, was visiting Omarakana village every night to sleep with her new friend. Her former Kwaibwaga lover got angry that she was sleeping with someone from another village. He and some other

[8] Although they were not "true" sisters, their mothers were sisters, which in anthropological terminology made them "parallel cousins." When two villagers call each other "sister," even if one of them is adopted or is a parallel cousin twice or three times removed, they both assume a sibling role with each other. This is a characteristic feature of Crow Kinship terms.

Kwaibwaga boys talked about fighting with her, but finally they did nothing. Her lover was Chief Vanoi's relative, and the Kwaibwaga boys were intimidated by Vanoi's power.

The choice of a lover can be difficult, and at times, one's freedom to have the person one wants is curtailed by public reprimands and peer retaliation. Certain limits are imposed on adolescent sexual behavior even though it may appear that boundaries and rules do not exist. High status and rank provide added support for exerting one's will, but even young people who are members of chiefly lineages face rejection. Magic remains the strongest support and also the most deadly obstacle. As young people get older, however, and their interests turn to marriage, their independence becomes more restricted. Not only peer pressure but also adult interference is more prominent because marriage is about adult productive concerns.

LOOKING FOR A SPOUSE

Whenever a man thinks that his son is becoming serious about a particular woman, he decides whether or not the woman is an appropriate choice. When Mark wanted to marry Mary, his father warned him that she was not a good worker, that she was lazy, and that he did not want Mark to marry her. He had another woman in mind for his son, so Mark followed his father's decision. A few years after his marriage, Mark told me, "Anna, I will always remember Mary. Whenever I see her on the Main Road, I always stop and give her betel nuts or some tobacco." Mark is a talented guitar player and he composed a beautiful, sad song about unrequited love.

In most cases men like Mark follow their fathers' advice and do not marry a first or even a second love. Despite all the emphasis on beauty and love magic during adolescent years, marriage is rarely considered only as a love match. It is an important political step that involves not just the two young people but many other villagers as well. Through each marriage new affinal alliances are formed or old ones are reestablished between the members of the new husband's and new wife's matrilineages. It is men as fathers who provide the critical link in these alliances since the marriage of a man's children has important political consequences for him.

To understand the kin and affinal connections that are linked through each marriage, it is important first to understand the *kumila*, a matrilineal clan composed of many matrilineages. In the Trobriands, as discussed in Chapter 2, each person born is a member of his or her mother's matrilineage (*dala*), tracing descent through women to named ancestors. Each person at birth is similarly a member of his or her mother's clan (*kumila*), but unlike matrilineages, there are no clan ancestors. Clans and lineages have different functions; a clan is not, as Malinowski reported,[9] merely a larger representation of a

[9] Malinowski (1922:71–72) glossed *dala* as "sub-clan" and *kumila* as "clan," and conflated the important differences between the two by assuming that the subclan was a local division of the clan.

lineage. Unlike matrilineages, of which there are hundreds, there are only four Trobriand clans: Malasi, Lukuba, Lukwasisiga, and Lukulabuta. Each clan has its own set of identifying totems, such as a particular animal, bird, tree, or flower, but it owns no property in common—for example, shell decorations, land, magic spells, or other valuables—nor does it have a specific place of origin, as a matrilineage does. Consequently Trobriand matriclans are of little overt economic importance to their members, who never unite for a specific cause or event. When discussions occur about clan membership, no one uses the expression "same blood," for this refers to lineage membership.

Yet so unchangeable is a person's clan identity that villagers believe the lines on a person's palms can show the clan to which one belongs. In the beginning of my fieldwork, whenever I visited a village that was new to me, someone always asked to see my hand to check my clan membership. At first, I thought curiosity made villagers want to identify me in this way. Later I learned that when a person travels to a village where he or she has no matrilineal kin or affines, the only villagers that can be asked for food are those who belong to the same clan.

Clans are also important in helping to distinguish whom a person can and cannot marry. Clans are exogamous; that is, a mate must be a member of another clan. Occasionally, two people do marry who belong to different lineages within the same clan. No one mentions this fact because marriage within the same clan is considered incestuous; public mention of such a case not only is considered shameful but may lead to fighting. When I was collecting genealogies, I was warned by my close friends not to question certain villagers about their clan membership because of their endogamous marriages within a clan. Clan membership, however, plays a more far-reaching role than the establishment of exogamous marriages rules. The best marriage for any villager to make is to marry someone who is a member of her or his *father's clan.*[10]

For example, Dabweyowa, a member of matrilineage A and the Lukwasisiga clan, married a woman who belongs to matrilineage C in the Malasi clan. Dabweyowa's father is a member of matrilineage D in the Malasi clan. By marrying this woman, Dabweyowa provides the link between the members of the two matrilineages, D and C of the Malasi clan which, as we shall see, has important consequences for his father. Dabweyowa's wife's mother and mother's brother are now related to his father almost as if they were members of the same lineage. They call each other *keyawa*, which means "like the same matrilineage," for the word *yawa* is a synonym for *dala*, the more common term for matrilineage. When visiting, villagers who are *keyawa* to

[10] Malinowski (1929:86–87) reported that informants told him that a man should marry his father's sister's daughter, but he found that no one followed this preference. I was told the same thing and also found that no one married one's true father's sister's daughter. When a man marries a woman from his father's clan, however, he calls her *tabu*, the kin term for father's sister's daughter, and therefore, most marriages do follow the preference that informants talk about. In fact in many cases, ego marries his patrilateral second cousin (see Weiner 1978b).

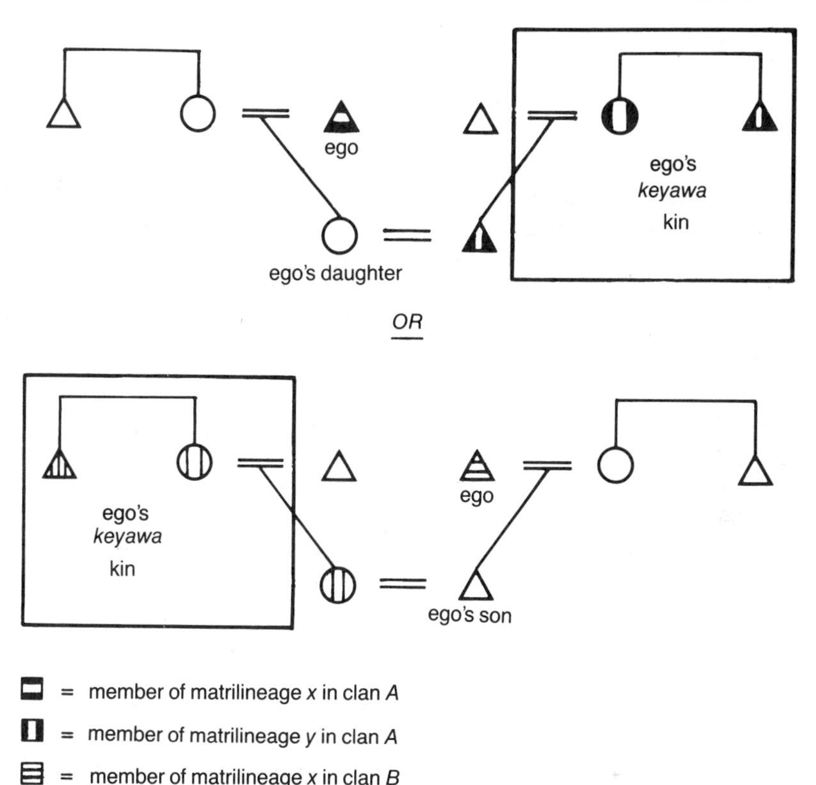

Figure 4. The clan relationships between a male ego and his keyawa *kin.*

each other are obligated to do much more than give each other food. They now must help each other when either needs to give away yams and other kinds of wealth for important exchanges. These *keyawa* kin, as Chapter 8 illustrates, are especially vital to the massive transactions of women's valuables that take place after someone dies. Therefore, a man's choice of a spouse is watched over very carefully by his father. If a man marries a woman in his father's clan, his children also will be members of his father's clan and the same close relationship between his father's matrilineage and his wife's will continue through his children into the next generation.

Figure 4 diagrams how these *keyawa* relationships are constituted and also illustrates how a man has the same opportunity for creating *keyawa* kin when his daughter marries. For example, if Ipukoya represents the ego's daughter in the figure, and she marries someone who is a member of the same clan as her father, her husband's mother and mother's brother will be *keyawa* kin to him. Each marriage with a spouse from ego's father's clan gives ego's father new close kin relationships with villagers who are members of different matrilineages within the same clan. With a daughter, however, a man cannot be as direct in discussing her choice of a husband because of the taboos associated with incest. An incest taboo prohibits sexual intercourse between a woman and her father or her brother, but the taboo equally prohibits a woman's father or her brother from having any discussion with her about her love affairs. Nor can other villagers say anything to either man about his respective daughter's or sister's sexual relationships. In the hamlet debate over Ruth and Esther, villagers felt even greater shame because both girls' fathers and all their brothers had to leave the village while the meeting took place. It was the burden of their shame that these men had to be privately told of the offense, so they could leave, that made the situation so unfortunate.

Initially it was difficult for me to recognize how deeply these taboos are felt and how far-reaching the restrictions extend. Once without thinking, I asked my neighbor, Helen, what girl Jacob was sleeping with, forgetting that Jacob was her parallel cousin and that their relationship was the same as if they were "true" siblings. When she heard my question, Helen stood up and without saying a word walked out of my house. Helen's mother finally explained that my mistake was so terrible that if I had not been "new," Helen would never have spoken to me again. After that incident, I was repeatedly reminded to be careful in my conversations each time two people visited me who called each other "brother" and "sister."

The sister-brother incest taboo is the most serious rule about social relations that exists in the Trobriands. Not only is the rule about mentioning sexual matters in front of a brother and sister an intensely dangerous one to break, but also infringement of the sister-brother sexual incest taboo is perceived to be so horrifying that its occurrence in a famous myth forced the couple to commit suicide.[11] Yet as the next chapter illustrates, the social relationship between a woman and her brother is extremely close. Once they each find a spouse, their relationship provides the foundation for a strong matrilineage. Even though a woman's marriage has great consequences for her brother as well as for the other members of her matrilineage, her brother plays no role in discussions and decisions about selecting a spouse. He only learns of the marriage after it happens, when his mother privately tells him. On hearing the news, he remains in his house or leaves the village and goes alone to the beach or into the bush for a day or two because he is shamed that his mother had to tell him about his sister's lover, even though she now is married.

The rule of incest between a woman and her father, however, follows a different pattern. Stories of sexual relations between a father and daughter are widely known, and villagers make fun of the men who found themselves overwhelmed by the beauty of their daughters. In fact, one of the songs chanted at cricket matches is about "the mistake" a father made when one night he entered his house in the dark and thought his daughter was his wife. He was ridiculed as "crazy" rather than ostracized because the incest taboo

[11] See Malinowski (1929:310) for a recounting of the myth.

between fathers and daughters is far less rigid than that between a sister and brother.[12]

Just as the incest taboo for a woman and her father is more loosely perceived, so too is a man's response to his daughter's marriage not at all like that of her brother. Politically, as discussed, it is to a man's advantage to have his daughter marry someone who is a member of his clan so that her husband's mother and mother's brother will become *keyawa* kin to him. A young woman's marriage is also of paramount importance to her matrilineage because once she has children, especially girls, the continuity of the lineage and its connection with ancestors is assured, as is a future economic base for matrilineage events. For these reasons, her mother and her mother's brother have a primary interest in her choice. A girl's mother plays the central role in decisions about her daughter's marriage. If she disapproves of her daughter's choice, she argues that "the boy is lazy and ugly." Until the couple tries to announce their marriage, she cannot, however, stop her daughter from continuing to sleep with him.

EATING YAMS TOGETHER

In the Trobriands, there is no traditional marriage ceremony. One day, instead of leaving her lover's house before sunrise, the young woman stays in his hamlet. In the morning, the two sit together and wait for the bride's mother to bring them cooked yams. The reason that such a strong taboo exists about lovers being seen together in the same house or eating food together is because these acts make a marriage official. The news that a couple is sitting on the veranda travels quickly, and only then do the girl's parents know that she wants to be married.

If the girl's mother and mother's brother approve of her choice, her mother quickly cooks yams and carries them to her. When she and her lover eat these yams together, the marriage is officially recognized. If the young woman's kin disapprove of the choice, her mother and father hurry to the hamlet and demand that their daughter leave with them. If the young woman refuses to go, they pull her out of the house and drag her away from the village. Yet the girl can still have the final word. In one such situation, I was told how one girl, Isupolu, stayed inside her parents' house like a widow, crying and refusing to eat any food until they acquiesced. In another case, the young girl Weteli finally agreed to marry a man that her mother chose, but she was so unhappy that after two months she ran away from her husband and returned to her own hamlet. Often, if a woman is determined to marry her original choice, she can arrange a secret meeting with him. Then together they go to the beach and live there for several days. Once they live openly with each

[12] Sexual relations between a woman and her son are also considered incestuous and no one ever recounted any incidents to me. Malinowski's (1926b) reports agree with mine that only brother-sister incest is deeply tabooed and feared. See Spiro (1982) for a reinterpretation and Weiner (1985) for a rebuttal.

Photo 20. Naugwayawa tries on the new skirts given by her husband's sister so they can be cut to the proper length for a married woman.

other, their parents must accept and respect the marriage. Even chiefs, whose marriages are arranged for political alliances, enter into some marriages for love in just this way.

On the day that a marriage is announced, after the couple eat yams together, the young man's sister brings three long skirts to her new sister-in-law. First she ties each one around her brother's wife's waist, and then with a knife she cuts the fibers until the length is just below the knee. No longer can the woman wear the short, provocative miniskirts that adolescents wear. Her days of adolescent sexual freedom are gone. Both she and her husband take off their red shell necklaces, for to continue to wear them indicates that they are still looking for lovers.

Gaining lovers is not merely a frivolous adolescent pastime. It is the first step toward entering the adult world of marriage; and as we will see later, it is no accident that on the first day of married life, yams and women's skirts figure centrally as the symbols of a couple's changed status and their life ahead. By analyzing the details of adolescent sexuality we begin to understand the kinds of constraints and limitations placed on individual behavior at the very time that individuals must come together in marriage. The struggle between individual independence and the demands of others is clearly articulated in the way magic is used to influence and seduce someone. Sexual freedom and independence of choice run counter to jealousy, pride, and the emotions of others. So important are the lessons adolescents learn about negotiating their intentions and desires against the will and longings of others that even as adults they return from time to time, as we will see, at harvests, in political endeavors, and even in the reversal of mourning taboos, to draw on the power of beauty and sexuality. After marriage, as the next chapter illustrates, sexual freedom is curtailed, but the style of social and political interactions for women and men remains the same.

5/Marriage and the politics of yams

When you are married you just go to live in your husband's house. Your parents then bring food, which in our terms, makes it official. The girl does not cook for one year, and this year is more of a trial. She can if she is hit or unhappy at any time go back to her own family. . . . Babies are said to come from Tuma, an island off of Kiriwina, which is where the soul goes when someone dies—although because the younger people have had some schooling, they don't really believe in it anymore. They still consider it a possibility though.

Linda Weiner

YAM GARDENS

One morning in early June, Bweneyeya sent a message inviting me to walk through the newly harvested yam gardens with him. He had a reputation as a fine gardener, and I was pleased to have him for my guide. I photographed the garden plots, each with their single pile of yams protected from the sun by a lean-to enclosure made from woven coconut leaves, and I thought how much everything still looked like the garden photos Malinowski took in 1915.[1] Bweneyeya told me it had been an excellent growing season, and the mounds of yams piled high under his lean-to were imposing. Against the back wall were the seed yams, sorted out for next year's planting. Bweneyeya pointed out that the huge yam heap in the lean-to across the path belonged to one of Chief Waibadi's wives. It was larger even than Bweneyeya's pile of yams, and the biggest yams were circled with white and black paint.

A few other mounds were almost as large, but some had only three or four circular rows amounting to not more than forty or fifty yams. None of these was decorated in any way, indicating that none was for a chief's wife. From Malinowski's study I knew that the yams displayed around me were not owned by the men who cultivated them. Men work arduously to grow yams. Their labor, however, is not for themselves but for others. If a man urgently needs yams because a relative has died, he cannot take any of the yams he has grown for himself. Malinowski, however, believed that the harvested yams

[1] See especially Malinowski (1935, I: Plates 55–57).

Photo 21. Sylvester inspects a huge pile of yams already painted with black and white circles that indicate the yams belong to Chief Waibadi's first wife.

were given "to finance the household" of the gardener's married sister. "It is because of her, for her and for her chidren's maintenance that the annual gift is given" (1935, I:190).[2] As we will see in this chapter and those following, the annual yam harvests are not meant to maintain a woman's children by feeding them. The reason for a man to give yams to a woman ultimately involves women's wealth. First, however, to understand the meanings that the mounds of yams represent as they stand on view in the gardens requires exploring all the many facets of yam production and distribution.

The harvest from most of the yam gardens belongs to particular women, and the garden plots are referred to by their names. Once the yams are on display in their lean-tos, the hard work in the yam gardens is over; during this time, the gardeners compare and appraise each others' productive efforts, and everyone gossips about which women will get the most yams. When it is time to carry the yams from the gardens, each mound is taken to the hamlet

[2] Malinowski reported that these yam gardens were called *urigubu*, but this term only refers to special exchanges of pork and betel nuts, which I describe elsewhere (see Weiner 1976:140). *Kubula* is the term that designates ownership of the mounds of yams in the garden. Someone asks, "whose *kubula* is that?" and the gardener responds, "Naseluma's *kubula*." Men also plant taro gardens for their married sisters, but these gardens are not associated with any formal harvest displays.

where the woman lives and there the yams are stacked in her husband's yam house.

During this time, talk about yams and the forthcoming harvest events inform most conversations. In September, after the new moon, the joy of yam harvests turns once again to the reality of hard work as villagers prepare for the onerous task of clearing new garden plots.[3] An area of overgrown land uncultivated for six or seven years is selected for each garden site. First, with large machetes, villagers begin slashing the weeds, bushes, and small trees, leaving only large trees whose branches they cut off. Then the debris from the clearing is piled up and burned on the garden plot, supplying the soil with needed nutrients, especially nitrogen.

This technique, called "slash and burn" or "swidden" cultivation, is practiced in most tropical environments throughout the world. It is an attempt to re-create the natural cycle of tropical jungles, where the decayed plants keep the soil fertilized. The method is much less labor intensive than hoe cultivation, but it requires extensive land because after a few year's planting, the plot of land must be left fallow. In Kiriwina, fallow time usually lasts from six to eight years. Recent population increases are putting more pressure on land use, and therefore some villagers cut new gardens on land that has not been left fallow for the optimum length of time. This is a poor solution, however, for the harvests from these plots are not as abundant.

Although growing yams is primarily men's work, when the gardens are ready to plant, married couples labor together in the strenuous work of preparing the soil. Early every morning for almost a month, men and women work in their gardens and return home only at dusk, tired and dirty. During the months ahead, as the yam tubers grow underground, the vines must be fastened around tall stakes. The most arduous work executed by the men is to fence the plot to prevent pigs from destroying the vines. Traditionally when making large yam gardens, extensive cycles of magic spells were chanted during each stage of yam cultivation.[4] Even today, certain kinds of magic spells continue to be employed, for example, to direct the yams how to move the soil so their growth will not be impeded by stones, to encourage the luxuriant growth of the vines, to make it rain when a drought occurs, and even to make the soil unattractive so pigs will not dig it up.

In addition to the work of yam cultivation, all men and occasionally women also plant taro gardens and, most important, a general food garden where sweet potatoes, tapioca root, greens, beans, squash, and banana and breadfruit trees are grown. Here no magic is employed, and the gardens are weeded and tended by women. The general garden, except for special occasions, supplies most of the daily food for the family throughout the year. Malinowski never emphasized the importance of the general garden because he thought

[3] In the southern part of Kiriwina, the time for clearing gardens and planting is about a month earlier.

[4] See Malinowski (1935, I and II) for extensive details on gardening techniques and magical spells.

Photo 22. Kilagowola chants magic spells into special leaves so that bush pigs will not break through the garden fences and spoil the growing yams.

that the purpose of the yam gardens was to feed a woman and her children. Of course, with so much attention focused on yam cultivation and the subsequent yam exchanges, one might wonder why villagers get most of their daily food from the taro and general gardens. To answer this question forces us to think about yams as objects other than food. Taken together, the piles of yams standing in the gardens reveal all the important matrilineal kin and affinal connections that dominate each harvest. As we shall see shortly, the yam piles are indicators not only of economic power but of political importance as well.

YAMS AS WEALTH

At the beginning of the harvest, the yams stay on display in the gardens for about a month until, with great ceremony, the gardener takes them to the owner, that is, a woman, where they are loaded into her husband's empty yam house. Early on the day that the yams are carried to the owner's hamlet, the young people come to the gardens dressed in their most festive traditional clothes: faces painted, hair teased, and bodies bedecked with flowers. The conical piles are then dismantled and the yams put into woven baskets. The young people, all of whom are related to the gardener, carry the baskets into the hamlet where the owner lives. As they enter the hamlet they sing out to announce the arrival of the yams, moving their bodies in time to their shouts and thrusting out their hips in a sexually provocative motion.[5] The rituals of bringing the yams into the village dramatically emphasize the relation between yams and sexuality.

The conical piles are re-created in front of the owner's husband's yam house; then, a few days later, the gardener returns to load them into the woman's husband's yam house. Now her husband is responsible for the yams and for repaying the gardener for his efforts. Typically, the day the yam house is filled should be a time of great feasting. The yam house owner provides the gardener and his young helpers with cooked yams and taro and with what everyone is waiting for—ample pieces of pork. Sometimes, however, no pig is killed. It may be that the yam house owner is disappointed in the size of the presentation, he may need a pig for a more important exchange, or he may be angry with the person who brought the yams because of some other problem. At one harvest the men who filled Chief Waibadi's wives' yam houses heard a rumor that the Chief would kill two pigs; but when they arrived in his village, he announced that one of the pigs had run away into the bush and no one could catch it. The men had to be content with one pig. Many wondered if Waibadi really had planned to have two pigs or was instead "tricking" them.

A man's yam house is not always completely filled. Some years a gardener may work very hard and the weather conditions may be excellent, so that a huge harvest results. Other years the harvest may be small because of bad weather, which is usually blamed on someone's magic. Sometimes a poor harvest reflects the gardener's choice not to work so hard. Even on the day when a woman's husband's yam house is to be filled, potential conflict rather then generosity lies just beneath the surface of people's interactions with each other. Overtly, everyone looks festive and happy—the brilliantly costumed young people, the presence of so many yams, and the temporary end of hard garden work—but there is also the danger of unspoken discontent and antagonism.

A man may comment to other villagers, "I was very tired this year and so I could not work so hard in the garden." Actually he may be very angry with the woman's husband. Perhaps the pig the husband killed the year before to repay him for his work in filling the yam house was too small. Maybe several years ago when he worked hard and made a very large yam garden, the woman's husband ignored his labors and did not give him a stone axe-blade, as is the usual custom for exceptional harvests. Both men have a fair amount of autonomy in their relationship, and both continually reevaluate how they

[5] In the film *Trobriand Cricket: An Indigenous Response to Colonialism* (Leach and Kildea 1975), the yam exchanges at the end of the cricket match illustrate the way young people look and act as they bring yams into the village at harvest.

feel about each other. With the yam display at every harvest reflecting the gardener's intent and the woman's husband's resultant full or empty yam house, the state of the relationship between these two men is on display. How the relationship of the two men directly involves the woman who is the titular owner of the yams is fully explored in Chapters 7 and 8.

Once the yam houses are filled, a man who knows the special magic spell to ward off hunger by making people feel full performs it for the hamlet. Malinowski thought it curious that at the time when food is the most plentiful Trobrianders resort to magic so that the yams are not eaten. When Bweneyaya took me through the yam gardens, he told me, "If a man has yams, he can find anything else he needs." When properly stored, yams will last for four or five months before they begin to rot. During that time, yams not necessary for food are used to purchase armshells; red *Chama*-shell necklaces and earrings; betel nuts; pigs; chickens; and other locally produced goods such as wooden bowls, combs, armbands, floor mats, and lime pots. Even some kinds of magic spells may be brought from others by payment in yams.

A yam house, then, is like a bank account; when full, a man is wealthy and powerful. Until yams are cooked or they rot, they may circulate as a limited currency. That is why, once harvested, the use of yams for daily food is avoided as much as possible. Even though today many of the things listed can be obtained with money, cash cannot replace yams for distributions to others following a death, and no amount of money takes the place of yams that are given to a woman's affines when she marries. Death, like hunger, can reduce a couple's stock of yams and interfere with their economic and political plans, but marriage is the foundation on which most of the yam displays and exchanges that take place at harvest time rest.

THE FIRST EXCHANGES AT MARRIAGE

When a couple eats yams together to announce their marriage, the cooked yams they receive from the wife's parents mark only the beginning of the way their future married life will be organized around yam production. First, the wife's parents quickly follow up the cooked yams with a large presentation of raw yams. Since yams are only in abundance from May through September, most marriages occur during these months. The raw yams are brought by the wife's father and her mother's brother. Both men organize the distribution by giving their own yams and adding to the presentation with yams collected from other men who are members of their respective matrilineages.

Meanwhile, in expectation of the yam presentations, the groom's father and his mother's brother, helped by their respective matrilineal kinsmen, have been busy collecting valuables to make up the husband's presentation to his wife's kin and her father. These valuables may include stone axe-blades (*beku*) or occasionally a *kula* shell, both of which have the highest value, or secondarily, if the men have neither of these two objects, they substitute large clay pots (*kuliya*) or money.

The valuables, such as axe-blades and clay pots, are not manufactured in the Trobriands. The stone for making axe-blades, generally referred to as "greenstone," was quarried on Muyua Island to the southwest, and large pieces were brought to Kiriwina and polished by specialists.[6] In the Amphlett Islands, southeast of Kiriwina, women manufacture cooking pots that measure 3 to 4 feet in diameter. The production of these pots has always been sporadic, and the quarrying of greenstone stopped sometime in the last century.[7] To get these valuables men have had to travel to the distant islands where they were made or obtain them through inheritance or exchanges.

The valuables are usually inherited by a man from his mother's brother or, sometimes, from his father. The objects are vital not only for marriages but also at deaths, especially for compensation payments. They are also essential as payments for the use of land, to buy seed yams from other men, and to pay experts who practice important kinds of magic—especially sorcery and the critical rain magic necessary for luxuriant gardens. As these valuables pass from one man to another, the names of their owners become associated with the object and this history adds to its value. Although the recent use of money as part of this category of wealth affords a substitute for traditional valuables, which are always in short supply, it does not carry the same historical associations with individuals and age and therefore has not replaced these deeper values.

The stone-axe blades vary in length, measured according to hand size, hand to elbow, and hand to shoulder. The largest size is rare, but these stones carry the most fear when they are presented to someone because they are used as payments for sorcery and as compensation payments when someone is killed. The largest and most prized axes are carried in beautifully carved wooden holders. Of all traditional wealth, giving someone a stone axe-blade is a solemn event. Like a formal contract, it binds the parties in a way that Kiriwinans both respect and, at times, fear.

In marriage exchanges, each person from the bride's side who contributed to the first yam exchange receives a valuable when they are collected by the groom's relatives. These valuables honor the marriage, creating an obligation on the part of the bride's kinsmen to take care of her husband. If, however, a woman rejects her husband, even her husband's kin may actively seek her return. Provided her husband wants her back, they may try to change her mind with strong love magic. If this persuasive technique fails, they visit her kin, offering them another axe-blade in hopes that her mother's brother will convince her to return. But the woman herself makes the final decision. If she is determined to divorce her husband, no amount of coercion can keep her from it. The original valuables are not returned, and the bond between all the parties associated with the marriage exchanges is broken. Distrust and suspicion replace caring and giving.

[6] In geological terms, the stone is dark green hornfelsed tuff or metarhyolite (J. W. Leach 1983a:26).

[7] See Lauer (1971) on pottery production and Seligman and Strong (1906:348–355; 1910: 517–521, 531–534) for more information on traditional axe production.

Photo 23. For the main meal of the day, women peel and then boil yams in trade store pots set over slow burning fires.

A man may also leave his wife, but if he does, no attempts are made by his wife's kin to repair the marriage. They still keep the valuables, but the fear now resides with the husband's kin. In most circumstances, a man leaves his wife to live with another woman. If his kin think that his first wife and her kin are hard workers or consider them to have high status, they may argue with him to return to her. Especially in the latter case, they may fear sorcery. If he finally decides that he wants his first wife back, which often happens, she still makes the ultimate decision as to whether or not she wants him.

The first year of a marriage is the most tenuous. As a marriage continues from year to year, however, divorce is less common, for as discussed later, the exchange relations that bind the couple and their affines become more politically prominent and economically essential. The first year of a marriage is a trial period to discover how well the couple gets along and, equally, how committed their kin are to the marriage. The way the couple eats yams together during this time signals again the significance of yams as a statement about their marriage.

YAMS AND SEXUALITY

During the first year the couple continues to live in the groom's house, which still has no cooking hearth. In the late afternoon, when women prepare the main meal, the groom's mother brings the couple a plate of cooked yams.

Husband and wife sit together and cut in half each yam to share it with each other. They continue to eat their meals in this fashion throughout the year. At the beginning of the next harvest, the groom's mother brings three large stones into the house to set up the hearth. His wife now is responsible for all the cooking, except for butchering and baking pigs in earth ovens and boiling taro pudding, all of which is men's work. The couple, however, never again share the eating of yams; thereafter, they eat separately for the rest of their married days.

By building the hearth, a mother transforms the small house that once was her son's adolescent retreat into an appropriate house for a married couple. Now the marriage begins in earnest; the sexuality associated with adolescence is submerged. From this time on, it is deeply shameful for anyone to refer to the couple's sexual life together. For example, children and young people often tease each other by shouting, "Fuck your mother" or "Fuck your father." But to say, "Fuck your wife" (or husband) to anyone is among the most dangerous verbal assaults. One evening I heard Thomas, a young Kwaibwaga man known for his difficult ways and temper, shout in a fit of rage at his mother's brother, "Fuck your wife!" His mother's brother threatened him so violently that he ran in fear from the village. A week later, some of his friends returned to Kwaibwaga and carried his small house to a village about 5 miles away, where he now lives with a fictive kinsman. Everyone believes that if he had stayed in Kwaibwaga, his mother's brother surely would have killed him.

Although a husband and wife do not eat together, raw yams dominate their life together. While sharing each cooked yam, the couple is waiting out their first year together until they receive the harvested yams cultivated by the bride's father and her matrilineal kin. When this next harvest begins and the hearth is in place, baskets of uncooked yams, this time numbering from fifty to a hundred or more, depending on the amount of valuables the groom's kin originally gave, are brought by the bride's kin and her father. Each man who originally contributed a valuable receives some of these yams to replace his loss. If a woman is married to a chief, her relatives will try to include one or two of the 10- or 12-foot-long *kuvi* yams, like those buried with Chief Uwelasi, that can only be displayed by chiefs.

These huge yams are extremely difficult to grow and demonstrate the knowledge, hard work, and allegiance of those who have the ability to cultivate them. The gardener must find garden areas where pockets of soil provide extensive depth to grow yams of this size. These gardens are usually separate from the regular yam gardens, and only those men who are most renowned for their gardening expertise attempt to grow the *kuvi* yams. Even the regular yam presentations that villagers make for all marriages must be attended to with great care, for the yams address the intention and the interests of the woman's father and her matrilineal kin. The yams also alert everyone to future presentations that will be made every year and will continue to support the most productive aspects of a marriage.

In public, married people never hold hands or touch each other with what

Photo 24. Two men on their way to Omarakana village with an exceptionally long kuvi *yam take a short cut through Kwaibwaga village.*

in American society we would read as signs of affection. Yet for most Trobrianders, marriage establishes an emotional bond that grows through time with the work and obligations that arise out of the necessity and complexity of yam production. With a new hearth in place, a married couple begins their productive lives together. The yams they ate openly, marking their marriage and their sexuality, now are the sign of their public separateness. Yet they are not quite like lovers, who also cannot eat yams together. For a married couple's life is now segmented into a public domain, where they must work for their own and each others' matrilineages and their private, sexual life, which must be kept concealed. Unlike lovers, yams direct and organize their

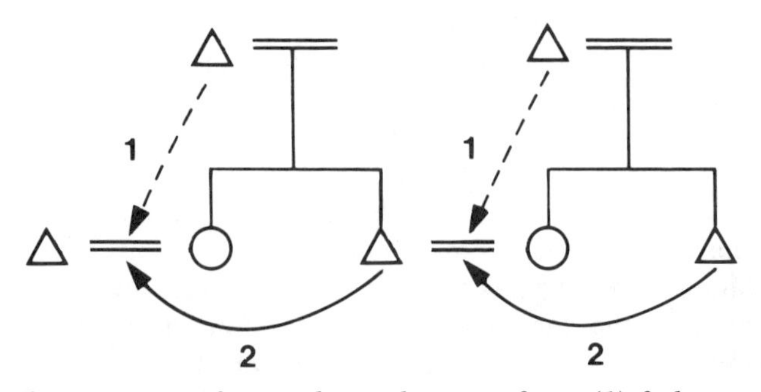

Figure 5. The sequence of annual yam harvests from (1) fathers to their married daughters and their husbands or (2) brothers to their married sisters and their husbands.

life together. This organization gives each of them a separate productive role. Men, by growing yams, and, as we will see in Chapters 7 and 8, women, with the production of their own wealth, make husband and wife independent to some degree. Yet their separation actually is complementary and critically interdependent.

WOMEN AND THE POLITICS OF YAM EXCHANGES

After the first year of marriage, a woman's father makes her a yam garden every year, as indicated in Figure 5. Five to ten years later, when her brother is ready "to work hard for his sister," he takes over his father's obligation, as the diagram also shows. Usually the oldest brother will make a garden for his oldest sister, the next oldest for the next sister, and so on. Adoption and fictive kin relations are quite common, and if a woman does not have a "true" brother, usually another man whom she calls "brother," such as an adopted brother or her mother's sister's son, will work for her. Bomapota had been married for six years, but she had two older sisters so her brothers did not yet make any gardens for her. One day, while thinking aloud about the future, she told me how she always gives things to her brothers when they come to visit. "Even if I only have a little cooked food or a few betel nuts," she said, "I always give what I have. Because I am generous like this, soon one of them will make a garden for me."

Malinowski did not recognize that men made gardens for their daughters, which contributed to his erroneous idea that men were not directly instrumental in their children's married lives. The garden a man makes for his daughter after her marriage usually is small in size unless she married a chief. She and her husband will not have their own yam house for many years, so until that time, the yams they receive are not accompanied with the spectacular displays and rituals associated with the filling of yam houses. Instead, a newly wed man must store his yams in the rafters of his house, enabling the couple to make small presentations at feasts and other important exchanges. Only with time and his own hard work will a young man be able to raise a few pigs or save some money. Eventually he may inherit or purchase a valuable. Except for chiefs, it takes ten or fifteen years before a man is economically successful enough so that his wife's brother recognizes his abilities and begins to grow yams in quantities that necessitate storage in a yam house. Men do not acquire yam houses automatically. Even a chief cannot build a yam house for himself. All men must wait until their wives' brothers decide they will construct it. Consequently, yam houses standing in the hamlet plaza express a significant political accomplishment; some men never achieve this goal.

Annual yam presentations not only represent marriages and economic potential but also the degree of political status that each man has achieved. By the time a man has his own large yam house built for him, his daughter probably will be ready for marriage and he will begin a garden for her, in addition to the gardens he makes for his sister. While a man is growing yams for his sister and daughter, his wife's brother and/or her father is growing yams for him. It is this complex network of men making gardens for their sisters and daughters and, at the same time, receiving harvested yams from their wives's brothers and fathers that forms the basis for all important kin and affinal relationships between women and men. For example, Towdoga, who controls and organizes his hamlet's affairs, now has a large yam house. Each year his wife's brother makes his wife a yam garden. If she needs yams before the yam house is filled, she herself can go to the garden and take them. They belong to her; therefore, even when these yams are stored in Towdoga's yam house, he cannot use them in place of his own garden for his married sister and a smaller one for his married daughter. Towdoga must make each garden separately, presenting each woman and her husband with their own yam display.

Towdoga, however, has other sisters who do not receive yams from him, for a man makes a garden for only one sister. Yet these other sisters also play roles, although more minor, in harvest exchanges. These include Towdoga's younger sisters, those women he calls "sister" who are his mother's sisters' daughters, or adopted sisters. To some of these women Towdoga gives a basket of yams from those that are to be stored in his yam house. The more yams Towdoga receives, the more "sisters" he can supply with small baskets of yams.

The way Towdoga creates this important exchange relationship with a network of "sisters" follows the same pattern of exchanges that takes place at marriages. For example, the first time Towdoga gives his "sister" a basket of yams, she and her husband later give him a valuable, such as a clay pot, money, or a small axe-blade. The yams and the valuable bind Towdoga and his "sister" and her husband into a new productive relationship, just as the valuables given from a groom's kin and the yams given by a bride's kin mark the transition of the married couple into a productive working unit. When Towdoga receives a valuable, he then takes yams each year to this "sister." Towdoga's sister's husband now must work for Towdoga as if they were affines. In Chapter 8, we will examine the importance of this relationship, because skirts and bundles—women's wealth—are connected in a primary way to all yam exchanges that men make to sisters and daughters and their respective husbands.

A man can develop political power only if he has strong support from his wife's relatives, and this support is primarily demonstrated through yam production. When a man reaches his forties, however, he develops a secondary source of yams that enables him to augment the yam garden harvest and the small baskets of yams that his wife's brother loads into his yam house. By then a man's own sons and his sister's sons are grown men, and they contribute in important ways to his additional accumulation of yams.[8]

[8] Malinowski noted that men make gardens for their fathers; but so strong was his conviction that in matrilineal societies men had to work only for their mothers' brothers that he minimized the importance of this garden, describing it as a harvest that a man gives first to his mother's brother, who then presents the yams to his sister's husband (1935, I:191).

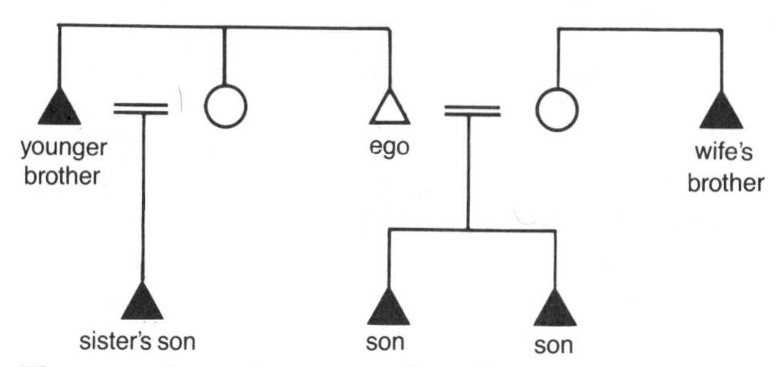

Figure 6. The men who make yam gardens for ego and his wife.

MEN AND THEIR YAM HOUSES

Towdoga, in addition to the yams from his wife's brother, also is given the harvest from yam gardens made by his two married sons, who still live with him in his hamlet, and from his sister's son, who eventually will inherit his position as hamlet leader. Therefore, on the day when Towdoga's yam house is to be filled, four pyramids of yams of varying sizes are displayed before they all are stored away together. Sometimes a man receives yams from his younger brother. For example, Modububuna makes a garden for his married sister, but his yam house is filled with yams given by his wife's father and also by his younger brother. Thus, in addition to the yams men receive from their wives' brothers or fathers, eventually (as Figure 6 indicates) they also may receive yams from their sons, their sisters' sons, and their younger brothers. Although Malinowski (1935, I:190–192) noted that sometimes men grow yams for other men, he thought this exchange occurred only under special circumstances and therefore did not recognize its importance. Unlike the yam gardens made by a man for a woman, those gardens made by a man for another man are not about marriages and affinal relationships. They revolve around rights to land and the political control of a hamlet.

Each matrilineage is associated with hamlet and garden lands that are believed to have been founded by the matrilineage's original ancestors. The origin stories describe sisters and brothers who first came to Kiriwina, either from a cave, out of the ground, or by canoe. Upon arrival they had to search for their own garden lands and a place to build their houses. Not all people came at the same time, and the details of the origin stories are explicit about the members of the matrilineages who came first and those from other matrilineages who came later. Once the ancestors decided on the hamlets' sites, along with the areas of bush and garden lands and, in some cases, beach fronts, these areas became the property of that particular matrilineage. The history of what happened to those lands from the time of the first ancestors is carefully guarded knowledge, kept by the hamlet owner and told to his successor. If there is a dispute over rights to a particular plot of land, those who know the most details of the land's history have the strongest claim to the land.[9]

In each generation, one man, as the head of the matrilineage, controls the land. When he dies, his younger brother assumes his position, until in the next generation the oldest son of his oldest sister inherits control. In practice these lines of inheritance and control often are not so simply executed. Jealousy and a struggle for power between two brothers may sometimes result in the split of a lineage into two segments. In other cases, as described in Chapter 2 with the death of Chief Uwelasi, there may not be any matrilineal heirs and the land is left in the control of a man's son. Even chiefly lineages die out or are replaced through time by another lineage.

When a man knows he is next in line to become the heir, it is still necessary for him to make a yam garden each year for his older brother or his mother's brother, who still controls the land. By giving yams each year, the younger man acts like an apprentice, as he now will learn the necessary secret knowledge about the origins of the land. He also learns the magic spells that are the property of the matrilineage, and when his predecessor dies, he then may inherit stone axe-blades or *kula* shells. None of these things is given to him without payment. If a man works hard for someone older than himself, that person may give him all the knowledge he has of magic and information about land. If he does not work well for yams, or if his mother's brother or older brother is "not generous," he may not learn everything the older man knows. As with magic, men transmit their knowledge "bit by bit," keeping younger men attached to them and working for them. Men sometimes die without passing on the full extent of their knowledge. Such are the limitations of oral traditions.

Only when a man is next in line to take over the control of his own matrilineage does he go to live avunculocally with his mother's brother. This move enables him to watch how his mother's brother (or his older brother) takes care of the hamlet's affairs and gradually to learn the stories and magic spells before his predecessor dies. Most of his younger brothers and the other young men who are members of his matrilineage, such as his mother's sisters' sons, remain in virilocal residence with their fathers after they marry. These men make yam gardens each year for their fathers, thereby fulfilling the obligation they have to their fathers who "took care of them" when they were small. If a man makes a yam garden for his father, when his father dies he will inherit some of his father's personal property, such as a stone axe-blade or clay pots. If he substantially supports the members of his dead father's matrilineage by giving them yams for his father's mortuary distributions, he may continue to live on his father's land and ensure that his own son eventually will have the right to use the same land.

Malinowski thought that because of matrilineal descent and the rule of inheritance, all young men moved from their fathers' houses to live with their

[9] See Weiner (1976:155–167) and Hutchins (1980) for specific stories about controversies over land.

mothers' brothers. Although he recognized that some men made gardens for their fathers, he found this puzzling (Malinowski 1935, I:191), especially because he did not believe that men inherited anything from their fathers. Yam exchanges between men assure that matrilineal control over land will be strongly entrenched generation after generation, but more than matrilineal relationships are involved in the relationships between men. The yam gardens that men make for their fathers create rights to the use of land and other property across matrilineal boundaries. These connections extend further into the next generation as men provide the same rights for their sons' sons. Men work to strengthen their own matrilineage through yam production and to build up resources and political allies through their children's matrilineages. Yam production is directed outward to others who are not related by blood ties. In this way, yams become the object that most frequently crosses lineage boundaries to make individual relationships into vital group support. For as each man creates kinship ties through yams, he is making himself and the name of his matrilineage strong. Yams are the nurturing element that leaves the matrilineage in order to eventually strengthen it, as we will see in later chapters.

A marriage sets into motion the elementary exchanges of yams and valuables that create the beginning of a man's, and eventually a woman's, political destiny. The first marriage exchanges suggest the potential of the relationships among a woman, her husband, and their respective kin. As the years go by, the strength of the marriage can be determined by the size of the yam gardens made for the wife and her husband. These yams are the organizing force behind the long-term obligations among a woman, her brother, and her husband. Just as cooked yams provide the signal that the sexuality between a woman and her husband has become a dynamic force, so too uncooked yams as wealth transform that sexual force into the most important relationships that each person has.

When Bweneyeya told me that a man can find anything he needs with yams, I first thought that he meant all the material things that yams can buy. But yams indicate much more than mere purchasing power, for they are the objects that transmit rights to land, property, protection, and allies. Yams secure places to live and garden land to use. Yams mark the transition from the sexuality of adolescents into the productive and reproductive energy that comes with adult marriage. With yams, villagers no longer need to influence each other only through the beauty of their bodies. The beauty and power of yams now express desire, intention and political seduction. With marriage, the political career of husband and wife begins with the displays of yams marked for them through the labor of other men. Yet that labor is only the beginning; with time, hard work, and the strong continued support of a man's wife and her kin, his political potential is given public recognition when his wife's brother builds him a yam house. That structure documents his generosity and capabilities, what Trobrianders call a man's "good customs." The yam house also proclaims a woman's value both to her husband and to her own matrilineage.

When a man dies, his yam house is dismantled. The productive partnership between husband and wife comes to an end. No one inherits a man's yam house, because its construction grew out of the unique relationship among a man, his wife, and her brother. Yams are food, wealth, and ultimately power. Yet basically, yams represent a weak source of power. Amassing yams depends on the work of others, work that must be repeated year after year. Within each year, yams must be eaten or they rot. No long-term accumulation is possible, and there is no way to escape the gardening cycle and the tie to the labor of others. Men who receive several large gardens from others are politically strong, but their hierarchical position of dominance still demands careful negotiation. They, too, must work continually to influence and "sweeten the minds" of those who labor for them, for such labor may cease at any time. Even chiefs only inherit positions that give them the *possibility* to amass more power than any other men. As we will see in the next chapter, they too are not immune to the exigencies of political loss and to the political role that women play in the lives of all men.

6/Chiefs and hierarchy

After the church service, which was dull, we went to the next village, Omarakana. This is where the two big chiefs live, Vanoi and Waibadi. Vanoi lives in the main part of the village and Waibadi lives in a small section a few hundred yards away with his close relatives. . . . Vanoi is the no. 1 chief and Waibadi is no. 2. . . . Waibadi is just as feared, if not more so. . . . When people not of the chiefs' clan enter into their presence or cross the path of one, they will ask them to rise and walk bent over as a sign of respect. Vanoi was seated on this rather large raised platform made of logs with a swamp grass roof. . . . Waibadi came up later. I wondered what the relationship was between them but I could not really tell.

Linda Weiner

A CHIEF'S VISIT

Immediately upon hearing the news that Chief Vanoi would be my guest, my neighbor Kila came over to supervise the arrangements. When I told him that I planned to serve tea and some English cookies I kept hoarded away in a tin box, he asked if I had any new cups. Tabalu chiefs cannot use dishes that others who are not Tabalu have touched; luckily, I still had a few that I had never used. Kila next decided where Vanoi should sit so that his head would remain higher than mine. He cautioned me that when I boiled water for the tea, I first must ask Vanoi to stand before I could walk in front of him to reach the Primus stove on the other side of the room. I had to remember to bow my head and hunch my shoulders over as I passed Vanoi, acting exactly the way other villagers respond when they are in the presence of a chief.

Only after Kila felt certain that I would not make any mistakes did he relax. If Vanoi were coming to Kwaibwaga for a formal occasion such as a feast or to adjudicate a court case, he would be accompanied by other Omarakana men. Before he entered Kwaibwaga, one of the men would announce the chief's arrival by blowing strenuously into a large conch shell, forcing the shrill sounds to echo throughout the village in the same way as when his yam house is being filled by his wife's relatives. But this was to be an informal visit, so Vanoi arrived alone without heralding. He quietly entered my house and, within minutes, other important Kwaibwaga men crowded into the room.

The occasion was unlike anything I previously experienced in the village. Despite the open sociability—everyone chewed betel and smoked together—a degree of tension permeated the gathering. The deference paid to Vanoi was heightened by a slight undercurrent of fear. The tension was further exaggerated by Vanoi's aristocratic demeanor as he sat upright on my metal patrol box, which made him higher than the rest of us, who were sitting on low chairs or the floor. Slim and straight, he elegantly chewed betel nut, using a lime stick made from a long daggerlike cassowary bone. His lime pot was a novel one, a tall, red Mavis talcum powder can. Each time Vanoi inserted the lime stick into the narrow opening, he deftly rattled the bone rapidly against the sides of the tin to shake off excess lime. The noise, though slight, was riveting, as it made clear Vanoi's stature and separation from the rest of us. No one else may chew from a chief's lime pot, and no one except a chief is permitted to tap the sides of the lime pot, making these sharp rattling noises.[1]

Empty talcum powder cans and the tins in which hard candies or peanuts are commercially packaged are now used as lime pots by many villagers. Others continue to carry the traditional small gourds, incised with handsome designs. These lime pots are only made by specialists, but often villagers sell them to tourists. Occasionally, a chief carries the kind of lime pot that marks his rank. Made from large gourds perhaps a foot in diameter, these lime pots are elaborately decorated with intricate designs. At the top, strong fibers are woven into a stopper with a pig's tusk stuck into the center from which beads and shells are suspended. Vanoi chatted and laughed with all of us, but when I finished preparing the tea, the others immediately departed from the house, leaving only my young friend Bulapapa. Although chiefs, like all villagers, eat privately, they should not eat alone. Since Kwaibwaga has no chief,[2] it was acceptable for Bulapapa and me to join Vanoi as if we, too, were high-ranking persons.

As we sipped our tea, I tried to turn the conversation to questions I had about Vanoi's predecessor, Mitakata, the Tabalu chief who died in 1961. At that time, Vanoi was only thirty-three years old, and I asked him how he felt when he took Mitakata's place. Vanoi's manner changed and his voice sounded serious, even confidential. "Anna," he said, "I was frightened to be chief. I did not know how to lead the people." Vanoi spoke about how tired he was after two days and nights of mourning before Mitakata was buried. Yet when he finally was alone in his house, sleep was impossible. His fears kept him awake. "Suddenly," he said, "a woman appeared at the foot of my bed and

[1] In the film *Trobriand Cricket* (J. W. Leach and Kildea 1975), there is a scene in which two chiefs explain to John K how Trobrianders changed the English way of playing the game. As they talk the chiefs chew betel and, using a traditional lime pot, tap the sides in the way Vanoi did.

[2] The last chief of the Buliyama matrilineage was Tonuwabu, who lived in Kwaibwaga and died in 1952. He had no heirs but his sons still live in his hamlet. Two of them act as the hamlet leaders, but because of the rule of matrilineal inheritance, neither one can become chief.

talked to me. 'Do not be afraid,' she whispered; 'remember you have the stones. They will keep you strong.' "

Vanoi knew of the stones, but struggling with his fear, he had forgotten about their power. "Those stones," he continued, "came from my ancestors. They now are in the bush near my hamlet. When the stones are upright in the ground, the yam harvests will be good. But if I turn the stones down, everyone's yams will shrivel up and die." When I asked the proverbial anthropologist's question, "Why?" Vanoi shook his head. "Anna, I only know that the stones are from our ancestors. When they are down, no rain falls; the yams will die. I do not know the name of the woman who came into my house that night, but she made me think about the stones and I felt strong." After Vanoi left, Bulapapa turned to me and asked, "Ah, Anna, did you write that carefully in your notebook? That man told you a very important story for Kiriwina."

WHAT THE ANCESTORS BROUGHT

The origin stories that document the first ancestors—usually a brother and sister—who founded the hamlet and garden lands that each matrilineage claims are not perceived as myths of primordial or legendary times. In the minds of Trobrianders, the stories recount the actions of real people who made decisions that continue to affect the affairs of each successive generation. Among all the ancestors who established matrilineages, only some of them came to Kiriwina with extensive food taboos and certain shell body decorations; these, from the beginning, ranked them as chiefly lineages (*guyau*) and separated them from the commoner matrilineages (*tokai*), whose ancestors came without these elaborate sumptuary rules (that is, rules about foods and decorations that are permitted or prohibited).[3] Whether expressed as taboos or prescriptions, these sumptuary rules sharply isolate the chief and define him and the other members of his matrilineage as different kinds of social persons.[4]

Each founding brother and sister did not arrive alone. Other sibling sets identified with other matrilineages in the same and other clans often came from the same place together. The lineage ancestors who came together continued to be allies, and today these same alliances continue. In the case of chiefly lineages, however, those who came with them as commoners worked for them by raising their pigs and growing betel nuts and coconut palm trees. From time to time, the chiefs rewarded them with stone axe-blades or shell valuables. Today, these obligations continue, so whenever the Omarakana

[3] The chiefly matrilineages are unevenly divided among the four clans. The Tabalu lineage is the only chiefly lineage in the Malasi clan.

[4] Elman Service (1962:155–156) pointed out the importance of sumptuary regulations in designating the permanent office of chiefdoms: because "Sumptuary regulations and customs have perhaps the most noticeable effects in creating separate classes of persons" (p. 156).

Photo 25. Before the harvested yams are brought into the village, a chief's yam house stands empty except for a few dishes of yams and betel nut which an affine brought for a small feast.

Tabalu chiefs need pork, coconuts, or betel nuts for a feast, they send a message to the men whose ancestors came with their ancestors from the same place of origin.

The ranking that the ancestors brought for the chiefly lineages was not established at the same time; some ancestors, as informants said, "came early"; others "came late." Some lineages arrived in two parts; the ancestors of each had to establish separate hamlet sites, the earlier ones retaining a higher rank over those who came later. In the Tabalu case, the ancestors came together from a cave in the northern part of Kiriwina, and they brought more food taboos and body and house decorations than anyone else. The Tabalu ancestors lived briefly in several villages, but finally they moved to Omarakana, where members of another matrilineage already lived. According to the story, when the Tabalu people entered the village, the residents got down from their verandas, thus acknowledging the high rank of the newcomers.[5] The former residents became the Tabalu's guards, and their descendants continue that tradition to this day.

Some years later, so the origin story relates, two Tabalu women broke the taboo on eating a certain kind of bony fish. Because they "made this mistake" they were forced to live elsewhere, losing their right to the most important of the Tabalu's decorations. Therefore, the Tabalu of Omarakana who did not break this taboo represent the senior lineage, and they sit higher than the rest. Today, even though the chiefs from these junior Tabalu lineages are politically important men, they all recognize the Omarakana Tabalu as "number one." Some villagers call Waibadi, as they did Vanoi before him, in English, "king."

What the origin stories make clear is that rivalry among chiefs always was a fact of life and that weaknesses are tested as one chief strives for an advantage over another. Chiefly decorations validate one's authority to claim the ranking brought by one's ancestors; therefore, it is no surprise that competition between chiefly matrilineages often is expressed in fights over these "kingly" regalia. For example, at the celebration in Losuia for Independence Day, a Tabalu woman from Gumilababa village, who ranked lower than the Omarakana Tabalu, wore the long cowrie-shell head decoration reserved only for the latter. When Botabalu, a woman from Omarakana, saw her, she took her knife and defiantly cut the string of shells right from her head, ending, she said, this attempt to usurp the Omarakana prerogatives. Although the rights to ranking as expressed in decorations appear to be inviolate, in every generation women and men seek to overturn them. Most often they fail; occasionally they succeed.

In the same way that decorations enhance a chief's physical appearance, the food taboos prohibit him from eating things such as wild pig, wallaby, stingray, certain other bony fish, shellfish, and garden greens and from drinking swamp water. These restrictions keep chiefs separated from foods thought to be physically debilitating. Thus, the continued enforcement of these sumptuary rules brought by ancestors ensures that those who rule will be physically attractive and strong and, therefore, influential. Like decorations, the food prohibitions are so important that other villagers often attempt to take them for their own, thereby claiming association with a certain rank. For example,

[5] See Malinowski's (1954:111–126) description of the Tabalu origin "myth." Malinowski claimed that the Tabalu were the first to appear on Kiriwina, but the stories of origin are much more complex than he supposed. See Weiner (1976:38–50) for more details of the Tabalu stories.

men who are commoners but whose fathers were chiefs sometimes practice the same food taboos as their fathers, putting others on notice that they, too, are entitled to the prerogatives of rank. In other cases, a chief from one ranking lineage may restrict himself to the same prohibitions that a higher-ranking lineage observes, asserting that no differences exist between the two.

Chief David, always competitive with another chiefly lineage whose ancestors came first, once told an elaborate story about men chasing a wild pig in the bush. When finally they caught the pig, he said, "Everyone ate pig, except me. I returned to sit in the village." Although no one said anything to David at the time, the other chiefs all knew "the truth." David's ancestors did not bring the prohibition against eating wild pig; he was "telling a lie," pretending to follow the "customs" of the higher-ranking lineage.[6]

The right to wear chiefly decorations and to follow chiefly food taboos extends to all members of chiefly matrilineages,[7] but the full measure of the sumptuary rules that define rank are condensed in the body of the chief. The top of a Tabalu chief's head should not be touched except by the members of the high-ranking Mwari lineage, who also are the only people permitted to enter the Tabalu chief's house. Traditionally, a chief did not even touch his food but was fed with long wooden forks by one of his trusted "guards." Not only does a chief's presence carry an aura of deference and fear, but even the hamlet of a chief represents a place of danger to those who are members of commoner lineages. Except for special occasions, a chief rarely wears all the body decorations to which he has title, but the painted and shell decorations that cover his house and his yam house stand as full testimony to these rights. Only a chief displays the long *kuvi* yams hanging in a prominent place around the house. Even his coconut and betel palms planted at the edge of the hamlet sometimes have shells hanging from the uppermost branches, which clink together like chimes in the wind, announcing to anyone passing that this is a chief's property.

Despite all the attention and emotion invested in each sumptuary rule brought by the ancestors, ranking is not equivalent with political power. The ancestors of each matrilineage established for all time the boundaries that separate those of rank from commoners. The ancestors' stories give authoritative sanction to the prerogatives of rank, making a person's birthright through matrilineal inheritance the primary criterion for chiefly actions. Yet from the very beginning of Trobriand time, the details of the origin stories record the loss of decorations and land and the gains that the members of one matrilineage made over others. A chief must work not only to solidify his arena of power and status but also to protect and prevent other chiefs

[6] Certain magic spells also have associated food taboos. Sometimes a villager will pretend that the food taboo he keeps is due to his chiefly lineage or his father's chiefly lineage. Others, however, always know that his lineage was not that high in rank and that the taboo is only from his magic.

[7] A chief may give his children his decorations to wear, but his children cannot transfer their use to their own children.

from destroying or diminishing his ancestral heritage. A few ranking lineages have died out, and also, over generations, some chiefs have been more successful in negotiating their own rise to fame at the expense of other chiefs. Today the competition continues, as chiefs of some high-ranking lineages have much less power than chiefs who are members of lower-ranking matrilineages.

A hierarchy of relations separates each ranking senior and junior matrilineal line, each major ranking lineage from others, and all those of rank from all commoner matrilineages. Historically, individual chiefs created differences in the ongoing political status of a lineage. A person's right to sit higher than the rest comes from his birth and the authority brought by his ancestors. How many people will actually sit under him comes from the authority he himself is able to summon. By authority I mean the right to claim legitimacy that is acknowledged by the members of the society. Trobrianders may not like a chief because, perhaps, he is ungenerous or too combative, but they still accept his right to be "chief" and to be accorded the appropriate deference. Power is the ability to act upon someone directly by carrying out one's will. A person may have the legitimacy of a chieftaincy, but he may not have the power to make others do what he wants them to do. Vanoi's story about the stones for yams was symptomatic of the difference between authority and power. Every person, including chiefs, must work to develop power in their relationships with others. Vanoi had the authority as chief, but the stones gave him a way to threaten and sanction others. The stones did not address an individual's fear of another person, such as sorcery does, but they controlled the yam harvest for everyone; and when a man begins to grow strong politically, his power is publicly expressed in yams.

THE DIFFERENCES YAMS MAKE

Whether villagers are members of ranking or commoner lineages, the organization of hamlets is fundamentally the same within each village. From two to eight hamlets, although these may vary in size, constitute a village, and each hamlet is composed of approximately six to twenty households. As described in Chapter 5, in each hamlet one man controls all the matrilineal land and other property originally established by his lineage ancestors. Within a village, intermarriage between hamlets is of political importance because these marriages create alliances between the hamlet leaders, generating close affinal and kinship ties. In some cases, marriage does not always play a unifying role because jealousy between hamlet leaders may create tensions that develop into animosity and distrust. The history of the ebb and flow of these encounters makes some hamlets, with or without chiefs, at particular times more dominant and powerful than others. Only a few members of a matrilineage actually reside in the hamlet, for example, the leader and a younger brother or his sister's son, who eventually will succeed him. Still, the hamlet represents the matrilineage, and the hamlet leader speaks with the authority of his ancestors when he organizes activities. Most members of a matrilineage live part of their lives in other hamlets: Women reside with their husbands and men often live with their fathers.

Therefore, although a hamlet leader controls the matrilineage's property, he also must try to retain some direction over the affairs of those members who live elsewhere. It is a leader's hard work and managerial skills rather than the actual makeup of the hamlet that ultimately gives rise to his power. A "generous" man attracts others to him, whereas a "hard" man makes others angry or afraid. For a truly strong leader, both characteristics are necessary. A leader's political sensitivity in judging when to be generous and when to be hard contributes greatly to the prosperity of a matrilineage, as well as to his own enduring authority. As described in the last chapter, some of the men who live in a hamlet may make yam gardens for the hamlet leader, but the most important yam contributions come from men who reside in other hamlets. If a hamlet leader demonstrates that he has the qualities necessary for becoming an important man, his wife's relatives eventually will build him a large yam house—which publicly establishes his status and gives him the possibility of achieving further power. Although the control of a matrilineage's land is inherited and validated by the hamlet leader's detailed knowledge of the origin stories, the political fame and forcefulness of the matrilineage depend primarily on the yams that move across matrilineal boundaries when they are given by affines.

From this perspective, a chief's position is organizationally much the same as that of any other hamlet leader. A chief has ultimate authority over the affairs of his hamlet, but his authority is limited in relation to the other hamlets that make up the village. Although a chief does not have full sway over the entire village, if he is a strong leader, his presence overshadows less powerful hamlet leaders and makes him influential in the organization of most village activities. Each hamlet leader continues to make decisions about land, marriage, and mortuary exchanges for the other members of his matrilineage, so even in a village where a chief resides, individual hamlets will have their own matrilineal concerns that exclude the chief. Trobriand chiefs do not have large retinues of kin, affines, clansmen, and allies over whom they hold uncompromising control, like we find in some African chiefdoms. Although Trobriand chiefs have prominence in the district where they live, they do not control everyone in that district. When conflicts over land or adultery occur in villages without chiefs, the most important chief of that district is called on to judge the case. Sometimes several chiefs listen to the stories presented and together make a decision.

Since colonization, the government has taken some of this legal power away from the chiefs by setting up a government court at Losuia. In most cases, villagers make thier own choices about whether to seek help from the government or from the chiefs. Especially over land disputes, because they involve the complicated histories of plots of land from the time of the first ancestors, chiefs remain the major adjudicators.[8] In all other respects, the power of a Trobriand chief is localized, only spreading out into other hamlets and villages through individual matrilineages, which either have a woman member married to the chief or whose ancestors came from the same place of origin. In the latter case, a chief inherits these relationships, but even then he must work to keep them strong.[9] In villages without chiefs, a primary goal for each hamlet leader is to establish and maintain alliances between hamlets within the village, so that a hamlet leader can depend on some of the other village men for support. A chief, however, tries to expand his links further by creating support with hamlet leaders in many different villages.

One of the prerogatives of chiefly rank is the possibility of having more than one wife. Polygyny enables a chief to enhance his economic situation. A chief with several wives receives annual harvest yams from the matrilineal kin of each one. Unlike women in monogamous marriages, each wife has her own personal yam house, built by her matrilineal kin when she first moves to her husband's hamlet. Only when a woman's relatives make her an exceptionally large yam harvest will the additional yams be placed in the chief's own yam house. When his yam house is full, he is indeed powerful. At the yam harvest displays, villagers always discuss the number and quality of yams each wife of a chief receives. They comment to each other about who, among all the chief's wives' kin, made the largest yam contributions. Will there be enough yams to fill completely the chief's own yam house in addition to the yam houses for his wives? Who did not work so hard this year? These evaluations are important for they act as an annual barometer assessing the strength of a chief.

The talk is subdued in years when the yam harvests are small. In the first years of John K's development schemes, Chiefs Waibadi and Vanoi received very few yams. Most of their affines initially supported John K. By not growing yams for the chiefs' wives' yam gardens, they showed their opposition. Omarakana's yam houses stood empty, in stark contrast to the huge amounts of yams that filled the yam houses of the chiefs who were on the side of John K. Only as Waibadi slowly gained back his supporters did the size of his yam harvests increase, until it was clear that he had beaten John K.

Yams give chiefs the possibility of enormous increments of wealth each year. With good harvests, chiefs can be generous, distributing large amounts of yams to many villagers as payment for their work—their services in building things such as houses or canoes—to secure valuables, and to take baskets of yams to their "sisters." When all individual needs and obligations are fulfilled, a chief may entertain the residents of other villages at feasts, harvest dances, or cricket matches. For a chief to have enough yams to "overturn his yam

[8] With the establishment of a local council, with elected representatives from each village, many court cases are now brought to the head of the council, who is Waibadi.

[9] Even in traditional warfare, when chiefs organized a fight against other chiefs, they each had to solicit villagers to fight for them by sending axe-blades to the hamlet leaders. Many times, however, the valuables were accepted and then the young men ran away when the fighting started.

house" for many guests is a splendid and politically advanageous event. The largesse of a chief is politically important since giving yams is a sign of fecundity, nurturance, and power. Yet chiefs do not achieve such bounty easily. They do not completely dominate the labor of others because a man may always show his dissatisfaction with a chief by not growing any yams for him.

FINDING WIVES

Since the ongoing political currency of chiefs is measured in yam production, the women that chiefs marry assume a role of great consequence in their political careers. As we just saw, polygyny provides chiefs with the opportunity to accumulate more yams than most other men. Before a marriage, the relatives of each woman agree to build her both a residential house and a yam house when she goes to live with the chief. Unlike men who are not polygynous, and who therefore must wait until their wives' relatives decide to build them their yam houses, marriage for a chief creates an immediate obligation on the part of affines to build this structure, not for him, but for his wife. At least four male relatives of a chief's wife—usually her mother's brother, her father, her brother, a matrilineal parallel cousin, or another brother—pledge to make yam gardens for her each year and place the harvest in her own yam house.[10] A woman, however, does not come to live in the chief's village until her own house and her yam house are built. Her relatives may accept her marriage, but they may wait a few years, until they think that the chief is powerful enough, to begin construction. Chief Vanoi had nine wives, and therefore a total of thirty-six men made yam gardens for them. He also had three other wives promised, but when he got sick no other yam houses were built.

A commoner, with only one wife, can never hope to outdo a chief in yams. Even if a hamlet leader is very strong and has five or six men making gardens for him, in addition to his wife's yams, his accumulation is limited when compared to what a chief can expect.

Some low-ranking chiefs are monogamous; most other chiefs have three wives; a few have six. Only the highest-ranking Omarakana Tabalu chief traditionally has been able to take many more wives than all other chiefs. At the turn of the century, for example, the Omarakana Tabalu chief had seventeen wives. The selection of a wife is handled by the chief's guards, who single out particular women who may be members of lineages from which previous chiefs have taken wives and whose kin may want to continue the chiefly relationships. These guards also select women who are members of lineages from which no other woman has married a chief. The imperative in either case is that the women's matrilineal kinsmen must be vigorous and hard-working so that they will make strong allies. Chiefs build on their pre-

[10] If a hamlet leader approves the marriage, he will find other men, even if they are fictive kin, to make some of the woman's gardens.

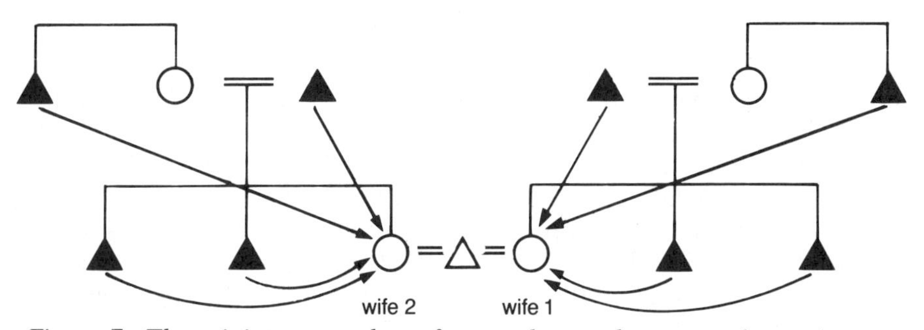

Figure 7. The minimum number of men who produce annual yam harvests for a chief's wife.

decessor's affinal relationships, but they also create new ones of their own.

In arranged marriages of this kind, no adolescent sexual intrigues usually take place. Sometimes the women selected are quite young, and the chief waits for five years or so until her kin decide to bring her to his hamlet and build her yam house. The announcement for arranged marriages is not made public by the couple eating yams together, as in the case of monogamous marriages. Instead, the chief's guards take a spear with four coconuts attached and present it to the hamlet leader of the woman's matrilineage. Each coconut represents one yam garden that her relatives agree to make for her. Figure 7 illustrates how a woman's brothers, her father, and her mother's brother each will make her a yam garden. Sometimes an adopted brother or a distantly related man will also make her a garden. If the hamlet leader accepts the spear, each man that assumes the responsibility of making a yam garden is given one of the four coconuts. The alliance is confirmed and the marriage is consummated when the woman's relatives decide it is time to build her house and take her to the chief's hamlet.

In some cases, when a chief dies, one or two of his youngest wives may be kept by the chief's successor. Often the new chief will already have been married, and his first wife will wield authority over his other wives. She is accorded much deference and respect not only by her co-wives but by villagers too. After a man becomes chief, in addition to his arranged marriages, he may take other wives for "love." Unlike villagers who are monogamous and are not supposed to take lovers, chiefs are expected to make new "friends." Since only a few high-ranking women may enter a chief's house, his adulterous relations take place outside his hamlet. At least in recent times, the wives of some chiefs are not always content to allow them to engage in these affairs, and some will fight with his lovers, often inflicting serious wounds. To be jealous like this, however, is not considered proper behavior by other villagers. If a chief finds a woman whom he wants to marry, he remains with her at the beach for several days, making the marriage public. Her relatives respond to the *fait accompli* by building her house and yam house and then planting yam gardens for her as long as she wants to remain with him.

Neither marrying "for love" nor "for yams" is easily accomplished. The commitment to a chief by his wife's affines is not taken lightly by villagers. Chiefs must be strong and attractive to find a woman to marry for love. Although chiefs' wives are always treated by other villagers with great deference, they also must share their husband with his other wives and negotiate their own hierarchical relations with his older wives. Not only must a chief demonstrate his political status so he continues to attract wives through the formal arrangements of yam gardens, but also he must continue to look young and handsome, using all the techniques of attractive dress and magic spells that young people use to seduce lovers. The power of such seduction must stay with chiefs, especially the Tabalu chiefs, throughout their lives.

To marry a woman by arrangement with her kin is equally difficult. A hamlet leader has the option to refuse the coconuts and reject the chief's request; the woman may resist the marriage or she may return home shortly after she takes up residence in the chief's hamlet. She may divorce him at any time. Before villagers agree to take the coconuts and assume the burden of yam production, they too must have some assurance of the strength and vitality of the chief.[11] Will he be able to pay them properly for their hard work? Does he have the power to support and protect them? For several years after Chief Mitakata died, Vanoi had difficulty finding wives. He was young and other men were uncertain about his future; the coconuts were refused. Only as Vanoi demonstrated his powers of sorcery through retaliation for Mitakata's death, as discussed later, and talked of the stones that could destroy yam harvests did he begin to obtain promises of wives.

POWER AND FEAR

Chiefs are not first among equals, nor do they pretend to be. With the beginning of Trobriand time, the ancestors established a permanent division between lineages that Trobrianders still acknowledge as an immutable fact of history. The sumptuary regulations that came from the ancestors create the office of chief. With decorations, food taboos, and ritual forms of etiquette, the person of chief is separated spatially from all other villagers. Since the authority for that separation is lodged with the ancestors, it remains an authority outside particular social and political actions. Individuals may strive to alter that authority, but the stories of the ancestors stand strong against distortions and changes. When Vanoi died, a lesser-ranking Tabalu chief from a hamlet near Losuia argued that his ancestors originally came from Omarakana and that he, and not Waibadi, should be the highest-ranking chief. Waibadi never replied, for everyone else knew that now he was "king."

There is another dimension to the power of a chief. The regalia of rank is underwritten by the exercise of authority that controls the seemingly uncontrollable. Important chiefs must demonstrate that they know formidable kinds

[11] As Lévi-Strauss noted, "Consent . . . is at the same time the origin and the limit of leadership" (1944:28).

of magic spells that successfully give them control over villagers' lives and the growing cycle of yams. In general, most important spells originally were brought by the ancestors, but some have been lost because they were not transmitted in part or in full before the last owner died. Such was the case with the yam-gardening magic once used by the Tabalu, which Malinowski described. It was not passed down to the next generation, and today the Tabalu chiefs rely on gardening magic that was purchased from villagers living in the southern Massim. Throughout the islands and the mainland of Papua New Guinea, there is a brisk trade in magic spells of all sorts.

The spells that are most talked about because they are so dangerous are those for sorcery and those that control the weather. These traditional spells are the property of certain matrilineages and known only by a few men. Not all chiefs own sorcery spells, but since they usually have more wealth than ordinary men, they can pay those who know the magic to accomplish their wishes. However, the specialist may not be willing to kill a particular person. Sometimes he may agree, take the payment, and then not perform the spell appropriately. A man's control can be unquestioned only when he can execute his plans himself. A few months after Mitakata died, a man from another village died suddenly. Many villagers believed that he had been the person who had killed Mitakata. While the mourning was taking place, Vanoi walked through the dead man's hamlet wearing bright clothes. By his style of dress he announced that this man was *his* victim. By his actions he made it clear that he knew traditional Tabalu spells for sorcery, and in his role as chief, he had the right to claim retribution for Mitakata's death. Only a chief can display his dangerous talents so publicly.

The power that chiefs have through their knowledge of sorcery breeds fear in others. Opposition to a chief or participation in such incidents as keeping a long *kuvi* yam rather than giving it to the chief or, worse, being suspected of adultery with a chief's wife, stay in the minds of those involved, making them fear the future. Sudden sickness or death points a finger at the mistakes made or the rules broken, making clear the price to be paid for autonomous behavior. Public accusations of sorcery are rare. No one except another powerful chief would dare to accuse a chief, and in all cases, those who want to prosecute must have proof—which is very difficult to find. Therefore, most deaths stir up fear inflamed by gossip and hidden suspicions.

Although chiefs walk with the authority that control over sorcery gives them, they themselves are not immune to its effects. Several months before Vanoi died, he said that he knew that another chief was planning to kill him. Even for chiefs, death comes in the same way, through the imposition of another person's desires on their lives. Yet fear of sorcery is not the most devastating psychic burden that villagers carry. Individual deaths are traumatic, sad, and distressing, but the anger and hostility that lead to the death cannot be confronted publicly and instead generate further misfortune and danger. One death in the past is linked to the suspicion of another in the future, but who might be the victim or the victimizer cannot be determined with certainty.

Although sorcery is always to be feared, nothing compares with the threat of a chief's magic over the weather, for then the very fabric of social life for everyone is torn apart. Yams symbolize the most sensitive and critical relationships that each woman and each man constructs between the members of one matrilineage and another. Yams are the public measure of a villager's power and the most significant statement of the political currency of a chief. Those few chiefs who control the magic spells that produce rain or sun are feared by everyone, for their power affects the lives of many.

Historically, the Omarakana Tabalu are known to have gained the most powerful spells that control the weather as well as the stones that ruin crops. In a public meeting of several hundred men, with tempers inflamed over John K's new economic association, Waibadi shouted a charge at everyone present not to follow John, reminding them that only he had the strongest rain magic, which could destroy all the yams. The stones in Omarakana were proof that only the Tabalu could effect changes on the entire society—at will.

Power is wedded to yams attained through marriage and allies. In that power lie the boldness and eminence of chiefs; but to achieve the supremacy of autonomy, chiefs, too, must destroy the very substance of their support. Pushed to the limits, political power unravels. Yam houses stand empty, not because they have been overturned in generosity or a chief's affines have expressed their disapproval or a chief has died, but because an angry chief has turned to the ancestral stones and caused the yams to die. The fear of the destruction of the growing cycle is a fear of the disintegration of fertility, social relations, power—the very breath of life. The highest-ranking chiefs hold that possibility in their hands. Their anger, if uncontrolled, becomes everyone's defeat, including their own.[12]

Sorcery and yam destruction are the negative weights against which individuals—especially chiefs—work, as Waibadi said, "to show who you are." The Tabalu, the highest-ranking chiefs, embody the ideals of fertility and prosperity and also must demonstrate their control over the reverse realities of death, decay and starvation. Their control does not free them from becoming their own victims. The degenerating aspects of nature are tampered with through their magic powers and knowledge, but these aspects are not eliminated. In the next chapter we see that as chiefs "show who they are" through spectacular yam harvests, death suddenly forces villagers to show not who they are but, as one villager said, "where you belong."

[12] See Young's (1983) sensitive analysis of how Goodenough Island leaders ultimately defeat themselves in similar ways. In a different part of the world, but in the same fundamental circumstances, Chinua Achebe's well-known novel about the Ibo from Nigeria, entitled *Arrow of God* (1967), illustrates how an Ibo chief, through his own vengeance against others, ultimately wreaks havoc on himself and his whole clan.

7/Men working for women

The next day was a sagali again for the mourners who came and also gifts were made to his wife. I was so excited when they kept calling my name for doba and food but felt guilty because I hadn't done much. We ended up with 3 chickens, two big trees of bananas, betel nut, and plenty of taro and yams.

Linda Weiner

HARVEST COMPETITIONS

The annual growing cycle of yams is so deeply interconnected with the social and political well-being of Trobrianders that even the months of the year are named for each stage of growth. Once the yams are stacked in the yam houses, however, a lacuna occurs in the calendar, which marks a two-month holiday. From July, after the yam houses are filled, until September, when new gardens must be prepared, the work for yams is finished and the time for "play" (*mwasawa*) begins. With exceptionally large harvests, the "play" becomes a competitive event in which the players receive rewards that announce their fame and renown.

When a chief or hamlet leader decides to show who he is by spreading his fame among many other villages, he organizes a yam competition (*kayasa*), a harvest event that requires extensive planning. First, when villagers begin to clear their new gardens, the chief or hamlet leader announces that after the next harvest he will hold a competition. To do so, however, he needs the close cooperation of other men in his village, who agree to plant additional yam gardens just for this purpose. His major supporters are members of his matrilineage and his *keyawa* kin. Sometimes, men from his village who are members of other clans may agree to help, making the harvest competitions appear to be a village affair. The organization and control of the competition is vested in the chief or hamlet leader, and his success reflects on the status of his matrilineage. The first part of the competition is between the gardeners. To the men who produce the most yams, the chief gives payments of valuables, such as stone axe-blades or money, as rewards for their work and expertise. Therefore, before a chief or a hamlet leader can think about sponsoring a yam competition, he first must be able to accumulate the necessary valuables for these prizes.

Once the yams are harvested and the chief rewards his kin who worked for him, these supporters carry the yams, several pigs, and betel nuts that the chief has bestowed to another chief or hamlet leader and his matrilineal kin who are members of a different clan. At a future harvest, the recipients are expected to stage a yam competition in return to prove their own equal or superior ability. Bulapapa told me that yam competitions are to "make good friends" with men from another clan. Making friends, as we saw in other kinds of activities, demands seducing people with things, proving one's influence and power. Lovers, too, are called "good friends," but only marriage stabilizes relationships between clans, shifting individual competition and seduction into permanent obligations. The outpouring of yams at harvest is used in the most dramatic way possible to emphasize and build on the seductive qualities of being young. Polygyny enables the highest-ranking chiefs to create affinal relationships among many matrilineages outside their own clans.

In addition to contracting marriages, all chiefs and hamlet leaders continually try other means to expand their networks of "good friends," finding them among men in other clans. Yams provide the wherewithal to create fame by politically influencing "friends" through enormous displays and distributions of yams. A chief or strong hamlet leader can spread his fame more broadly among other clans if, instead of a yam competition, he decides to hold a competition with dancing. For these events, young unmarried Trobrianders from different villages are invited to nightly dances in the host's hamlet throughout the months of "play." Today, the dances are attended not only by young people from twenty or thirty villages but also by curious tourists anxious to witness the sexual excitement touted by travel agents as the high point of the "Kiriwina yam festival." They are not disappointed. The dancers never look more extraordinarily beautiful in their traditional styles than when they walk in groups along the road to their nightly rendezvous at the host's hamlet, where they "play" until dawn.

To outside spectators, the scene is a night of sexual revelries—a bacchanal of sorts. As the evening progresses, young people chant and shout in the center of the hamlet plaza, slapping their hips as they thrust the lower part of their bodies forward in a highly provocative way, similar to the way they bring yams into the village when the yam houses are ready to be filled. While older men steadily tap their drums in a traditional percussion beat and other adults sit talking on their verandas, the dancing gets faster and the participants aggressively chase and grab each other. Couples disappear into the bush to make love. This night of sexual "play" is decidedly indiscriminate when seen against the more usual roles governing adolescent behavior throughout the year. In these competitions there are no messengers carrying betel nuts to arrange meetings and no demands for village propriety. The exaggeration of sexuality when the yam houses are the fullest goes hand in hand with the general harvest themes of prosperity and fertility. These competitions are a

Photo 26. With feathered headdresses and beautiful skirts, villagers dance to the traditional drums that mark the end of the harvest period.

victory, at least for that one year, over death and loss—the dangers that undermine these political aspects and sense of well-being in yam production.

When these two months of nightly dancing finally end, the hosts conclude the competition with spectacular traditional dancing held during the day. Many dances are believed to be hundreds of years old. Some villagers are renowned for their knowledge of dances brought by their ancestors and loaned to others for a price. Adults and young people from many villages attend this grand finale to watch the dancers, who are men, and in some dances, women and men. Wearing traditional dress, face painting, feather headdresses, and magical preparations for beauty, adults are transformed into youthful, seductive performers.

Monobogwa, a young man, told me that when he saw his mother dance, he said to her, "I always thought you were old, but today you are young and beautiful." To mark the end of the dancing and the competition, the yam houses are metaphorically "overturned" and emptied of their harvest. Pigs are chased, tied up, and hung on poles; and wooden crates 10 or 15 feet tall, fastened against coconut palms, are filled with yams; one crate and one pig are divided among the residents of each hamlet who participated as guests and dancers. By the end of this event, by hosting nights of dancing and giving food to hundreds of people, a chief or hamlet leader demonstrates that he and his matrilineage are "the best."

The missionaries have long tried to stop the overt sexual practices associated with these competitions but with little success. Early in this century they

Photo 27. At sunrise before the start of a cricket match, Kwaibwaga men carefully paint their bodies and help each other apply special designs.

introduced cricket playing as a substitute for village fighting and as a sport that would replace the harvest dancing and open sexuality. Over the years, the game has changed dramatically from the staid British rules and style to the Trobriand way. Instead of inviting dancers each night, a chief or hamlet leader decides to arrange a tournament in which each village with a cricket team is individually invited to play the host team. Contrary to the missionaries' hopes, concern with sexuality has not disappeared; it has merely emerged into new expressive forms. The cricket players are as sensually dressed and magically decorated as if they were attending a dance competition. With cricket, however, young women are no longer equal dance partners but dress in all their traditional finery as spectators. Cricket is played during the day, and the game, with fifty players on each team, continues for eight or nine hours. Each side is known for their chants and dance formations, which they perform at the beginning and end of each inning. The words are sexual metaphors, used as one team taunts the other and exhibits their physical and sexual prowess to the appraising eyes of the young women on the sidelines.[1]

The cricket competition continues week after week until the matches are

[1] In the film *Trobriand Cricket: An Indigenous Response to Colonialism* (Leach and Kildea 1975) these chants and dance formations are dramatized. The film emphasizes the way cricket was introduced by the early missionaries as a substitute for warfare, but, in fact, the missionaries thought that cricket also would replace adolescent sexual "promiscuity" during harvest dancing. Because the cricket match in the film was performed expressly for the filmmakers, the yam exchanges at the end of the matches do not accurately show their full magnitude. See also Weiner (1977 and especially 1978a) for further discussion of this film.

completed; then the host village holds a huge feast, distributing pigs, yams, and betel nuts in the manner of the dancing competitions. The significance of this day, like the other kinds of harvest competitions, broadcasts the host's fame as he and all his relatives demonstrate their ability to organize and pay for the event by extravagantly feeding everyone attending. Public displays of power not only carry the fame of the hosts but also ignite the possibility of resentment and envy. There is a Trobriand saying: "When you give too much, people worry." Although the lavish displays of yams "make people happy," they also fan jealousy. As the guests recount enthusiastically to each other the chief's largesse, many are jealously thinking how to proclaim their own fame the following year. Thus friendship may slide dangerously into covert enmity.

In cricket matches, these problems are exacerbated because the hosts, who organize and give away so much, by common consent must always win. Often the losers, who actually are winning, get angry at the umpire's calls. When they return to their own village, they tell everyone that they "in truth" won. Luckily, during this time of year rain showers frequently occur in the afternoons, so that often a match is called in the final innings of play. Even though cricket was introduced to stop fighting, as with many sports played throughout the world, fights still erupt. In 1918, Malinowski reported that the losers created an unforgivable situation by confronting the hosts with demands that they in fact won. In 1981, fighting over the score by a guest team became so intense that several men burned down some village houses in retaliation and only their subsequent arrests restored the calm.

The Australian government's annual reports from the turn of the century to the 1970s note again and again that the harvest months are the most precipitous time for village fighting. The most dangerous fights, however, lead to another kind of yam competition, that is, the actual measuring of large yams. These challenges (*buritilaulo*) provoke such hostile feelings that other villagers do everything they can to stop one from taking place. One day, as I walked along the main road on my way back from visiting another village, I saw men running and shouting to others to follow them. Two men had fought with each other over their yam gardens. They were so verbally abusive in their criticisms of each other's yam-growing abilities that one had challenged the other to a yam-measuring contest, and now their matrilineal kinsmen were bringing their largest yams to confront one another. The men I saw running were trying to stop the challenge, but they were too late. A winner was announced, and without speaking, the men of the rival matrilineages separated. So awesome is the fear and the expectation of reprisals from a yam-measuring competition that to win is really to lose.[2] All parties believe that the losers, having been publicly humiliated, will try to destroy the members of the other lineage through sorcery, a fear that lasts for generations. This challenge to show "who you are," made in anger rather than in the acceptable

[2] See Malinowski (1935, I:plates 68, 70) for photographs of a yam challenge. On Goodenough Island, southeast of Kiriwina, these yam fights occur much more frequently as one clan politically challenges another (see Young 1971).

context of generous giving, throws light on the underside of power—its fragile and perilous nature and the thinly veiled hostility underlying hospitality and friendship.

For all these reasons the harvest competitions draw together all the positive elements expressed when yam houses are full—youth, sexuality, fertility—in order to project without seeming to boast about the competitive renown of chiefs or hamlet leaders and their kin. Yet the positive elements are transitory. People grow old; postmarriage sexuality, except for chiefs, is disguised; one's renown is overtaken by others; fights breed formidable desires for revenge; and death claims a final justice. Hovering over the excitement of any successful harvest is the knowledge that such losses may result. A chief or hamlet leader rallies others to witness his success, but each occasion contains the seeds for counteractions. However, the intense and deep-seated emphasis on youth, beauty, and sexuality helps to overcome the negative destructive possibilities that lead to death.

DEATH AND WOMEN'S WEALTH

Not all harvests become arenas in which a chief attempts to establish his renown. A death in a village interrupts such plans, proving once again that fear of others' autonomous behavior is well founded. With a death, instead of yam houses being "overturned" to spread the fame of a chief, they are emptied to feed mourners. Drab-colored skirts replace those of bright red. Bodies that would be glistening with coconut oil are now washed, then rubbed with the blackened, charred husks of coconuts. If a death occurs during the year, the entire village is closed to all "playing," out of respect to the hamlet where the dead person lived. Regardless of when the person died, the mourning lasts until the final wealth distribution (*lisaladabu*) of skirts and banana-leaf bundles organized by the women.[3]

Like all important occasions these distributions take place only during the yam harvest season. Therefore, if someone dies during the year, yam competitions are replaced by competitions in women's wealth. In contrast to the former celebration, where the hamlet leader or chief is in charge of all the work of distributing yams, the women "owners," that is, the dead person's kinswomen, are in control. The women are helped by their *keyawa* kin and the married daughters of the men who are members of the dead person's matrilineage. Each woman works individually to accumulate vast amounts of skirts and bundles until the day of the distribution—similar to the one I described when I first went to live in Kwaibwaga—when they disperse all their wealth. Like a chief who overturns his yam house when guests come to his hamlet for dancing or cricket matches, the women owners with their

[3] The word *lisaladabu* refers to the payments people receive for cutting their hair in mourning, although the actual distribution involves many other kinds of payments. The distribution is also referred to as a *sagali*, a general term that means "to distribute things to many people."

Photo 28. While everyone watches, Kasenai counts the bundles of banana leaves that she is arranging for the women's mortuary distribution the following day.

helpers distribute the equivalent of four or five hundred dollars to all the villagers designated as "workers," who engaged in some act of mourning for the deceased. The woman who overturns the largest number of baskets to distribute more wealth than anyone else is the leader and is called "a wealthy woman." It is she who proclaims the political message that, as with a chief, expresses her power. She, too, makes the larger claim that her matrilineage is strong.

Each woman who gives away her wealth is in direct competition with her sisters, her mother, and even her brothers' daughters, as each one individually tries to become a "wealthy woman." Part of a woman's success depends on her own hard work and ability to produce large amounts of bundles and skirts. While the spouse and father of the dead person are secluded in mourning and all their kin keep their heads shaved and their bodies blackened, the women owners work for months, stocking their own individual stores of women's wealth. Only when they have enough and the yams are harvested will the distribution take place.

First, the women need to find huge numbers of banana leaves to begin producing the fibers for the skirts and bundles. The lucky ones are those who own many banana trees.[4] After a death, it is not unusual to see five- and six-

[4] Banana trees are planted in the gardens and in the village, usually in back of the houses. They are easily propagated, and a woman will inherit banana trees from her mother or her sister.

year-old girls sitting together, working on the first stage of bundle preparation. With the sharpened edge of a shell, they scratch the green outer fibers off the leaves. After these pieces are left to dry so that they whiten in the sun, the next, more intricate step is always performed by women. Cutting each piece into narrow 1-inch strips, a woman places about twenty-five strips together, making a thick bundle that she tightly ties at one end. The bundle looks flat, but it is only half completed. With the tied part in one hand, the woman then pulls each strip outward, as if she were stretching the petals from a crepe-paper flower. When she pulls the strips back into place, they remain puffed out, making the bundle wide and full, much like the shape of a whisk broom.

"New" bundles (*yawovau*) made in this way are the most highly valued, and a minimum of several thousand are necessary for the women's mortuary distribution. Even though bundles have no utilitarian value, extensive labor is invested in their production, creating out of a plain banana leaf a specialized object with unique material properties. This detailed labor gives exchange value to each bundle. During the day's distribution, other bundles, designated as "clean" (*migileu*), "dirty" (*yapagatu*), and even "old" (*yabwabogwa*) are used. I might not have recognized the different exchange values in this range of bundles had I not participated in the distributions myself. When a neighbor, Kulumwelova, died, I was given bundles by the women from his lineage because I sat up all night and mourned before he was buried.

A few weeks later, in preparation for a women's mortuary ceremony for someone else who had died five months earlier, Imkitava, Weteli, and a few other Kwaibwaga women came to check over the bundles I had. They wanted to make certain that on the following day I would not make any mistakes at the distribution. Fascinated, I sat and watched them examine each bundle. I was proud of the amount that I had been given, but disappointed when they told me my bundles were either "old" or "dirty." "Don't worry," Imkitava said; "we will make you some 'clean' ones." Deftly, they cut apart each bundle, retied it, and then pulled the strips apart to puff them out as if they were making new ones. It took about fifteen minutes to transform each crushed bundle into a clean one.[5] Imkitava warned me, "If you give those women dirty bundles that are flattened out, they will scream at you: 'You only want to eat; you do not care about the customs for bundles.' "

Making skirts takes even more time and attention as only the most beautiful red-dyed skirts are given away as wealth. The banana leaves are cut into long, narrow, fringelike fibers; after drying, they are colored red with commercial dyes purchased in the trade stores. Traditionally, local dyes were produced from special roots, making the labor process even more arduous. Each piece of prepared leaf is threaded through three thick fiber cords to construct the waistband. The decorative ruff below the waist is further elaborated and puffed

[5] See Weiner (1976:239) for a more detailed description of making bundles. When old bundles become too torn and frayed to be used at all, they usually are thrown away. Sometimes women will dye the banana-leaf strips and reuse them when they weave skirts.

Photo 29. After dying the banana fibers, Iloweya laboriously weaves each piece between three heavy fibers to make the waistband.

out with pieces of dried pandanus cut into designs. For women of rank, tiny white cowrie shells are woven into the band.[6] The technology for making skirts demands far more production time than that for bundles. In Kiriwina, with a large population and competition in the rank and power of individual chiefs, bundles provide more wealth with less labor. But when a woman needs a sizable accumulation, she still cannot make enough by herself.

THE NEED FOR BUNDLES

The key to finding large amounts of bundles is a woman's husband. For example, when Isoba's mother's brother died in 1980, her husband, Modu-

[6] See Weiner (1976:240–241) for a more extensive description of making skirts. In many parts of Papua New Guinea, traditional women's skirts are used as trade items, and in the southern Massim, skirts are important in mortuary exchanges (see Battaglia 1981, 1983; Lepowsky 1981). On Vakuta Island, to the south of Kiriwina, women use skirts, but not bundles, for the women's mortuary distribution (Campbell 1981).

bubuna, took one of his pigs to his friend in Omarakana. The man accepted the pig and agreed to pay Modububuna 30,000 new bundles.[7] When a woman needs bundles in large amounts, her husband must take his own things and purchase (*valova*) bundles for her. Not only pigs but also yams and various other kinds of crafted objects are used to buy bundles. Only seed yams, stone axes, and shell valuables cannot be used in this way. Today many men use money to buy rice, tinned fish, or tobacco in the trade stores; they then sell these things to other villagers for bundles. Women make bundles not only for someone's death but also to buy things from others who need bundles. Since colonization, inflation has increased the demand for bundles because, with trade store goods, it is easier to find villagers who are willing to give up their bundles, especially if they do not have money to buy things they want in the trade stores. But each time store prices rise, the cost of bundles increases because bundle currency is tied to national inflationary trends.

One day while I was riding in a truck to Losuia, I chatted with Joshua, an unmarried Kiriwina man who had just returned from medical training in Port Moresby. As we talked we passed near a village where a woman's mortuary distribution was taking place. I nodded in that direction and commented about the distribution. "Ah," he said smiling, "you already know about women's wealth." His smile faded as he told me that women had to stop giving away bundles. "If women stopped needing so many bundles, then men would have plenty of money for other things."[8] In his shrewd comment, Joshua put his finger on the vulnerability of using such bundles as currency. From a capitalist perspective, he was right. Men take money, which can be used to purchase all sorts of things, and turn it into bundles. Yet despite the demanding need for money to pay school fees, government taxes, trade store goods, and even airfares to the capital, men continue to spend their money on bundles. Why women's wealth has not diminished in importance over the past one hundred years is a serious question, which Joshua, in his own way, was asking. But Joshua was not married and so his interest in the cost of bundles was limited. Had Joshua lived in a village where his wife's brother produced yams for him each year, he would not have framed his comments in Western economic terms.

Because a woman and her husband receive yams from her brother every year, her husband must help her find bundles whenever someone dies who was a member of her matrilineage. In this way, a woman's large accumulation of wealth is intimately tied to yam production. This is the key to the exchange relations among a woman, her husband, and her brother. By giving yams each year to his sister, a man secures women's wealth from someone in another matrilineage for his own matrilineage. In this way the exchange relationship between yams and bundles and the circulation of bundles as a limited currency operate within a system of precise checks and balances.

[7] As the price of pigs increase so does the number of bundles. In 1971, for example, 18,000 bundles equaled one pig.

[8] I originally discussed Joshua's conversation in Weiner (1980). This essay also includes more extensive information on colonialism and its effects on women's wealth.

Photo 30. Neighbors evaluate the bundles and skirts that Isoba received from her husband after he was paid for the large pig he gave away.

When men give yams to their sisters and their sisters' husbands, they are crediting a debt that can be repaid only in women's wealth. When someone dies, the women of the dead person's matrilineage need bundles, as we have just seen. Because their husbands receive yams from their wives' brothers each year, they must take their own things and get more bundles for their wives. Women draw on their husbands' resources to make their own matrilineage look strong. Since almost all deaths are thought to be the result of sorcery, it is important to demonstrate strength, not only to commemorate the dead person, but also politically to confirm the wealth and vitality of the matrilineage in the face of its loss. When women give away substantial amounts of bundles and skirts, they establish their own wealth and also make their brothers and all other members of their matrilineage appear politically unaffected by what everyone assumes has been a sorcerer's success.

Because of the men's support to their wives who are the dead person's kinswomen, the wealth and vigor of the dead person's matrilineage is made more publicly prominent. Yet a woman can draw on her husband's support only because her husband received yams from her brother. Therefore, if a man says he is "tired' and does not support his wife when she needs bundles, as sometimes happens, then her brother does not make a large yam garden the following year because his garden work is measured against the needs of his matrilineage each time someone dies. The negotiation between yams and women's wealth is always being evaluated by each party, so that when a man's affines build him a yam house, the message conveys that he is and will continue to be a strong provider for his wife when she needs bundles. In this process, men's resources in food, pigs, and now money are continually being drained, as Joshua saw so clearly.

Regardless of how formidable a chief may be, his wealth, too, is subject to the same exigencies brought on by a death. If a chief like Vanoi has nine wives, the death of any member of those nine matrilineages to which his wives belong means that he must help with bundles. Although, through their polygynous marriages, chiefs have an advantage over monogamous men in getting many more yams during the harvest, the need to demonstrate their largesse during good harvests, or to use their yams and money to get bundles for their wives during harvests when mourning takes precedence, levels any extensive buildup of wealth. To "show who you are" in yam competitions is essential for chiefs and hamlet leaders who aspire to high status and power. Before these men can draw on other supporters to grow yams for them, however, their personal aggrandizement first depends on their wives, whose brothers support them strongly with yams. Behind each man's economic eminence and growing political stature is his wife and her brother, members of another matrilineage. Although the debt created through yams enables a man to become more dominant as a leader, there is a price to be paid. Because a man cannot fill his own yam house, he is always dependent on other men. Supporting relationships through yams demands constant effort and attention. Furthermore, yams have short time limits to their use as wealth because they must be eaten before they rot. There are no substitutes and no room for neglect. A longevity of sorts is given to yams, not in the objects themselves, but in the most important debt they produce.

Yams given by a man to his sister create a return of bundles and skirts. This is the underlying purpose of all the work and display of yam production. Women, however, are not totally dependent on either their husbands for bundles or their brothers for yams because they can and do make bundles and skirts themselves. Unlike yams, the exchange of bundles and skirts does not create debt but rather removes the debts that accrue throughout the life of a person. So vital and deeply meaningful are these bundles and skirts that in the process of their circulation, they subsume all of men's resources, except for shells and stone-axe blades. The most central relationships between women and men are continually evaluated and negotiated in the public arena of yam harvests and mortuary distributions.

In this way, the production of yams forces a check on the intent and strength of relationships among individuals—for example, a woman, her husband, and her brother—while at the same time the yam harvest and distribution of women's wealth reflects on the relative power of individual matrilineages, connected to each other through affinal relations. In the center of these individual and group relationships and obligations are women, for the economic role they play enforces the productivity of men. Men work for women both in their gardens and in their purchases of women's wealth. As we will see in the next chapter, so important are the bundles and skirts controlled by women that, politically speaking, when a woman "shows" who she is, she even more profoundly shows where everyone belongs. The relationships that are accounted for in the mortuary distributions of banana bundles and skirts go far beyond the core affinal connections among a woman, her brother, and her husband; they include the relationships between women and their fathers and all patrilateral relationships that encompass those who are *keyawa* (like true matrilineal members) to each other. Women stand as the representatives of the matrilineal group, dispersing their wealth in all directions to the widest network of relationships that the individual members of a matrilineage have. In these distributions, constituting hundreds of individual relationships, we can see how individual actions also represent a group's strength.

8/The regeneration of matrilineality

> Today we went to a big *sagali* in another village. For six hours, starting around 8 A.M., all the women present exchanged *doba* [skirts and bundles]. A name would be called and certain people would run out and give *doba*, making a pile, and then the person whose name was called would run out and take it. One of these exchanges takes a minute, so you can imagine how hard it is for an observer to figure out what is going on—and I haven't.
>
> Linda Weiner

THE WOMEN'S MORTUARY DISTRIBUTION

Early on the morning of a *lisaladabu*—the women's mortuary distribution—the paths and the main road are filled with women carrying the large baskets to the dead person's hamlet, where they will arrange their huge piles of bundles and skirts in the plaza. First the women "owners," that is, the dead person's matrilineal kin, take the most prominent places around the plaza. Then in preparation for the day's events, they arrange their heavy baskets of bundles and skirts. The women carefully count out "clean" bundles and place them in small baskets, which they stack on top of each other. The "new" bundles they pile high onto separate large flat baskets, which they display prominently so that everyone else notices how many new bundles each owner has been able to obtain. If it promises to be a rainy day, as is often the case during the harvest season, men from the hamlet drive some stakes into the ground to support woven coconut-leaf mats that create individual canopies over each group of owners.

Around each owner are her *keyawa* kin and the daughters of the dead person's matrilineal kinsmen, all of whom have their own baskets of bundles and skirts. Each owner and helper are waiting to give away everything that they have been accumulating for the past four to eight months. Behind them, the women "workers" seat themselves, but the baskets they bring are not very full. These workers are the women whose relationship to the dead person is through affinal, patrilateral, or *keyawa* kin and cross-clan friends. On this day, they will be paid bundles and skirts by the owners because they attended to the dead person, the burial, and all the mourning restrictions. Some of them "carried the dead person" and still "carry the dead person's things," that is, the hair or fingernails inserted into cowrie shells; the skirt of a woman or a man's purse; and traditionally, the skull, jawbones, or long bones (see Chapter 2). Most of them have shaved their hair, painted their bodies black, wear mourning skirts, or in the new custom, have tied a piece of black cloth around their arms.

Men workers, that is, the dead person's affinal, patrilateral, and *keyawa* kin, and cross-clan friends also receive bundles and skirts for their work in carrying the dead person to the grave, digging the grave and now caring for it, shaving their heads, blackening their bodies, or wearing black clothes or black armbands. The men are not seated around the plaza because only women carry out the distribution. They sit on the verandas, away from the center, where women dominate the day's events. Their payments are retrieved by their wives or sisters, depending on which mourning activity the payment represents.

Some women come to the hamlet only to purchase bundles for their own forthcoming mortuary distribution. They sit among the workers, but their baskets are filled with tobacco or lime for chewing betel nuts, which they want to exchange with other women in payment for bundles. Because many children attend the distribution, some women buy candies or chewing gum in the trade store; one enterprising woman usually brings balloons. Just as elsewhere in the world, when children see these treats, they run to their mothers and ask for them. Only in Kiriwina, the payment is in bundles.

Just before the distribution begins, a line of women forms on the side of the plaza. The women walk in single file to one of the women owners whose husband is their "brother" and either makes them a yam garden or gives them baskets of yams. Each woman carries twenty to forty bundles or a skirt that she presents to her "brother's" wife, as women say, "to help her" with her distribution. If the woman's husband has a large yam house, he of course will have many "sisters" (see Chapter 5) who walk in the procession and add to her collection of bundles and skirts. As the women present their help to their sister-in-law, they show off their "brother's" strong position and demonstrate what an important help he has been, because of all his yams, to his wife and her matrilineage. A separate line of women attends to each woman owner in the same way, emphasizing the connections that underwrite the day's distribution—yams and women's wealth, women, their husbands and their brothers, and one matrilineage linked through these objects to another.

The general direction of the distribution is like the men's yam competitions, in which members of one matrilineage give wealth to members of other matrilineages from other clans, but the actual details of the distribution are far more complex. Although Malinowski (1922: 54; 1929: 36–38) mentioned the important role women play in mourning rituals, he never wrote anything about women's wealth.[1] He briefly mentioned the exchanges of food following

[1] Malinowski (1929:plate 20) photographed women with their wealth, and in his field notes he mentioned that bundles are distributed when someone dies.

Photo 31. Masawa gives his sisters yams each year and they in turn bring his wife bundles and skirts just before the official women's wealth distribution begins.

each death, emphasizing that it was difficult to understand the rationale behind these events because the same villagers who brought food received food. What is initially confusing but important about those who both give and receive bundles is that these women illustrate the close dependency the members of one matrilineage have with another. The yams that a woman's brother gives to her and her husband in relation to her husband's support for her bundles are a primary example. During the women's mortuary distribution another set of similar relationships is prominently shown.

FATHERS AND DAUGHTERS

The women of the dead person's matrilineage are helped in the distribution by their brothers' married daughters, who are members of other clans. Yet these women give away their wealth with the owners. If a matrilineage is small, these women, in terms of the manifest distribution, make the dead person's matrilineage look stronger than it might be. It is obvious that they are not the dead person's matrilineal kin because their heads are shaved and their bodies blackened. Not being "true owners," they still must observe the mourning taboos for those in the worker category. During the day's distributions, they not only give their wealth as owners, but also receive bundles and skirts because they are workers. It is very shameful, however, to remark to anyone that these women are not "true owners" because to do so publicly marks a matrilineage's dependence on outsiders.

The daughters' presence as owners shows the deep bonds that men have to their daughters, demonstrating the vitality of patrilateral relationships. As emphasized earlier, a man underwrites the economic interdependence between his sister and her husband through his yam production for them. In the same way, he also underwrites the economic link between his daughter and her husband because he gives them yams annually during the early years of their marriage. Even though his yam garden for her may now be replaced by her brother's garden, a yam garden once made for a woman obligates her and even her daughter to assist the women of her father's matrilineage when they are the organizers of a distribution.

Women, along with their husbands, not only work for their own matrilineages but for their fathers' as well. In this way, marriage and all the exchanges of skirts, bundles, and yams creates obligations to and through one's father, which make patrilateral relationships significant for matrilineal activities. The binding tie between a man and his children affirms how each matrilineage can be enhanced by these relationships, as his daughter, and often her daughter as well, work for him and for his kin even after he dies. All the nurturing care and the things from his lineage that a man lends his children are grounded in the help his children eventually give to him.

A Trobriand father is the first and most important relationship through which a child gains access to resources controlled by another matrilineage in another clan. A person's spouse is the second relationship that provides resources from another matrilineage in another clan. The significance of these two relationships and the two stages in a person's life are highly visible during the women's mortuary distribution. Throughout the distribution, the father and spouse of the dead person receive the major payments of the day. Their bundles, totaling in the thousands, must be new ones—those of the highest value—honoring their intensive work of mourning and the care they gave the dead person throughout her or his life.

THE BUNDLE DISTRIBUTION

Every person who in some way was associated with the dead person and a member of another lineage is given bundles. With each subsequent payment, the expanding network of the dead person's connections can be traced to friends, affines, *keyawa*, and patrilateral kin. When a man dies, even the men with whom he participated in *kula* exchanges are given bundles. These distributions are truly the recapitulation of each social and political relationship that figured in the dead person's life. As noted earlier, most of these villagers will have done one or more of the following: shaved their hair; blackened their bodies; carried the dead person's things; prepared the grave; brought

Photo 32. The "big" woman of the day calls out each recipient's name as she makes the first presentation and then other owners quickly add to the pile.

yams to the earlier burial distributions; or cooked food for the spouse and father, who were secluded since the death occurred. Each person is paid with bundles and sometimes skirts for each act of mourning. So many payments are involved, especially if the dead person was important or had powerful kin, that now villagers often record some of the names in notebooks to prevent quarrels when someone is forgotten during the distribution. When a child dies, the distribution is much smaller, as only the father and his kin will be the primary receivers of bundles and skirts. The one woman who stands as the leader of the distribution is the "wealthy" woman of the day because she has been able to collect more skirts and bundles than anyone else. Sometimes two women share this role because both have amassed equally imposing quantities of bundles, especially new ones. During the months between the burial and the women's distribution, all the women owners have been competing against one another to take this leadership role. Just as a chief's exceptional economic power in yams is equated with the strength of the men who make gardens for him, so, too, the women who achieve this leadership position reflect the economic resources of their husbands.

On the day of the distribution, the leader is easily recognized by the special

Photo 33. Only a few women have enough bundles for each individual exchange, and so most make careful decisions about how much to give when each name is called.

long skirt she wears. A few weeks before the event, when it is apparent who will have the most wealth, the skirt is woven for the leading woman.[2] The distribution is under her control as she must make the first payment for every single distribution by throwing bundles on the ground in the plaza center while she calls a worker's name and the reason for the payment. "Bomapota, *lisaladabu*," she shouts, as she throws ten or fifteen bundles to reward Bomapota for shaving her hair. Then other women owners, plus their helpers, each add five or ten more bundles to the pile. Finally, Bomapota gathers up the bundles and puts them in her basket. If the owners are successful in showing their strength, they contribute bundles when each name is called. If a matrilineage has many women and many helpers, the piles each time will be larger than if a matrilineage has been reduced to a few women. Wise women carefully plan their strategies: If they do not have large reserves, they conserve their bundles by not adding too many to each outlay or they withhold bundles from certain payments. What makes a woman wealthy and a leader is her ability to disperse her wealth generously to every single person whose name is called. Even during the distribution, women owners still compete among themselves to gain recognition for their contributions.

Throughout the day, the individual payments vary, depending on the owners' accumulated wealth, the particular reason for the payment, and the status

[2] Usually when the skirt is finished, several women will actually fight with each other to be the one who will wear it. See Weiner (1976: 97–103) for details about the skirt weaving and the competition associated with its ownership.

of those who receive the wealth. Important women and men who have wide networks of relationships receive many more bundles when their names are called than younger people or those adults who are not economically strong. Some payments are made with old or dirty bundles, such as those given to villagers who shaved their heads. Each of these payments never amounts to more than sixty bundles. But some payments require clean bundles. These are the distributions Imkitava warned me about, for they are "for yams."

All the dead person's matrilineal kinsmen and their *keyawa* kin, who helped them by contributing yams to the earlier distributions following the burial, receive bundles and skirts. This is another example of how the owners who give their wealth away also receive wealth. When a man's name is called, any woman for whom the man makes a yam garden or gives baskets of yams, regardless of whether or not she is an owner or a worker, must add additional bundles and skirts to his pile. The men who work hard to grow yams and have many "sisters" may find as many as a thousand bundles and ten or more skirts heaped up in the plaza center when their names are called and these are claimed by their wives, emphasizing again the complementary connections between women and men, yams and bundles.

All together there are seventeen categories of mourning services for which villagers may receive payments.[3] Finally, after anywhere from five to eight hours of continual transactions, each of which takes only a few minutes, the bundle distribution draws to a close. The women owners now attend to the special workers, that is, the closest matrilineal kin of the dead person's father and spouse, who carry the dead person's things. Earlier in the distribution, each of these women received extensive amounts of clean bundles for each act of mourning she performed. Now the owners cut the black fiber cord that each woman has around her neck and remove the two strands of long black mourning necklaces of dried seeds that each woman wears. The owners then drape a beautiful red skirt around her drab-colored mourning skirt.

Today, some of the more sophisticated owners sprinkle talcum powder over the women's heads, the white in stark contrast to their shaved and blackened heads, emphasizing their return to beauty and sexuality. Their elaborate mourning garb is a negation of their sexuality, their removal from sexual activity. As onerous as their mourning taboos are, when the owners approach them with new skirts, many of the women begin to cry and pull away out of grief for the dead person. Even though they now let their hair grow, dress in bright colors, and look attractive again, the full extent of their work is not completely finished. As we will see, they still carry the shells with the dead person's things.

The women owners return to their places; and then, suddenly, they run into the plaza center with small empty baskets, shouting, "Give some bundles for my husband!" Women workers who are related in some way to the woman or her husband throw a few bundles into her basket. Although the workers were the major recipients of bundles, they now show their appreciation for

[3] See Weiner (1976: 104–116) for explanations about each of the seventeen categories.

Photo 34. When a woman does not have fine enough red skirts she substitutes trade store cloth for the final march to the spouse and to the father of the deceased.

the men who helped make it possible for them to receive so much. Now the bundle distribution is finished, but it is not the conclusion of the exchanges.

THE END OF *LISALADABU*

The activity shifts as the women owners and their helpers form a long line, each one carrying a beautiful skirt. The skirts should be new ones that were dyed red but have not yet been cut short. Occasionally, if a woman does not have a fine enough skirt, in the trade store she buys cotton cloth, which she ties to a long pole and carries like a flag. It is not surprising that in the most modern women's mortuary distribution, held for Chief Vanoi in Port Moresby (see Chapter 1), most women brought yards of cloth because in the city they had no access to large numbers of banana leaves.

The women walk in a single-file procession to the house veranda, where the bereaved spouse is secluded, and deposit the skirts. Forming another line, they carry equally fine skirts or cloth to the house where the bereaved father is staying. After the women present all the skirts and cloth, the men owners, that is, the dead person's matrilineal kinsmen with their sons and *keyawa* kin, enter the proceedings. They leave the house verandas where they had been sitting while the bundle distribution was taking place; for the first time during the day, they take an active part in the distribution, carrying their own prized valuables—such as an axe-blade or a *kula* shell, or as lesser substitutes, a large clay pot or money—all of which they, too, leave with the father and the spouse.

The men owners are not done with their part in the distribution because they next sort out piles of yams for each hamlet that has been represented by all the women in attendance. Just like the women leaders, the men stand in the center of the plaza, where the yams are arranged, and call out, "Obulabula hamlet, your yams!" The wife of Obulabula's hamlet leader then gets the yams and redistributes them to all the other women from her hamlet. When each hamlet's name has been called, the men leave the center. *Lisaladabu* is now finished, and as everyone prepares to return home—many with far more women's wealth than when they arrived and many others with empty baskets—the value of the owners' wealth is made clear. Because the baskets of the women owners have been overturned successfully, they have handsomely repaid all the work of mourning for the dead person. Yet they do not leave the hamlet empty-handed; not only do their "brothers" participate in the presentation of valuables to the dead person's father and spouse and give away their yams, but also they have been cooking since sunrise. They now bring their "sisters" large pieces of pork, taro pudding, and cooked yams to "thank" them for working so hard. Even though men also participated by giving away their valuables and yams, the day belongs to the women. In giving this food, men show their respect for what their "sisters" have done.

I always had a special feeling of accomplishment when, at the end of a long day of distribution, I received some food from a "brother" because I gave away my own bundles. When in 1980 I helped the women owners in a very large distribution for Tomuwa, a middle-aged Kwaibwaga man who was thought to have died from European poisons, my performance that day sparked an unusual conversation. After the distribution was over and all the women were leaving Kwaibwaga, Bilagola, a woman from Mutawa village who had never seen me at a distribution before, stopped to tell Bunemiga that he should not let me return to America. "She knows how to do *lisaladabu* very well," she said. "Make her stay in Kwaibwaga." That was the best compliment I ever had.

Once *lisaladabu* is finished, the mourning hamlet returns to all usual activities, and all the workers let their hair grow and put on good clothes once again. It will be six months or another year before the spouse and father of the dead person are completely freed from their seclusion and mourning attire. At the appropriate time, the women owners take them both to the beach, and in a special ceremony (*winelawoulo*) at the water's edge, the owners wash off the black paint. In a final flourish, they cut the thick, blackened fiber necklace that traditionally was made from the dead person's hair. This necklace is called a *kuwa*, the same term used for the bright-red shell necklaces that young people wear to symbolize their sexuality (see Chapter 4). As the red *kuwa* necklace is removed when young people marry, symbolizing the end of their adolescent sexuality, so at death the black *kuwa* is the last element of mourning removed, symbolizing the end of the marriage and, for the father, the end of his role in the life of his child.

Even after this final ceremony with the spouse and father, the ties to the dead person's kin are still not lost. Additional distributions take place once a year during the harvest season, continuing for five or ten years after the women's mortuary distribution. These events are organized by a hamlet leader or a chief for his dead kin, but they commemorate other villagers, members of the same clan, who also recently died. Their matrilineal kin join with the organizer to present the distribution, which must be one kind of food only, such as yam, taro pudding, pig, fish, betel nut, or a large *kuvi* yam. The same elements of competition occur throughout the day's event, as each group of owners tries to outdo the other owners. In these distributions, huge piles of food are given by each group of owners to the father, to the spouse if he or she has not yet remarried, and to those of their kin who carry the dead person's things or take care of the grave. Only when one distribution for each kind of food has been held will the owners take back the dead person's things. By then, marriages or other deaths will have started new sets of connections linked to these former relationships.

Traditionally, when a chief died, the last distribution took place when his skull, decorated with red paint and cowrie shells, was carried to the top of the limestone ridge and left there, overlooking the sea. Before this event could take place, the new chief had to be able to sponsor a massive distribution of large *kuvi* yams, proving that his authority and power now equaled or surpassed his predecessor's former stature. It might take fifteen or twenty years to carry out this final farewell. The death of chiefs or important hamlet leaders precipitates for their successors not only widespread mourning and exhaustive work—to accumulate and give away massive amounts of all kinds of wealth—but also, politically, the start of building new marriages and expanding power relationships. A successor assumes his new status because of his birthright. Most of his predecessor's movable wealth has been given away in all the mourning distributions. Little, if anything, is left except the inherent force and authority embodied in the matrilineage itself. This is what Chief Vanoi was reminded of by the woman who appeared in his room after Mitakata's death. Remember the stones from your ancestors, she counseled him. Remember them because your ancestors are your strength.

THE REGENERATION OF MATRILINEAL IDENTITY

In Kiriwina, the work of death is far more burdensome and costly than any exchanges associated with births or even marriages. It is easy now to understand why Becky complained to me that with one death "we work so hard." What we see is that out of each death comes the regeneration not only of all the complex relationships that went into the life of the person who died but also of the matilineage's strength. Beyond everything that a villager might become throughout his or her life, there is always the necessity to make others know where one belongs. Although through women and the *baloma* spirits, matrilineal identity is thought to be inalienable, the authority conveyed by that identity is subject to jeopardy. Ancestors were the original providers of significant sumptuary paraphernalia, such as the stones, shell decorations, magic spells and food taboos, but right from the beginning they also lost some of these things to others. The Tabalu ancestral story describing the loss of status through the breaking of a food taboo (see Chapter 6) speaks directly to these failures.

To show who one is and to show where one belongs are the two sides that constitute hierarchical relations. To make unassailable who one is politically and where one belongs ancestrally, one must establish some measure of control over others outside the matrilineage. For men, yams are the key to this control, but as we have seen, control even for chiefs is difficult to sustain. As a leader or chief gains power, these goals become even more essential. For this reason, the work of projecting one's fame and one's matrilineal identity can never cease, for ultimately the two are tied together. Lasting individual fame is dependent on those same outsiders, whereas they themselves need to have constant proof that the person to whom they are attached is building fame for the name of his matrilineage.

Unlike any other Kiriwina event, the women's mortuary distribution details both these processes as the exchanges register the strengths and weaknesses of individuals in their endeavors to build toward these goals. The bundle presentations by the women owners not only point out where villagers belong in their kinship and affinal connections with each other but also expose the political positions of those they reward. At the same time, the distribution gives the women of the deceased's martrilineage the center stage to show who they are individually. In the day's competition, a woman owner, like any chief, marks out her own status and that of her husband and brother. Beyond individual politics, the women owners en masse define the eminence and vitality of the matrilineage itself. The day marks a political challenge enacted by women to those who think that the matrilineage owners are weak. By distributing enough wealth to look strong, the women of the matrilineage "untie" the dead person from all her or his relationships, paying back each villager for the care and attention that constituted the relationship, so that with the close of the bundle distribution, the deceased is separated from all past obligations.

In the process, the women of the dead person's matrilineage pay the price of each relationship that was created with villagers in other clans. By *cutting* these ties, women momentarily suspend these relationships and expose the authority of the matrilineage as an inalienable force requiring nothing from anyone else. Yet this moment is short-lived because the members of the matrilineage realistically must return to their dependence on others. The trauma associated with each death is the disjuncture it causes in the hundreds of relationships that cross clan boundaries. The measure of how difficult it is to regenerate these relationships through time can be seen in the devotion and hard work that is expended as one person in a matrilineage throughout his or her life tries to make his or her matrilineal identity strong while building bridges to long-lasting relationships with villagers in other clans.

From a societal perspective, the process of building up a person by creating relationships among others in different clans is potentially an expanding one; but as we have seen in the previous chapters, it is a process that demands unending attention and work. Death deflates this buildup, puncturing the expanding possibilities by destroying one person in the web of all these relationships. The difficult work of creating extended networks of relationships is far too important to be lost. Women with their wealth, by "untying" the deceased, revitalize these relationships by showing for the future where people belong. Women's wealth circumscribes not only the standing of each person vis-à-vis others but also where each person belongs in terms of future rights and obligations. Free of debt, the matrilineage, like puffed up new and clean bundles, can expand outward again, regenerating these relationships with renewed strength. As bundles are given to five hundred or more villagers, they mark the intergenerational, ego-centered networks that link husbands to wives, fathers to children, *keyawa* kin to *keyawa* kin, and cross-clan relatives to cross-clan relatives. At the center of this ongoing reaching out across marital, lineage, clan, and generational boundaries is a woman and her brother —the primary relationship that constitutes each matrilineage.

Although bundles repay the most extensive range of debts, it is the skirts of the women and the valuables of the women's brothers that begin the regenerative process. In the march to the father and the spouse at the end of the women's mortuary distribution, each woman carries a new red skirt— the ultimate women's valuable—symbolizing sexuality and fertility, the active components of matrilineal autonomy. After the women come their "brothers," with their traditional valuables of stone axe-blades or *kula* shells. Unlike the women's valuables, the most important of the men's valuables are those that are old. Men's valuables, made from hard substances, last for generations, and each valuable is recognized by the history of its circulation. These histories, however, are of individual men and their relationships with other men in other matrilineages. Thus, hard valuables symbolize the connections between one person and others, whereas soft valuables symbolize the inalienability of matrilineal identity.

The full range of a matrilineage's movable valuables is presented in this distribution to the members of the two matrilineages most closely related to the dead person. These valuables together express the two dimensions of hierarchical relations: who one is and where one belongs. This occasion is the only time when men's and women's valuables are presented in tandem; at all other times their exchange values are mutually exclusive. In the mortuary exchanges it is the women's soft wealth of bundles and skirts and the men's valuables of hard wealth that together show the strength of the matrilineage and the effort the members now make to restore a measure of the social and political relationships, among others, that the death has left in question. Hard and soft valuables, representing the men and women of a matrilineage, come together in this final moment of the women's mortuary distribution, showing clearly the political necessity to redefine and reestablish individual status *and* matrilineal authority.

Photo 35. Looking brilliant against the drab browns and greens of the village, women's red skirts are spread out in front of the deceased's spouse's house where they will be divided up among the spouse's matrilineal kin.

When women walk before men in this procession, they carry in their hands the wealth that gives them a socially preeminent and politically forceful role in Kiriwina society. Through their distributions of bundles and skirts, they represent the stability of the matrilineage; and in the beliefs associated with conception, they and their ancestral spirits are the connecting agents through which conception occurs. Their wealth not only is marked in symbolic ways as an object of sexuality and fertility but also has economic value, as it subsumes men's wealth and keeps men dependent on women. In this way, women are the major conservative figures, drawing everything back to the importance of expressing the inalienability of matrilineal identity when that identity is most under attack.

Although Kiriwina women control an activity that has economic and political importance, making them unusual in comparison with women's status and power in many other Papua New Guinea societies,[4] there are limitations to their power. These boundaries are illuminated in the differences between women's soft valuables and men's hard valuables. In Kiriwina, as we have seen, men's valuables are used to repay other men for their exceptionally hard garden work, to buy additional seed yams, to purchase important magic

[4] Compare, for example, the role of Melpa women in the New Guinea Highlands (A. M. Strathern 1972), the Kewa (Josephides 1985), the Enga (Feil 1984), and the Baruya (Godelier 1986); see also the essays in Brown and Buchbinder (1976), A. J. Strathern (1982), and Poole and Herdt (1982).

spells, to give to the bride's kin at marriages, and even to pay a sorcerer. In each case, hard valuables provide the wherewithal to obtain the kinds of increasing resources that are necessary to make men politically dominant. The effort to retain this wealth so one may increase one's productive control over others is undercut by the equally destructive role that death plays. In the final march to the house of the spouse and father of the dead person, men's valuables are given away *without any material return*. Just as each death drains the men's other kinds of wealth, when they must provide women with bundles, so, too, death drains their hard valuables.

As the next chapter illustrates, finding hard valuables is the most difficult pursuit of all. In these endeavors, men travel far from their place of authority within their matrilineage to pursue *kula* activities. Men's dependency is of a different sort since they are free from the demands of women's wealth and from the demands that matrilineal identity produces. In *kula*, men think of themselves as independent actors, but as we will see, if women's power is circumscribed by the form of their wealth, men ultimately fare no better.

9 / *Kula* and the search for fame

After a quite boring church service we went to the beach for a picnic. The traveling was rough—climbing up and down slippery coral rocks for about a mile, but it was worth it. I just laid in the sand and the coconut trees seem stretched miles out over the water that goes on infinitely. It's another story when you walk into the water. It is all coral. Even holding on to someone a wave knocked me down and I'm covered with bandages from coral cuts.

Linda Weiner

"ARGONAUTS" ON *KULA* VOYAGES

To anthropologists the word *kula* conjures up large outrigger canoes with intricately carved, brightly painted prows and great pandanus sails rigged and trimmed by handsomely decorated Trobriand men, voyaging from Kiriwina with hopes of exchanging the ornate, white *Conus* armshells (*mwali*) or the finely chiseled red *Chama*-shell necklaces (*bagi*). Since Malinowski first described these voyages in *Argonauts of the Western Pacific*,[1] anthropologists have puzzled over the precise value concentrated in the famed *kula* shells—a value so intense that men travel for weeks or months, often under difficult sailing conditions, to another island, where they camp on the beach until finally, using all their powers of persuasion and magic, they "turn the minds" of their *kula* partners to release the prized shells. Returning home, their waiting kin profess to hear thunder roar and feel the ground shake—nature's witness to the success of the voyage and the spreading fame of the men.

In its barest essentials, *kula* can be described as the exchange of an armshell to which cowrie pendants, beads, and string have been attached for an equally valued necklace, from which gold-lipped oyster shells and other trinkets hang from either end. In *Argonauts of the Western Pacific*, Malinowski documented that the acts of giving and receiving shell valuables, associated as they were with myths, rituals, and magic practices, could not be happenstance occur-

[1] Malinowski published an earlier essay on *kula* in 1920.

Photo 36. The canoes are beached at the edge of the water, while men sit on the house verandas and discuss Kula *business.*

rences. Here was a *system* of exchange that operated with specific rules and obligations over wide distances and among people with different, although related, languages and traditions. No other ethnography has had a more lasting impact on the development of ideas and theories of "primitive" economics.[2] Once *Argonauts* was published, scholars could no longer characterize such societies as functioning without economic principles, and no longer could "primitive" exchange be associated with people with "primitive" mentalities.

Still, even for Malinowski, there was something incomprehensible about how this "simple action—the passing from hand to hand of two meaningless and quite useless objects" could become "the foundation of a big inter-tribal institution. . . . so vast, complex, and deeply rooted" (1922:86). From recent research in the Massim, we know that *kula* is an exchange system of such complex magnitude that Malinowski never fully comprehended the intricacies

[2] Marcel Mauss (1954) devoted a major part of his classic work on exchange to the *kula*. Reo Fortune's *Sorcerers of Dobu* (1932) discussed *kula* from the perspective of Dobu Island, southwest of Kiriwina, where men from the southern part of Kiriwina and Vakuta Island travel to do *kula*. J. P. Singh Uberoi (1962) reanalyzed the *kula* from Malinowski's findings, focusing on local and interisland politics. Malinowski's study played a substantive role in the theoretical work of, for example, Dalton (1977), Raymond Firth (1967), Claude Lévi-Strauss (1969), Karl Polanyi (1958), and Marshall Sahlins (1972). See J. W. Leach and E. R. Leach (1983) for recent studies and discussions of *kula* from Malinowski's time to the present decade. See Macintyre (1983b) for a comprehensive *kula* bibliography and J. W. Leach (1983a:1–14) for a review of the history of *kula*.

of the way the shells move around the islands and the meanings associated with their exchange.[3]

Contemporary studies from other parts of Papua New Guinea also illustrate that complicated exchange systems are not a Massim anomaly. For example, among the Melpa who live in the New Guinea Highlands, pigs and pearl shells (the latter now replaced by money) are strategically and laboriously amassed by powerful clan leaders, who hold huge distributions, called *moka*, for members of other clans.[4] In these exchanges, the use of magic, ritual dress, and speech are important to attaining success. As Andrew J. Strathern (1983) pointed out, *moka* does not operate with the same basic principle of equivalency found in *kula*. In *moka*, the intent is to make each distribution incremental to the previous one, so that a "big" man gains more than he previously gave. Of course, each time he gets more, in a future distribution with the same person he will have to return more. It is against this incremental competition that clan leaders, helped by their wives, cognates, and affines, gain status as they oppose each other in exchange.

In *kula*, however, the main thrust of the exchange is to *match* the size and value of one shell exactly for another. Members of a clan are not in competition with other clans in a corporate way, as in the New Guinea Highlands. *Kula* men individually compete with each other to acquire specific partners, or "friends" as they are often called, living on a continuum of islands, who exchange serially with each other and usually are not relatives.[5] Individual partners constitute a "path" (*keda*) along which ideally particular shells are passed from one partner to another. Men from one village or several nearby villages join together under the leadership of a chief or hamlet leader to sail to another island, where they meet their *kula* partners who are resident there. A few months earlier, these partners sailed to another island, where they brought back their *kula* shells from their partners in residence on that island. The armshells move in a counterclockwise direction, linking each partner with the next. The necklaces move along the same paths, but in the opposite direction, being passed to the same partners. In each trip, the *kula* men sail with empty hands to bring the shells back to their own homes, where eventually their partners from the next island will come to take them. Six months or a year later the voyages are reversed, and the men who before as hosts

[3] There are regional variations in the details of *kula* activities, especially in the western part of the Massim (see Macintyre 1983a, 1983c, Thune 1983). See also Battaglia (1983), Lepowsky (1983), and Liep (1983) on exchanges of shell valuables in the southern Massim where *kula* is not practiced. Although the view I present is essentially an overview, my primary focus is from Kiriwina. For discussions of *kula* from the perspective of other northern Massim islands, see J. W. Leach and E. R. Leach (1983), especially the essays by Campbell (pp. 201–248), Damon (pp. 309–344), J. W. Leach (pp. 121–146), and Munn (pp. 277–308). See also Damon (1980), Munn (1977), and Weiner (1983b:147–170).

[4] Both the *moka* for the Melpa and the *tee* for the Enga have undergone changes with pacification. For extensive accounts of both systems, see A. J. Strathern (1971) on the Melpa, Meggitt (1972) and Feil (1984) on the Enga.

[5] Within one local area, however, a few men who are kin or affines may be partners, and then they are both part of the same overseas path. See Malinowski (1922:464–477) on inland *kula*; see also Campbell (1983b), Damon (1980), and Macintyre (1983a).

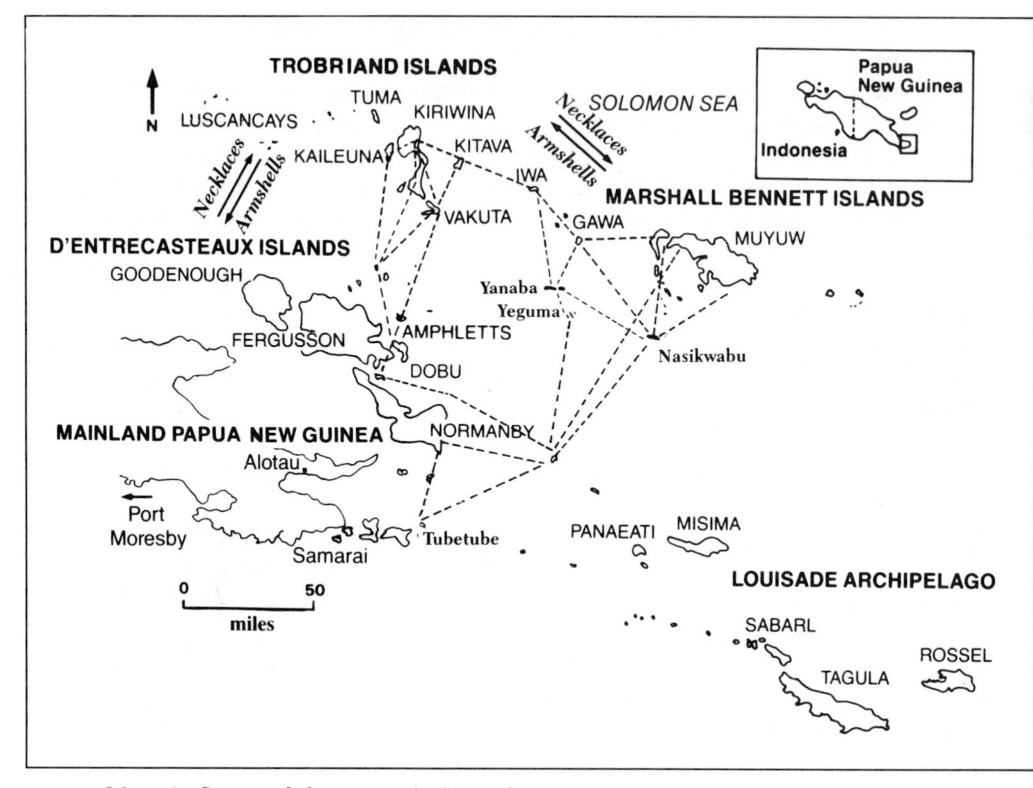

Map 4. Some of the major kula *paths.*

received their partners in their own village now are the ones to travel as guests to their partners' island to get their necklaces.

In this way, from one location to another, the shells move through those Massim islands where particular villagers engage in the exchanges (see Map 4).[6] For one shell to travel from the beginning of its path to its return takes a minimum of two to five years, often longer. In some islands, almost all villagers participate, so that, for example, in one southern Kiriwina village and on Vakuta Island, to the south of Kiriwina, most men are active in *kula*. Traditionally, in northern Kiriwina only men from high-ranking lineages or their sons engaged in *kula*. Since colonization, when the pearling industry brought more wealth into the local economy, a measure of democratization occurred and commoners, too, took up *kula*. Currently in northern Kiriwina, only the most politically prominent men, whether members of a ranking

[6] See J. W. Leach (1983a:18) for a list of all participating *kula* communities throughout the Massim during the 1970s, and J. W. Leach (1983b) for a discussion of who participates in Kiriwina *kula*.

Photo 37. A Sinaketa man measures two of his prized kula *necklaces.*

lineage or not, form a *kula* community. Generally, Kiriwina women do not *kula* on their own, but on Kitava Island, to the east of Kiriwina, and elsewhere in the Massim, some women are important players in these strategic games.[7]

Once while discussing *kula* roads with a few Kwaibwaga village men, Bweneyeya went to his house and returned with a piece of paper listing the names of his *kula* partners. He personally knew those who live on the closest islands, where he himself travels to *kula*, but he had never seen his other partners from more distant places. Bweneyeya said proudly, "They never see my face, but they know my name."

A *kula* man's fame (*butura*) is created through the circulation of his name in relation to the largest and the most valued shells that he has obtained. Armshells and necklaces are ranked according to their size, color, and fineness

[7] Throughout the Massim, women represent a small percentage of participants. Although they are often players of great renown, they seldom travel on the overseas voyages because an intermediary carries out their transactions for them. See details from Tubetube Island (Macintyre 1983a) and from Kitava Island (Scoditti with J. W. Leach 1983). On Kiriwina, if a young boy inherits his mother's brother's *kula* paths, his mother will do his *kula* exchanges for him when men from other islands or other Trobriand villages come to make their transactions; but his father will go on the sailing voyages until he is old enough to participate.

Photo 38. An armshell is valued when it is large and exhibits striations of dark color indicating its age. This prized shell also is inscribed with the names of the partners who possessed it.

of the shell's polishing; with these criteria, the best ones are categorized into named rankings. For example, in judging the value of a necklace, a person will examine the length, the fineness of grinding, and the dimensions for each individual shell. Then the color is evaluated, and the speed with which a person's hand slips along the full length of the necklace is noted (Campbell 1983a:229–248). Through the years that a shell is passed around the Massim, it accumulates a history of its circulation. Although a new, large, finely polished necklace may be highly ranked, its value and fame increase as the accounts associated with it accrue. Just as a man gains renown through the circulation of his name with particular shells, so too, as the shells continue to move from one partner to another, they likewise gain value from their association with particular men.

Because the movement of the shell garners value and fame, *kula* partners must attend to *kula* transactions with great care and expertise. For example, the farther the shells travel away from Bweneyeya, the less influence he has over their direction and the intent of those partners he never sees. Fame in *kula* is difficult to achieve. Unlike kinship relations within a Kiriwina village where, for example, yam production and women's wealth provide continual checks and balances on each person involved in these exchanges, *kula* partners are much freer agents. Usually only men who have been doing *kula* for many years manage to become the experts whose fame circulates widely.

THE BASIS OF *KULA*: CEREMONIAL OR UTILITARIAN

To those anthropologists who link causality to material production, the motivation to create history seems an improbable reason for *kula* actions. Unlike the *moka*, in which huge numbers of pigs must be cared for and fed by many relatives until they are grown and then killed and distributed to large numbers of people, *kula* requires little in the way of local intensive garden production or husbandry. Although a *kula* man usually presents his partner with a piece of pork, some taro or yams, or even crafted goods—such as pandanus mats, clay pots, or woven baskets—these small gifts are not given to claim fame. Like the exchanges of betel and tobacco among lovers, they are the means to influence, to "seduce" a *kula* friend to part with his shell. Although each shell should follow its particular path, passing from one partner to another, a person may divert a shell to another path or delay giving his partner a shell for several years, sometimes even longer. To be generous with food and other things conveys good intentions and expresses a partner's future trustworthiness in passing the shells to the appropriate partner.

The custom of giving the initial small gifts in *kula* transactions—as well as Malinowski's (1922:99–100) report that men engaged in "secondary trade" or barter for other things while they were visiting their partners—prompted many anthropologists to hypothesize that *kula* exchanges merely constituted the "ceremonial" umbrella under which "utilitarian" trade of scarce resources took place. Archaeological data indicate that extensive trading of foods, craft goods, and valuables occurred for hundreds of years throughout the Massim and from as far away as the mainland of Papua New Guinea.[8] Objects used for wealth, such as clay pots, stone axe-blades, and even *kula* shells, are produced from raw materials found only on certain islands, and therefore they always had to be transported from their source of production to the islands where they were needed. Yet evidence from a large-scale trade network that still operates illustrates that overseas trade can be undertaken without the necessity for the "ceremonial" exchanges of shells.

The Siassi, who live on one of the offshore islands in the Vitiaz Straits, north of the Trobriands, are renowned canoe makers and sailors, who travel from their island homes to the mainland and then across to the coastal villages of New Britain where, as sea-faring entrepreneurs, they trade what is scarce in one place for what is abundant elsewhere (see Harding 1967, 1970). In this way, clay pots, coconuts, food, pigs, and dogs are shuttled across the straits, providing local villagers over a wide area important valuables necessary for marriage and mortuary payments. The Siassi are middle men, trading without "ceremonial" rituals. Nothing like the solitary giving of one kind of shell for another occurs in their transactions, so that it is not necessarily the case, as some anthropologists have argued, that the friendship created through "ceremonial" exchange provides safety for men whose primary mission is to trade their wares.

[8] See for example, Allen (1977), Egloff (1972), Irwin (1978), and Lauer (1971).

Malinowski argued the reverse: The "ceremonial" exchange of the shells themselves produced such emotional feelings on the part of the participants that *kula* had to be understood as a unique system of exchange. The "utilitarian" aspects were secondary to the exchange of shell valuables; he further conjectured that *kula* would continue as a dynamic institution even without the necessity to barter for other things. Even before Malinowski, however, Gilmour (1900), a Methodist missionary stationed in Kiriwina at the turn of the century, described long overseas trading expeditions from the Trobriands; but he also noted that other canoe trips "were principally concerned in the exchange of the circulating articles of native wealth," that is, armshells and necklaces. It seems more than likely that before the arrival of Europeans in the Massim, both trade expeditions *and kula* voyages were active simultaneously. Even now, long-distance canoe voyages expressly for the purpose of trading, without any *kula* participants, still take place in the Massim. Perhaps we will never know if *kula* began in this way. What we do know is that the basic feature of exchanging one kind of valuable for another in opposite directions has remained surprisingly constant over the past one hundred years, and in *kula* expeditions today, secondary trade is almost nonexistent, bearing out Malinowski's first observations.

KULA IN HISTORICAL PERSPECTIVE

The general form of *kula* exchanges and the emotional attachment to *kula* transactions, as Malinowski saw, have such deep cultural meanings that they have withstood considerable modification and variation. Archaeologists report that armshells and necklaces have been in the region for 2,000 years, although the institution of *kula* may be only about 500 years old.[9] Yet *kula* is not a static system; its most dynamic qualities are expressed through its vitality and accommodation to change. Long before Europeans settled in the Massim, access to *kula* objects, shifts in local participation, and interisland warfare, especially in the southern and western Massim, forced alterations in *kula* activity.[10] In the last century, many other articles of value, such as boars' tusks, stone axe-blades, *Chama*-shell belts, elaborately decorated lime spatulas, and canoes, were an integral part of *kula* transactions. These objects, however, were not all equivalent to each other nor were they haphazardly exchanged. Specific criteria were used to distinguish their values, which determined their role in particular *kula* transactions.

From archaeological research, we know that places where shells, as well as pottery and stone axe-blades, were produced have shifted, illustrating that long before Europeans discovered this area, technical specialization was never permanently localized geographically.[11] Even in the historic period, produc-

[9] Irwin (1983:71).
[10] See Macintyre (1983a).
[11] See especially Egloff (1978), Irwin (1978), and Lauer (1971).

tion of *kula* shells would drop off in one place only to flourish in another. For example, in Kiriwina, men from Sinaketa village in southern Kiriwina used to make red shell necklaces, but by the 1930s, no one produced the shells, and now the technology is lost. Not only technical skills but also the locations for *kula* exchange shifted as some villages, even entire islands, ceased to be part of the *kula* circuit in prehistoric time. These alterations in local *kula* participation continue today as *kula* transactions diminish or disappear in one place and "new" men or women enter the *kula* in places where no one remembers any *kula* activity in the past.[12]

In general, the colonial situation expanded the opportunities for *kula*. Large quantities of newly made armshells and necklaces were bought by European traders and resold in their stores to villagers. By far, the most inflationary trend was created when shells were given by Europeans to villagers as payment for their labor. When local Kiriwina men were needed as divers for the lucrative exports of pearls and *bêche-de-mer*, traders paid them with stone axes and armshells to entice them away from work on their yam gardens. With more wealth available and with the cessation of warfare, throughout the Massim more women and men engaged in *kula* activities, so that the inflation in the volume of shell valuables eventually served to accommodate these new players. As certain rare valuables like boars' tusks and stone axe-blades were no longer being produced, the increasing volume of armshells and necklaces kept the total number of *kula* valuables from declining, further stabilizing the exchange system.

One of the most significant changes that colonialism brought was motor-driven boats and commercial fishing and shipping. Communication between islands was no longer dependent on sailing canoes, and often a local man working on a government or commercial ship could visit a *kula* partner on his own without waiting for a *kula* expedition to be launched. Travel by ship for *kula* is much preferred since it is faster, safer, and easier, but in the beginning there was some resistance. For example, in the early 1930s, a European trader took a group of Kiriwina men on board his trawler and ferried them to Dobu Island for *kula*; but the Dobuans made fun of the men because they had not come by canoe. When a colonial government officer stationed on Kiriwina heard of the trip, he became adamant about keeping *kula* "pristine," and he tried to make it illegal for *kula* travel in anything other than canoes. The law was never approved and today, whenever Kiriwinans can go by motorboat, they do so. In the latter 1970s, Vanoi and Waibadi crossed to Kitava Island for *kula* on a government launch. A few years later, John K took Sinaketa men to Dobu Island on a cabin cruiser. Yet Kiriwinans still build *kula* canoes, although fewer in numbers than in Malinowski's time. With the continual decline in Australian commercial shipping in the Massim since World War II, many *kula* partners still rely on outrigger canoes, at least for now and the near future.

Whether *kula* partners travel by canoe or motorboat, interest in *kula* has

[12] See Chowning (1983:411–430), Macintyre (1983a), and Thune (1983: 345–368) for details.

not subsided with national independence. In 1964, when the first national elections were held for seats in the House of Assembly, Lepani Watson, a Trobriand candidate for the electoral district that included several other islands, based his campaign on his *kula* expertise. Watson's father had been a chief who was renowned in *kula*, and important village leaders on these distant islands remembered Watson from his younger days when he traveled with his father on *kula* expeditions. Ultimately, it was this *kula* fame that gave him the winning edge over his five opponents.[13]

Usually young men begin their *kula* training under older, knowledgeable men. In the Trobriands, a *kula* man may take his sister's son or his own son with him on *kula* voyages, introducing him to his partners and allowing him to listen to their conversations. A *kula* person's partners and paths are inherited. Often, however, after a man dies, his partners do not have much confidence in the younger man because of his inexperience. For example, although Peter's father was a chief and he left him three *kula* paths when he died, he lost two of them and his *kula* shells; his closest partner did not believe that Peter was "strong" enough so he diverted Peter's shells onto a different path. If a man has a well-known valuable, other men who are not partners on a valuable's present path will try to convince the holder of the valuable to change its path by putting it on one of their paths. As we will see, diversionary tactics abound among *kula* players. On the one hand, a person faces many temptations; on the other hand, he or she may become the focus of others' enticements.

Today, young Trobrianders who hold important business and government positions in Port Moresby enter *kula* as the means to spread their fame throughout the Massim and enhance their political careers. Some of them, away at school while they were young, have had little *kula* training. Lepani Watson summed it up when he complained about the young men with salaries in Port Moresby who take several hundred dollars and buy a fine necklace. When they return to Kiriwina, they want to enter *kula*. They think that all they need is one big valuable. But they quickly lose it because they forget "that *kula* takes a lot of work—all the time you must take care of your friends. These boys do not understand about the work."

WORKING FOR *KULA*

In Malinowski's account of *kula*, his descriptions of shells and their circulation made the acts of receiving and giving seem automatic. He emphasized that a shell could be diverted and given to another man instead of the intended partner, but he did not understand the principles of debt that operate in *kula*, nor did he recognize the importance of how *kula* paths are constructed and how they collapse. His major emphasis was on the circularity of the shells'

[13] See Fink (1965).

movements as they passed from one man to another, with a timelessness dictated by custom.

When I began to collect information about *kula* transactions on Kiriwina, I discovered a singularly important aspect that Malinowski did not report. Any armshell or necklace called a *kitomu* is a shell that is the property of its owner.[14] A *kitomu*, unlike shells already moving on *kula* paths, does not have to circulate for *kula* exchanges. It can, for example, be used as wealth for payments at marriages and deaths or for an expert to build a canoe. Like stone axe-blades, it, too, can be used to purchase seed yams or pigs. On Kiriwina, a man will often travel with yams to Kaileuna Island to pay for a newly fashioned armshell that will become his *kitomu*. On Muyua Island, to the southeast of Kiriwina, men receive many *kitomu* shells from villagers from other islands who pay them for sea-faring canoes. On Tubetube Island, southwest of Kiriwina, *kitomu* shells are exchanged for pigs. Today, *kitomu* shells are sold for cash by Rossel Islanders, who make fine *Chama* necklaces.[15] The basis for *kula* playing, much like the way Kiriwina women obtain their wealth from the sale of banana-leaf bundles for pigs or trade store foods, is the straightforward payments of *kitomu* shells for other things.

If the owner of a large *kitomu* wants to enter it into *kula* circulation, with luck and skill he will attract new partners and ultimately new wealth. The circulation of a *kitomu* in *kula* differs from other *kula* transactions, and for this reason, owning a *kitomu* shell, especially a large one, is extremely profitable but dangerous. Once a shell is acknowledged to be on a path, ideally its movement is through a prescribed number of partners. Any one of the partners, however, may keep the shell for a long time. If a number of shells are temporarily withdrawn from circulation in this way, such loss may seriously weaken the path; for paths are perceived to be strong only when many shells are moving along them. If only a few shells circulate, partners become discouraged and try to become partners with others whose paths are more dynamic.

Yet "strong" partners do *kula* slowly; younger villagers tend to be in a hurry and move their valuables too fast. High-ranking valuables undergo long delays as they move from one person to another; small valuables move quickly. It is the strong *kula* players who create the fame of a path. Thus, there seems to be a problem at the very basis of *kula* exchanges: how to keep a path, as *kula* partners say, "alive," while the best shells are moving on it very slowly.

High-ranking *kitomu* shells are the key to the gains to be had and the dangers to be faced in playing *kula* well. The most crucial step in the circulation of a *kitomu* shell is how its particular path is established, because the path publicly proclaims the value of the shell and, eventually, the talent and fame

[14] Since my first description of *kitomu* valuables in Weiner (1976: 129), other Massim field researchers have reported their importance in all *kula* areas. See Campbell (1983b) on Vakuta Island; Damon (1980, 1983) on Muyua Island; Macintyre (1983a, 1983c) on Tubetube Island; and Munn (1983) on Gawa Island.

[15] See Damon (1980, 1983), Liep (1981, 1983), and Macintyre (1983a) for details.

of its owner. When a man owns a *kitomu* shell and decides to find a *kula* path for it, his news circulates to others. When Bunemiga took ten baskets of yams to Kaileuna Island and returned with a large armshell, three men from Sinaketa, an important *kula* village in the southern part of Kiriwina, were interested in obtaining his shell. Each gave him a small necklace as an initial enticement. Bunemiga put the necklaces onto *kula* paths by passing them to his partners on Kitava Island, but he still sat with his *kitomu* shell.

The necklaces Bunemiga received are called *vaga*, to signify that they are the opening or initial shells that begin a *kula* path. Bunemiga explained the process as analogous to the first time a man sees a woman with whom he wants to sleep. He tries to become "good friends" with her so he gives her gifts of tobacco and betel and may even resort to magic spells that will "turn her mind" toward him. Even then, she may still reject him. So, too, with the shells Bunemiga received. He now thought carefully about each man who, having given him a small necklace, signified that he wanted his *kitomu* shell. How big is his name? Is he trustworthy, or does he sometimes take the shells directed for his partners and give them to other men for other paths? How reliable are his partners around the other islands? How big are their names? Should he decide on an old partner who has been "a good worker" for him in the past? Or should he decide on a "new" man, someone he never had as a partner before? Like a woman looking over the men who want to sleep with her, Bunemiga had to decide which man he wanted for his partner. His decision was important, for his objective was to get a good return for his *kitomu*.

All this time, Bunemiga kept his large *kitomu* shell, knowing he had something others desired. He could hold on to it as long as he wanted, soliciting interest from many men until he found someone he truly trusted. At this stage, there are many ploys that can be used, both by him and by those who want the shell, especially if it is large and fine. Men bring him food and other valuables, even money. They give him other *kula* shells to interest him in themselves. When they come to his village for *kula*, they have long conversations with him and his wife, hoping to convince his wife of their strength and sincerity so she will influence her husband. Bunemiga can play out his own strategies as well by keeping several men on the line, deciding on one, while making another think he will win the shell. Of course, if he plays off too many men against each other, some become angry.

Months later, Bunemiga sent an armshell back to two of the men who each gave him a *vaga* necklace, as a closing return. When they received the armshell, they knew that they had not been chosen. Bunemiga rejected their interest in his *kitomu*. They wanted the *kitomu* but they lost it. For the recipient of his *kitomu* shell, Bunemiga finally decided on Emmanuel, a man with a strong *kula* partner on Gumasila Island. Emmanuel had convinced Bunemiga that when he went to Gumasila, his partner there would find a large necklace to match Bunemiga's *kitomu* armshell. All this time, Emmanuel had been working to attract a Gumasila man who had a large *kitomu* necklace. Before Bunemiga would release his *kitomu*, he tried to get the best assurances

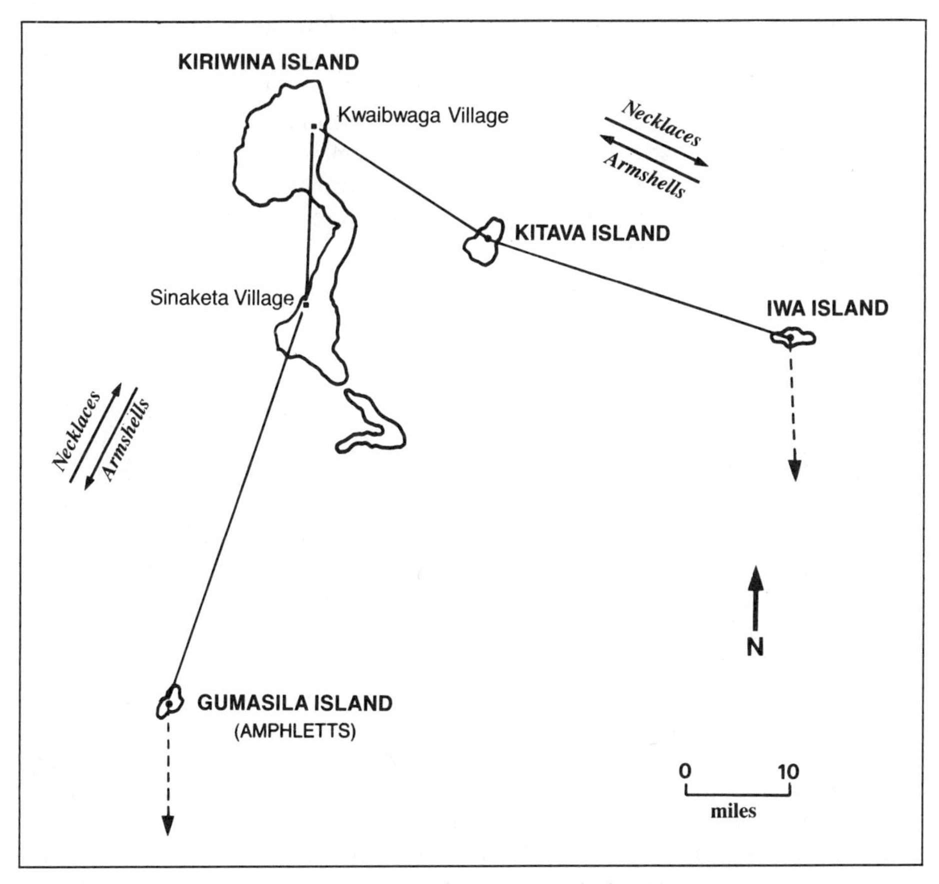

Map 5. Bunemiga's four closest kula partners.

that he would receive an equivalent valuable for it. There are many stories of men who are disappointed and feel cheated because, when they release their *kitomu*, the shell they get back is not a good match. This time Bunemiga was lucky. Emmanuel kept his word about his Gumasila partner, and within six months Bunemiga received a fine necklace as a replacement for his original armshell *kitomu*.

The necklace was now Bunemiga's *kitomu*. All his work and that of his partners so far was to secure an equal replacement of one *kitomu* for another. Now with the large *kitomu* necklace in hand, Bunemiga turned to Kitava Island and looked for a good partner there. The same exchanges of small shells took place, as quite a few men tried to interest Bunemiga in making them his partner. When Bunemiga selected his Kitava partner, he then gave him the important *kitomu* necklace. Bunemiga is now fully engaged in a new *kula* path with a partner on either side: a Sinaketa village man to whom he gave his *kitomu* armshell and a Kitava Island man who received his *kitomu* necklace (see Map 5). These two men will continue to be very important to

Bunemiga for they are the ones who work for him, the one traveling to Gumasila for necklaces, and the other to Iwa for armshells. Each ego-centered node of *kula* activity includes two partners on either side of Bunemiga. The Iwa and Gumasila partners likewise have their partners on the next islands, and in this way, the path of the necklace *kitomu* shell is expanded and strengthened. Only now do the exchanges associated with Bunemiga's *kitomu* begin in earnest. Once he has sent a *kitomu* in each direction, many more shells will begin to move along his path.

THE CIRCULATION OF A *KITOMU*

Bunemiga's original armshell *kitomu* is now the *kitomu* of his Gumasila partner, who replaced his own *kitomu* necklace for that armshell. He can keep the armshell as his own property or he can enter it into another *kula* path at any time. For the moment, however, the Gumasila partner's strategy involves his hope that the necklace he sent to Bunemiga will attract a well-known armshell from the partners on the other side of Bunemiga. This is Bunemiga's hope as well. Everything now depends on the success of the partners from Kitava and Iwa to find the appropriate armshell.

The final destiny of Bunemiga's necklace is never totally secure, for one partner somewhere on the path may be influenced to give someone else on a different path the large shell. Others hear about the fine necklace and desire it. If a man diverts the shell, he must work very hard to find an equivalent one to return to the original path or he cannot continue his participation with that path. He may not care about restoring his place on the path because his "new" partner may hold out the hope for a better path with more valuables. Then only fear of sorcery may make him rethink his plans. As Reo Fortune (1932:210) was told by Dobuan men about the danger of valuables, "many men died because of them."

Each time a man or a woman passes a large shell to a partner, he or she is taking a chance about its replacement. Bunemiga was in that position when, after putting his *kitomu* shell into circulation, he had to wait for a very long time before he received a replacement for the necklace *kitomu* he sent to his Kitava partner. While the Kitava and Iwa partners were trying to find a large enough armshell that would replace Bunemiga's necklace *kitomu*, they sent him smaller shells, some of which were classed as *vaga* (so he could start other roads while waiting) and some of which were called *basi*, an intermediary shell that Bunemiga said means we are "now sleeping together, but not yet married." These shells informed Bunemiga that his partners were working hard to find the large matching shell for his *kitomu*. They were keeping their segment of the path "alive," making certain that Bunemiga retained his confidence in them. Bunemiga understood well the danger that existed.

When finally the news circulated that a large armshell that would match his necklace *kitomu* was now linked onto the path segment from Iwa to Kitava, his partners on the other side from Sinaketa and Gumasila began to pass

Bunemiga several shells at a time. Like the other shells, these were meant to keep the path active so that no one would divert this forthcoming large armshell, which everyone knew would move slowly. Bunemiga's Gumasila friend wanted that shell to come to him, and so he began to send more valuables along the path through Bunemiga in the direction where the large armshell would be. In this way, the eastern part of the path through Kitava and Iwa was being strengthened and linked directly to Sinaketa and Gumasila. First the Gumasila partner sent two necklaces to Bunimega, which he passed on to his Kitava partner and then to the Iwa partner. The next year, three armshells came back from the Iwa side; and two years after that, four necklaces came from the Gumasila side. These increments were divided into three categories: (1) *vaga*, enabling Bunemiga to open additional exchanges with his same partners; (2) the intermediary shells called *basi* to keep the path "alive"; and then (3) a few shells called *kudu*, which matched the earlier *vaga* shells in value and marked the end of that set of exchanges. Shells called *kudu*, Bunemiga said, "are like a marriage" because when they travel along the path it is "truly strong." If no one thinks that the path is "alive," no one sends a *kudu* shell in reciprocation for the original *vaga*. Why waste a shell when there is little hope for later success?

Each one of these shells had nothing to do with matching the *kitomu* shell. Their purpose is to keep the path of the *kitomu* shell active and to build increasing confidence among all the partners on the segment of the path on either side of Bunemiga and further to the east, where the large armshell *kitomu* resides. This is the way segments of paths are linked to each other and then strengthened. If few valuables flow along a segment, the hoped-for large valuable will probably be diverted onto another path segment, with other, more active players who claim they know how "to work hard" for *kula*.

After eight years, Bunemiga finally received the large armshell that came from his Kitava partner as the replacement for his *kitomu* necklace. This armshell was now his *kitomu*, but because his Gumasila and Sinaketa partners had worked so hard Bunemiga knew that they wanted this armshell. They did not want Bunemiga to put it onto a different path segment, nor did they want him to use it to buy a pig or pay a mortuary obligation. They wanted that shell to continue on to them; they wanted it to remain in *kula*. With the armshell however, Bunemiga was also sent an additional shell, called *kunivilevila*, meaning "to turn," in the sense of turning a corner. The debt of the *kitomu* was fully repaid, not only with an equivalent shell, but also with this extra shell, which is considered a "profit" (*katumukolava*). According to Bunemiga, the complete yet slow circulation of his *kitomu* for its matching equivalent "gave birth" to this additional shell, but the gestation period took many years. This shell was sent as profit because the partners along the various path segments performed well and the Kitava partner wanted to keep the path from "dying." Once the final debt of a *kitomu* is repaid, nothing else flows along the path segments, unless this increment is sent "to wake up" the path by keeping the partners interested in future transactions. The partner of someone with a *kitomu* works hard to find the right shells, but all the time he knows that eventually, even though it may take many years, that shell will become his *kitomu*. For if Bunemiga keeps his armshell *kitomu* in circulation, it will go to his Sinaketa and Gumasila partners. All this time, they have worked for Bunemiga while looking toward the future for themselves.

THE MEANING OF *KULA*

If we multiply the number of exchanges on the single path segment just described by all the other paths and their segments operating in *kula*, and realize that some famous *kula* players have ten or more paths, we see the complexity in the exchanges just from an ego-centered perspective. When we think about *kitomu* and *kula* exchanges from the perspective of all the Massim islands that participate in *kula*, we see that despite some *local* variations, *kula* is a system of exchange that momentarily removes men from their own local exchanges, which are anchored in kinship, marriage, and deaths. Only very strong men have the ability to exchange along the best paths and obtain the most valuable shells. Once a man commits himself to a set of partners, he is no longer autonomous and must depend on them. Only men with both acumen and luck seek out and obtain the best shells for their partners. It is not surprising that the metaphors used to describe each category of *kula* exchanges speak about seduction, marriage, and birth. And it is equally not surprising that *kula* partners must use the most powerful means at their disposal to ensure success. In *kula*, a player uses magic and actively identifies with symbols of youthful power—for example, body painting, traditional dress, the wearing of flowers, and the scenting of the body with mint and ginger—to influence a partner and his spouse. A partner must have at his command not only magic spells to expedite a *kula* voyage—for example, controlling the wind and the rain or making the canoe lashings tight and the boat fast—but also spells for love magic that will "turn a partner's mind."

At the center of *kula* are the illusions that exist. A basic premise that underlies *kula* exchanges is the notion of equality, that is, the exchange of an armshell for a necklace equal to it in value. Yet in practice, partners reach toward the opposite, to gain ever-larger shells that consequently create hierarchy and profit. Players dream of gaining a famous shell, of having their names circulate as "the best."[16] So in *kula* relationships, as in romantic ones, a player's goal is to have "many friends," to sleep with "many lovers," to "marry" many times, and to "give birth" often. Although the lure of personal fame is a strong motivation to participate in *kula*, rare is the person "whose fame climbs to the top of the mountain." There are stories of other kinds of

[16] See Nancy Munn's (1977, 1983) accounts of how men from Gawa Island create fame in *kula*. See also Munn (1986) for an important analysis of fame as a motivating principle in Gawan social interaction.

dreams, told in myths and legends, where fame results in jealousy and death.[17] No one forgets that in *kula*, lying, deception, and the threat of sorcery may undermine any attempt to build fame and power.

In each *kula* area, only a few villagers rise to the top, exhibiting the ability to control their *kula* destinies more than others. In the final analysis of any *kula* path segment, dependency on others still overrides any one person's autonomy. Each *kitomu* is linked to path segments that stretch out beyond its owner's reach, and increments are difficult to obtain. In *kula*, a debt is easily created by accepting a *vaga*, but when the debt must be paid, the path may be beset with obstacles.

The foundation of *kula* is not simply reciprocal returns, nor is it incremental returns, that is, two shells given and three returned. It is a system whereby *kula* exchanges may move shells from reciprocal transactions to unequal increments and, finally, to a "profit," where no return is necessary. Like the conical piles of yams displayed in Kiriwina gardens, in *kula* there are many more shells at the bottom, passing from one partner to another to keep the path "alive"; within that circulation only a relatively few transactions produce incremental returns, and even fewer still at the very top of the heap culminate in the goal of profit for their owners. For someone to gain a profit, a loss had to occur someplace else. Men lose their shells because other *kula* men are strong. Shells again and again must be lost so that others can sustain increments and profits. From a systematic perspective, the losers are as essential to *kula* as are the winners.

Reciprocal returns produce the illusion of stability, generating the possibility for gain, whereas gain itself creates a rupture in continued reciprocity. The shell classed as *kunivilevila*, which on the one hand is a "profit" born out of the original exchange of one *kitomu* for another, is at the same time a shell that marks, as informants say, "the death" of the *kula* path. All the obligations that began this particular path are over when Bunemiga receives the shell called *kunivilevila*. Bunemiga's momentary hierarchical success over his partners, that is, his profit, shatters the very path that brought him his fame. That "profit" can be thought of as a "death" in another way because somewhere it represents another person's loss. This shell was someone's *kitomu* or was diverted from someone else's path. The desire to win, so easy to feel but so difficult to attain, results in the loss of shells for others, illustrating that while the essence of *kula* psychology is based on winning, the essence of the actual *kula* system demands losing.

Kiriwina *kula* players often told me that doing *kula* is "like having a bank account." For a long time I wondered what they meant; then I read R. K. Narayan's novel *The Financial Expert* (1952), set in India. In this tale, Margayya dreams of becoming a rich and famous financier. He begins his career by telling villagers that he will pay enormously high interest rates if they

[17] See the *kula* myths collected by Malinowski (1922:290–333), in which the achievement of getting a famed *kula* shell, often through devious means, results in the victor's death.

"bank" their savings with him. His renown and fortune grow beyond even his imagination until the day when someone circulates the rumor that money is not safe with him. A run on his self-styled "bank" destroys him in a few hours because of course, he cannot meet the outraged villagers' demands. So too, in *kula*, if someone suddenly stopped all *kula* activities so that all debts had to be paid immediately, the losses of many would be fully exposed.

When Kiriwina men journey from their islands in search of shells, they compete with their sailing companions to win more shells than anyone else. Not just any shell will do. The competition lies in finding a big shell and then seducing its owner to send it along a particular path. Some players succeed and are unrivaled. Winning, however, involves intense competition and the ability, when necessary, to engage in diversionary tactics. The real *kula* work lies in seeking out the best shells and then having access to many other shells to support one's long-range intentions. Although hundreds of shells may pass through a person's hands, only a very few, if any, may constitute a profit; and only occasionally may a partner have the opportunity to gain increments in the size and quantity of the shells exchanged. Knowledge, high status, and even sorcery help some *kula* players claim success and circulate their fame. Small wonder that the attainment of these most coveted shells that themselves, encrusted as they are with the histories of other players' failures and successes, inspires a person with emotional feelings for the shells themselves. Malinowski (1922:513) wrote how *kula* shells are held in front of a dying man as if "to inspire with life; and at the same time to prepare for death."

The histories of shells written through *kula* participation are of individuals' talents and exploits, of partners often long dead or whose faces were never seen. Through the shells, a villager transcends the history of his or her own ancestral lineage and becomes a part of *kula* history. What is of consequence is that this *kula* history legitimizes a person's right to win while others lose. In Kiriwina, *kula* participation enables players, if they are "strong," to create long-standing debts, to hold on to valuables for years, and to keep these shells free from kin-related obligations like marriages or deaths. In this way, *kula* allows individuals to protect their wealth from the exigencies of everyday social and political life. Of course, for some there are times when the situation if reversed. Without a stone axe-blade or money, a man may be forced to use his *kula* shell for a kin obligation, removing it from its *kula* path and losing it. Therefore, the ability to hold on to a *kula* shell allows a person to store wealth, even if only momentarily, in the face of continual kinship or affinal obligations.

Kula success, however, is limited. A player may keep a shell for five or ten years before giving it up to others, but finally it must be passed on. Further, each "profit" is slow in coming and, therefore, accumulation of *kitomu* shells is difficult. Even when a man takes his own *kitomu* out of *kula*, he becomes limited in the kinds of *kula* transactions he can continue to undertake. Without a *kitomu* moving in his name, a man finds that no one is seducing him or working hard for him. This is the paradox on which playing *kula* rests.

In the end, the goals of wealth in shells and individual fame do not free

Kiriwina men from the continual involvement in their own hamlet exchanges. The importance of lineage identity and the obligations to keep that identity strong and vital hold Kiriwina men in check. Hard valuables, symbolizing men's individual histories, are difficult to find and even more arduous to keep. Soft wealth—the wealth of women—symbolizing the collective unity of the matrilineage, although more easily attainable, because of death is impossible to conserve. "The world of *kula*," where men have the freedom to pursue their individual fame, remains deeply tied to "the world of born," where yams and women's wealth demand continual production and care. The never-ending need to participate in both worlds catches men between the exigencies brought on by a death and unrequited desire for individual renown.

As the concluding chapter illustrates, in the final analysis, neither Kiriwina women nor men completely realize their destinies. A man's role in *kula*, with its direct engagement in individual political action, is ultimately as frustratingly bounded as is the role of a woman in her guardianship of matrilineal identity. The attainment of *kula* shells provides the means to realize fame, but such fame must still be attached to a more elementary kind of immortality—that of the lineage. *Kula* holds out the possibility that a person with negotiating skills can build fame into a permanent hierarchy that, like Vanoi's powerful stones for yams, will establish his omnipotence over all other players. Yet the prospect and the reality of loss and death make clear the fragile nature of such success.

10/Conclusion

THE POWER IN OBJECTS

There is a brief episode in *Gulliver's Travels* in which Gulliver visits the Academy of Lagado and learns of an experiment that will abolish the use of words. The Lagado professors believe that since words are only names for things, people should carry with them those *things* necessary to engage in discourse with others. Gulliver describes two men, sinking under the weight of their sacks of *things*, who meet in the street. Opening their packs, they "hold Conversation for an Hour together; then put up their Implements, help each other to resume their Burthens, and take their leave" (Swift 1726/1970:158).

In this incident Swift, writing over 250 years ago, ironically reminds us how much we use objects to make statements of our identity, goals, and even fantasies. Through this human proclivity to endow objects with meaning, we learn at an early age that the things we wear convey messages about who we are or seek to be. In the dress codes of 1986, for example, just the mention of a three-piece men's suit, patched jeans, or a man's gold earring draws an image for us of different personalities. We are intimately involved with things we love, long for, and give to others. We also mark relationships with things—a wedding band, a birthday present, a Christmas gift, a cemetery marker. Through things we craft our self-image and cultivate and enhance relationships. Yet things also keep the past vital for us. An antique car, old letters, a favorite doll—each infuses our memory with rich details of other times. Things not only take us back in time but also may become the building blocks that link the past to the future. Philanthropists, monarchs, and dictators, each in their own way, construct monuments to themselves in an attempt to make their names a part of history.

Thus it should come as no surprise that Trobrianders, like people in other parts of the world, give meanings to things that make them worth more than their cost in labor and the material of which they are made. Long yams, bundles of dried banana leaves, and strings of polished red shell discs all occupy a deep and meaningful place in Trobriand life. These are the things that cross boundaries between people, that connect one villager socially and politically with another. Malinowski wondered why men give so much attention to their yam displays. Yams, we now know, are the objects that create relatedness as they cross clan boundaries, establishing long-term relationships between individuals that lead to other advantages, such as land rights, protection, assistance, and other kinds of wealth. Only from this perspective can we understand the political implications of a chief's yam house standing empty or yams becoming weapons as men measure them against each other in a fight for dominance.

Yams take on many meanings in the lives of Trobrianders, but their ability to function as a multivocal symbol rests in the way yams express the basic dynamics of what it means to reach out to others. Making claims on others is always surrounded by danger. Although relationships in all societies can involve feelings of love, generosity, and caring, they also can expose one to rejection, anger, and loss. Objects not only bring people together into a relationship but also mark off one person from another with explicit boundaries expressive of dominance, authority, fame, and power. Making these boundaries permeable is not an easy matter. In the Trobrianders' unremitting attention to the exchange of things, we see how individuals try to control others, while at the same time, they attempt to manage their own self-images, autonomy, and political destinies.

Expanding outward into the lives of others who are not members of one's own matrilineage is a process that eventually has political consequences, but these affairs follow precedents that begin with conception and continue throughout each person's life. As we already saw in earlier chapters, food, earrings, beauty, and magic are things given to children that are emblematic of how a person's social self undergoes enhancement. The most elementary mode of expansion occurs through one's father, the first presence of an outsider in an infant's life. This relationship is followed by one's father's sister and other kin. Later, when married, one's spouse and spouse's kin provide the next stage of expanding potential; and finally, one's own children, when grown and married, enlarge one's range of relationships. Through the interconnectedness of affines and patrilateral relations, the matrilineal boundary that sets off the self from others is penetrated.

Although this expanding process is primarily ego-centered, and ultimately political, it also has consequences for the matrilineal group. As villagers build up networks of relationships and their fame "climbs higher," the matrilineages to which they belong also gain renown. In this way, individual actions have an effect on a group's image and status. The objects that pass between people, securing relationships with members of other matrilineages, equally serve through time to make the roots of one's own matrilineal identity strong. From this view we see how the political domain is essentially and inseparably fixed in kinship relations.

Individuals link themselves to other individuals in what appears to be never-ending strategies, obligations, and desires. Success, for example, culminates in seductions, marriages, births, alliances, more yams, women's wealth, and *kitomu* shells. Some individuals fail in reaching such goals, whereas others have an initial advantage because they were born into a ranking lineage. Even those with such advantages may ultimately stumble, as Vanoi's decline dramatically illustrates. The work of expanding outward occurs continually in the face of counter exigenicies that prevent or even invert these broadening possibilities. The loss of shells or seed yams, anger, divorce, adultery, or destructive magic spells are examples of how things and people subvert growth potentials. The tension between autonomy and domination, desire and refusal, can never be fully resolved without entering into a dangerous confrontation in which security and retreat are no longer possible.

Death induced through sorcery stands as the final confrontation. In the destruction of a person, the entire group is threatened. In response to a death, the members of the matrilineage must overturn all their yams and women's bundles and skirts. Death always is a group affair because the matrilineage stands as the reference point for all those "others," that is, the members of other matrilineages, who have contributed to the cultural identity of the dead person. Because of the expanding possibilities in a person's life, each Trobriander represents her or his matrilineal identity—originally conceived through a woman and an ancestral *baloma* spirit—as well as the accumulation of all the other relationships that parenthood and marriage made possible. Therefore, a death demands attention to this full totality, as the members of a matrilineage seek both to repay all "others" for their past care and to hold on to them now that this death has occurred.

At a death, attention to these cultural charges is imperative—to repay and regenerate, to end and reconstitute, to close in and reach out. These oppositional acts exemplify the eternal struggle between the autonomous individual and societal demands. Some Massim societies repay, end, and close off all others at a death, thereby effectively severing all relationships among the dead person, the members of his or her matrilineage, and all those from other matrilineages connected to the dead person.[1] In Kiriwina, all efforts are made to avert these breaks with the past. Only a few things, such as a man's yam house, absolutely end. But even in this case, the boulders that supported the edifice stay in the ground, a visual reminder of past relationships waiting to be regenerated. In Kiriwina, even the bones of the dead person are cared for and carried by "others" for ten or twenty years, extending the period of repayment and regeneration for the members of the dead person's matrilineage.

To achieve this goal of lasting expansion, enormous amounts of wealth are demanded, wealth that must be given away to make a matrilineage look strong in the face of death and to continue the repayment and regenerative processes for many years. Banana bundles, women's valuables, constitute the means by which the oppositional processes of repaying and regenerating are ameliorated. By giving away thousands of bundles to hundreds of "others" beyond the deceased's matrilineage, Kiriwina women metaphorically "untie" the dead person from her or his attachments to "others." Shells, stone axe-blades, even yams are never sufficiently owned in large enough quantities to make such a massive distribution possible.

[1] See, for example, Fortune (1932) and Thune (1981).

Bundles are not rare items, like *kitomu* shells and stone axe-blades. Their production is "home-grown," limited only by the number of women and banana leaves available. However, production itself is not confined to the women of the matrilineage that need bundles. By exchanging other things such as pigs and trade store foods for bundles, the labor of many other women may figure into the total wealth of a matrilineage. Because of its relative accessibility, this form of wealth can be bestowed in hundreds of directions to villagers related to the dead person in as many ways. For example, among the Northwest Coast Tlingit Indians, blankets traditionally circulated as wealth in mortuary distributions; there were times when valued ones were torn into smaller pieces so that many people could receive payments, but even these small pieces were highly esteemed.[2] In the Marquesas Islands of Polynesia, during the naming ceremony for a newborn child, its genealogy was chanted over a 20-foot strip of barkcloth, which then was torn into smaller pieces and given to all the child's relatives.[3]

Clearly, the dismemberment of these cloths for bestowals to large numbers of people had an important bearing on the validation of social relations. Bundles of banana leaves, made from the same raw material as women's valued skirts, are as an object far less time-consuming to make. As the skirts' extension, they expand one's capabilities to repay everyone who had a relationship with the dead person as well as all the interconnected relationships between and among other members of the matrilineage. Thus at the deaths of high-ranking people, chiefs are able to maintain the processes of repayment and regeneration for their vast networks of relationships.[4]

In earlier chapters we saw how women's needs for bundles drain men's economic resources. When men must find bundles for their wives, they exchange food, pigs, manufactured goods, everything except their stone axe-blades and shell valuables. Even with these additional resources, women still must produce much of their wealth themselves. Women's valuables add new, critical resources to the entire wealth pool. Although the necessity for this wealth continually drains men's resources, such as food, pigs, and money, it does not subvert men's valuables, such as axe-blades and shell valuables. These hard valuables, although necessary to some degree for mortuary exchanges, are not used exclusively because of the presence of women's wealth. Even at a death, they continue to dramatize the political prominence of high-ranking men and their individual deeds.

In this way, in contrast to banana bundles and skirts, men's shells and axe-blades remain more specifically and individually political. The banana bundles and skirts, however, reveal the political state of a matrilineage. By showing where villagers are in their relation to the deceased and her or his matrilineage,

[2] See Emmons' (1907) essay on the Chilkat blanket.

[3] See Handy (1923) on the Marquesas.

[4] On Vakuta Island, to the south of Kiriwina, only skirts are exchanged in a mortuary distribution that commemorates many people who have recently died (see Campbell 1981). On this island, however, there are only six villages, and chiefs here have no political power or autonomy over others, as occurs among Kiriwina chiefs.

bundles act as the linchpin between individuals and groups, between the core of matrilineal identity and the network of relationships associated with that identity. If we could document each women's mortuary distribution over many generations, we would see the flux in the strength and weaknesses of matrilineages: more or less wealth given to larger or smaller number of people by the full complement of members of a matrilineage or rival branches, or only by a few surviving members of a matrilineage that is dying out.

Regardless of the current political situation, the women's mortuary distribution must be held. Unlike *kula*, in which the most expert players try to hold on to their large shells for many years, the object here is to give away as many bundles as possible. In this sense, women's wealth fundamentally expresses the immortality of the group. What we see in these actions is an attempt to create a matrilineal dynasty of sorts. At birth, the regenerative part of a *baloma* spirit re-creates human life in women, and at death, women re-create these beliefs materially by acknowledging and removing all the debts that went into the work of making a social person.

THE PATHOS IN OBJECTS

In the contrast between women's and men's wealth we find exposed the human condition of how one expands outward into the lives of others descended from different ancestors while keeping one's own ancestral identity intact. Loss, decay, and death continually attack the cultural semblance of wholeness and the vision of immortality. For these reasons, the loss of things and the death of people translate into political action—because such losses are a threat to all that went before—expressed in the creation and regeneration of identities, ancestors, and rank. Without a past that is given a concrete existence in time and space, it is difficult to control the future. For example, in ancient Hawaii, kings held sway over vast retinues of people and huge estates. When a monarch died, all his personal possessions, except for his chiefly regalia, were burned because they were now polluted. But the feathered cloaks that marked him as a chief were never destroyed. The regalia inaugurated his successor because the cloaks represented much more than any one individual chief. They symbolized the dynasty itself.[5]

The Hawaiian example lends a comparative perspective from which to view not only the power in objects but the limitations as well. In Kiriwina, the only objects that symbolize the group rather than any individual person or individual sets of relationships are banana bundles and skirts. In this society, where chieftaincy is far less stratified than in Hawaii, we see how bundles and skirts represent an elementary form of an object that at a minimal level touches on the dynastic power encompassed in Hawaiian feather cloaks.

Yet this comparison also reveals how limited banana wealth is. Although they are an absolute necessity, bundles are not sacred. They are not inalien-

[5] See Valeri (1985).

able like Hawaiian regalia. Age does not increase their value; it only makes them decayed and dirty. Thus, their value is seriously circumscribed by the limits of time, just as in economic terms their accumulation is restrained by the frequency of death.

In yams, too, we find the same short life, for finally yams must be eaten or they rot. Holding onto yams, bundles, and skirts for years, as a *kula* player does his shells, is physically impossible. The making of bundles and skirts, like the making of yam gardens, must be renewed year after year. There is no way to make these relatively ephemeral objects into heirlooms, inalienable properties of a lineage or dynasty, so that, like Hawaiian regalia, they attest to a lasting history beyond any one individual.[6] Only stone axe-blades and shell valuables have the durability that enables them to last for generations. But as scarce resources they, too, have their own culturally imposed disadvantages. Only those of the highest value represent fame, and they only convey the renown of individuals, not the preeminence of a lineage.

From this perspective, we face the limits inherent in this very complex system of exchange. Gains in shells are hard to obtain, yams rot, and death and decay deplete the stocks of bundles and skirts. Like all social systems everywhere, there are no ultimate solutions to subvert time. Still, Trobrianders make enormous efforts to do just that, to create something lasting out of every personal loss. It is an awesome task that keeps matrilineages defined through time and makes the ranking of matrilineages historically more consequential than elsewhere in the Massim, where the form, quantity, and economics associated with skirts as wealth is minimal.[7] Such achievements, however, take their toil in preventing accumulations of wealth and in the limitation of chiefly power.

These distinctions between objects are significant because they reflect broader cultural and sociological issues regarding the differences between gender relations and the more primary struggle between individual deeds and the group's interests and purposes. Each gender plays out its own role, roles that are at once complementary and confounding. Each gender makes its own contribution to the workings of a social system, but the solutions are always thwarted and contravened by the more pressing interplay between the search for immortality through one's own personal deeds and the deep-seated need to find recognition and acceptance from the group. How societies culturally construct these themes shows us how far they succeed in regenerating individual and group identities through time. In small-scale societies, where one group is ranked over another, the regeneration of ancestral identities at a death is essential. In this way societies like that of the Trobriands sustain hierarchical relations between chiefs and commoners.

Thus the objects in Trobriand exchange are more than economic in value and more than sociological in content. The meanings embedded in these objects direct our attention to the existential values that are both the animating

[6] See Weiner (1986) for a discussion of the importance of heirlooms and inalienable wealth.

[7] In the southern Massim, skirts are also used as objects of exchange, but they are not considered currency (Battaglia, 1981; Lepowsky, 1981). See also footnote 4, above.

armature and the fuel of all social activity. Malinowski dismissed these existential aims of human behavior in his attempts to show that practical needs, like metabolism and reproduction, were at the root of individual behavior and extended to the way institutions, such as *kula*, functioned. Even though Malinowski believed that emotions, magic, and the search for fame had pragmatic consequences, he never felt that these forces were directed toward such rational motivations as immortality and the control of time. In the Trobriand case we recognize how the attempt to achieve a degree of permanence against everything that tends toward destruction is the driving force in the constitution of the social system.

TRADITION AND CHANGE

It was not just a sentimental gesture that prompted Trobrianders to hold a women's mortuary distribution for Chief Vanoi in the distant national capital of Port Moresby after his death. Trobrianders who had moved to the city took their paychecks and spent them on cloth, transforming a village tradition into a heritage that withstands time, geographical distance, and Western beliefs. Vanoi's urban mortuary distribution pointedly documents the resiliency of traditional cultural values as they continue to resurface and to override any long-range, externally imposed changes.

By traditional, however, I do not mean an unchanging, monolithic, "primitive" way of life. On an untended plot of land about 2 miles from Losuia, the rusted and cannibalized remains of trucks and buses lay half buried under weeds and other debris. In one corner of this vehicular graveyard lies the Australian colonial government pickup truck that met me at the airstrip when I first arrived in Kiriwina in 1971. On the other side are the remnants of the Trobriand Hotel buses, newly purchased in 1972 to drive weekend tourists around the island. Here also is the rusty remains of the once new truck proudly owned by John K's village development corporation, organized just prior to national independence. Standing there, one is quick to remember how young men opposed to John K's group threw stones at the truck when it was only a few days old. Further on is the tractor, owned by those who were in opposition to John K's ventures, that was burned one night in retaliation for the stoning. The history that the trucks tell is one of change and aborted schemes, yet the failures cannot be tied to lack of interest, lack of understanding, or lack of risk. In response to these Western-styled economic collapses, Modububuna said, "They are just like our gardens. If we make only one garden, what happens if the garden fails? So we make three or four gardens. If one fails, we have the others. That is why we always try something new."

The rebuffs to development plans and strong resiliency to Western forces of change for over one hundred years can only attest to the failure on the part of colonial, and now indigenous, administrators to recognize how potent are the cultural meanings embedded in traditional wealth that organize villagers' lives. As we have seen, yams, bundles and skirts, stone axe-blades, and shell valuables each play a significant role in villagers' access to each other and to the projection of their group identity and individual fame. Money, important as it is in contemporary life, has not replaced any of these objects. At times, men use money in place of a stone axe-blade for exchanges at a marriage or at a death. But politically strong men still "show who they are" in traditional style. In other ways, money has simply been used to inflate women's bundles, making women even more competitive with each other, because money buys trade store goods, which then can be used to purchase bundles. Some people, like Joshua in Chapter 7, recognize that the women's needs for bundles siphon off the small amounts of money that villagers manage to get. So primary is the sanctioning power of bundles and skirts that it has withstood colonial rule and development schemes.

What Trobrianders proclaim today, as they have since the first missionary and colonial officer arrived on their shores, is that they regard themselves as active, dynamic individuals in control of the critical features of their interactions with other villagers and with the Western or Asian outsider. Trobrianders have not been passive pawns manipulated by "experts" on religion, government, law, or economics. Throughout the world, colonialism brought expatriates, missionaries, government officers, explorers, and business people, whose justification for their actions, regardless of individual differences, had a unified focus. As the harbingers of Wester progress, their interventions were couched in the rhetoric of "doing something" to and for the "natives"—giving them God, law, writing, clothes, soap, and whatever else was considered necessary to uplift their "primitive" status.

Anthropologists, too, were also part of the colonial scene. What they came to "do," however, was very different. Their task was to study and explain unfamiliar cultures, not only for a scholarly audience, but also so those in positions of colonial power could at least become more sensitive and insightful in their treatment and rule of their subjects. Anthropologists hoped that their studies would serve to caution interventionist agents of governments, missions, and businesses that villagers' lives were not to be tampered with arbitrarily and that Western economic progress often resulted in destructive rather than constructive change.

What the colonial period inspired more times than not, however, was an opposite view, which advocated the depiction of village people as passive subjects to whom and for whom things must be done. As a result, anthropologists' claims for the rights of villagers to their own priorities and actions were misinterpreted and appeared merely as a defense of all that is labeled "primitive." In contemporary times, this same colonial ideology still exists in the dialogue and controls between industrial nations and third-world countries. The anthropologists' claims all too often are subverted by international political expediency, the economic strategies of multinational corporations, and short-sighted national development projects.

To date, Trobrianders have fared better than many other societies, where, for example, the discovery of oil or gold opened the way for high-level Western technology and economic control, benefiting the "discoverers" but never the local people. Still, their traditional perspectives continue to be altered and reshaped by forces fostering change. Yet neither Western money, education, religion, nor law has uprooted the constancy and attention given to yam cultivation, the production of women's wealth, and *kula* activities. These remain the principle acts through which Trobrianders continue to define themselves and their relationships with others. They constitute the warp of Trobriand life, its strength and resiliency.

Across this warp, change has been woven in; but in coming from internal and external demands, from nationals and Europeans, and in the name of God, Country, Cash, and Independence, it is change that Trobrianders continually refashion in their own image. This cultural vitality is summarized in a scene from the film *Trobriand Cricket*. When a young Trobriander asks a chief about the game, he replies, "We rubbished [the missionary way of playing cricket and now] it is *our* game." With masterful zeal, Trobrianders make manifest who they are through what they exchange, thus making them expert at transforming into their own Trobriand style whatever encumbers or encroaches on their resolute sense of self.

Glossary of Kiriwina words and anthropological terms

affine: An individual who is related to another by marriage.
avunculocal: Residence of an unmarried man or a married couple in his mother's brother's hamlet.
bagi: A shell necklace made of ground and polished discs from red *Chama* shells and decorated at either end with beads and pearl shells. It is exchanged in *kula* transactions for an armshell or used as wealth in village exchanges. Also called *soulava*.
baloma: Matrilineal ancestral spirit that is thought to live on the island of Tuma.
basi: Term given to an armshell or necklace that circulates on a *kula* path to keep the path active during the intermediary stage of *kula* transactions.
beku: A stone axe-blade necessary, for example, for compensation payments, for marriage exchanges, to buy seed yams, and as payments for the performance of magic.
butura: Renown, fame.
buwa: The nut of the areca palm (*Areca catechu* Linn.) that is chewed with the leaf or fruit of the betel plant (*Piper Betle* Linn.), mixed with a small bit of slaked lime made from coral and seashells.
bwagau: The practice of sorcery by poisoning the victim.
cognate: Relative by blood.
dala: A unilineal descent group in which all members trace their descent through women (matrilineage); also called *yawa*.
doba: Colorful skirts made from banana leaves and used both as clothing and as a form of women's wealth; also used collectively to refer to banana bundles (see *nununiga*).
endogamy: Marriage within one's descent group.
exogamy: Marriage outside of one's descent group.
guyau: A chief; also any person who is born a member of a ranking lineage.
katuposula: A hamlet of a village. The affairs of each hamlet are controlled in most cases by the most important member of the matrilineage.
kayasa: A competitive yam harvest organized by a strong hamlet leader or chief.
keda: The path or segment of a path along which *kula* armshells and necklaces are circulated.
keyawa: Reciprocal relationship term between ego and his son's wife's mother and mother's brother, or his daughter's husband's mother and mother's brother when members of the same clan.

kitomu: Armshells (*mwali*) and shell necklaces (*bagi*) that are individually owned.

kopoi: To nurse, feed, or otherwise take care of an infant or child; also the act of caring for a dead person by sitting around the body until it is buried; also the long yams that men present to chiefs.

kubula: The annual yam garden made by a man for his married sister or daughter.

kudu: A larger armshell (*mwali*) or necklace (*bagi*) sent along a *kula* path to repay the owner of the shell that originated the *kula* transactions.

kula: The overseas exchange network that includes many islands in the Massim, where armshells (*mwali*) and necklaces (*bagi*) are exchanged for each other through complex sets of transactions.

kumila: A matrilineal clan.

kunivilevila: An armshell (*mwali*) or necklace (*bagi*) given in *kula* as a "profit" after the final return has been made for a large *Kitoma* valuable.

kuvi: A species of yam (*Dioscorea alata*) in which one variety grows as much as 6 feet in length and another grows as large as 2 feet in diameter.

kuwa: A short necklace made from red *Chama* shells worn by young children and unmarried adolescents; also the black neckband made from plant fibers (traditionally of human hair) worn by a dead person's spouse and father.

lisaladabu: The women's mortuary distribution where banana bundles and skirts are distributed four to eight months after a person has died.

Massim: A term first used by A. C. Haddon in 1894 and continued by C. G. Seligman to distinguish the people living along the eastern tip of the Papua New Guinea mainland and the islands that extend out into the Coral Sea. The Trobriands are located at the most northern part of this island ring.

matrilineal descent: A principle of descent in which individuals are related to each other from a common female ancestor through women.

mwali: An armshell cut and polished from the *Conus leopardus* or *C. litteratus* and decorated with white cowrie shells and beads. It is exchanged in *kula* for a necklace (*bagi*) and also used in village exchanges.

nununiga: Women's wealth made from strips of dried banana leaves tied in a bunch at one end.

patrilateral kin: Ego's relatives through his or her father.

polygyny: The marriage of a man to two or more women.

sagali: The collective term for all mortuary distributions.

sibububula: The combination of a woman's blood and a *waiwaia* spirit child, believed to cause conception.

sigiliyawali: The first of a series of a mortuary distributions, which takes place on the day after burial.

Tabalu: The highest-ranking chiefly matrilineage in the Trobriand Islands.

tadabali: The second major mortuary distribution, held two days after a person has been buried.

taytu: A species of yam (*Dioscorea esculenta*) that is a major source of food and the most important yam for exchange.

tokai: "Commoners," that is, villagers who are not members of chiefly matrilineages.

toliuli: The members of a dead person's matrilineage who act as the "owners" during the mortuary distributions.

toliyouwa: The members of clans other than the dead person's who are the "workers" and take care of the burial and the mourning.

vaga: An armshell or necklace used in the opening transaction for further *kula* exchanges.

valu: The congregation of two or more hamlets into a village.

virilocal: Residence of a married couple with the husband's kin.

waiwaia: The spirit child that comes from a *baloma* spirit and is thought to cause conception.

References Cited

Achebe, Chinua

1967 Arrow of God. New York: John Day.

Allen, Jim

1977 Sea traffic, trade and expanding horizons. *In* Sunda and Sahul: Prehistoric Studies in Southeast Asia, Melanesia and Australia, J. Allen, J. Golson, and R. Jones, eds. Pp. 387–417. London: Academic Press.

Austen, Leo

1945 Cultural Changes in Kiriwina. Oceania 16: 15–60.

Battaglia, Debbora

1981 Segaya: Commemoration in a Massim Society. Ph.D. thesis, University of Cambridge.

1983 Syndromes of Ceremonial Exchange in the Eastern Calvados: The View from Sabarl Island. *In* The Kula: New Perspectives on Massim Exchange, J. W. Leach and E. R. Leach, eds. Pp. 445–466. Cambridge: Cambridge University Press.

Beidelman, T. O.

1971 The Kaguru: A Matrilineal People of East Africa. New York: Holt, Rinehart and Winston. Reprinted 1985 by Waveland Press.

Boas, Franz

1888 The Central Eskimo. *In* Sixth Annual Report of the Bureau of Ethnology. Pp. 399–669. Washington, D.C.: Smithsonian Institution.

Brown, Paula, and G. Buchbinder, eds.

1976 Man and Woman in the New Guinea Highlands. Spec. Pub. American Anthropology Association, No. 8.

Brunton, R.

1975 Why Do the Trobriands Have Chiefs? Man 10(4): 544–558.

Campbell, Shirley

1981 A Vakutan Mortuary Cycle. Paper presented at the Second Kula Conference, University of Virginia.

1983a Attaining Rank: A Classification of Shell Valuables. *In* The Kula: New Perspectives on Massim Exchange, J. W. Leach and E. R. Leach, eds. Pp. 229–248. Cambridge: Cambridge University Press.

1983b Kula in Vakuta: The Mechanics of Keda. *In* The Kula: New Perspectives on Massim Exchange, J. W. Leach and E. R. Leach, eds. Pp. 201–228. Cambridge: Cambridge University Press.

Chowning, Ann

1983 Wealth and Exchange Among the Molima of Fergusson Island. *In* The Kula: New Perspectives on Massim Exchange, J. W. Leach and E. R. Leach, eds. Pp. 411–430. Cambridge: Cambridge University Press.

Clifford, James, and George E. Marcus, eds.

1986 Writing Culture: The Poetics and Politics of Ethnography. Berkeley: University of California Press.

Dalton, George

1977 Aboriginal Economies in Stateless Societies. *In* Exchange Systems in Prehistory, T. K. Earle and J. E. Ericson, eds. London: Academic Press.

Damon, F.

1980 The *Kula* and Generalized Exchange: Considering Some Unconsidered Aspects of *The Elementary Structures of Kinship*. Man 2:267–292.

1983 What Moves the Kula: Opening and Closing Gifts on Woodlark Island. *In* The Kula: New Perspectives on Massim Exchange, J. W. Leach and E. R. Leach, eds. Pp. 309–344. Cambridge: Cambridge University Press.

Egloff, B. J.

1972 The Sepulchral Pottery of Nuamata Island, Papua. Archaeology and Physical Anthropology in Oceania 7(2):145–163.

1978 The Kula Before Malinowski: A Changing Configuration. Mankind 11(3):429–435.

Emmons, George

1907 The Chilkat Blanket. *In* Memoirs of the American Museum of Natural History 3:329–409.

Feil, D. K.

1984 Ways of Exchange, The Enga Tee of Papua New Guinea. Queensland: University of Queensland Press.

Fink, Ruth A.

1965 The Esa'ala—Losuia Open Electorate. *In* The Papua New Guinea Elections, D. G. Bettison, C. A. Hughes, and P. A. Vander Veur, eds. Pp. 284–298. Canberra: Australian National University Press.

Firth, Raymond, ed.

1957a Man and Culture: An Evaluation of the Work of Bronislaw Malinowski. London: Routledge & Kegan Paul.

1957b The Place of Malinowski in the History of Economic Anthropology. *In* Man and Culture, An Evaluation of the Work of Bronislaw Malinowski, R. Firth, ed. Pp. 209–228. London: Routledge & Kegan Paul.

1967 Themes in Economic Anthropology: A General Comment. *In* Themes in Economic Anthropology, R. Firth, ed. Pp. 1–28. London: Tavistock.

Fortes, Meyer

1957 Malinowski and the Study of Kinship. *In* Man and Culture: An Evaluation of the Work of Bronislaw Malinowski, R. Firth, ed. Pp. 157–188. London: Routledge & Kegan Paul.

Fortune, Reo

1932 Sorcerers of Dobu. London: Routledge & Kegan Paul.

Gilmour, M. K.

1900 A Few Notes on the Kiriwina (Trobriand Group) Trading Expeditions. *In* British New Guinea Reports. Pp. 71–72.

Godelier, Maurice

1986 The Making of Great Men. Cambridge: Cambridge University Press. Original publication in French, 1982.

Handy, E. S. C.

1923 The Native Culture in the Marquesas. Honolulu: Bernice P. Bishop Museum Bulletin No. 9.

Harding, Thomas

1967 Voyagers of the Vitiaz Strait. A Study of a New Guinea Trade System. Seattle: University of Washington Press.

1970 Trading in Northeast New Guinea. *In* Cultures of the Pacific, T. G. Harding and B. J. Wallace, eds. Pp. 94–111. New York: Free Press.

Hogbin, H. Ian

1946 The Trobriand Islands, 1945. Man 66–69:72.

Homans, George C.

1941 Anxiety and Ritual: The Theories of Malinowski and Radcliffe-Brown. American Anthropologist 43:164–172

Homans, George C., and David M. Schneider

1955 Marriage, Authority, and Final Causes: A Study of Unilateral Cross-Cousin Marriage. New York: Free Press.

Hutchins, Edwin

1980 Culture and Inference: A Trobriand Island Case Study. Cambridge: Harvard University Press.

Irwin, G. J.

1978 Pots and Entrepots: A Study of Settlement, Trade and the Development of Economic Specialization in Papuan Prehistory. World Archaeology 9(3):299–319.

1983 Chieftainship, kula, and trade in Massim prehistory. *In* The Kula: New Perspectives on Massim Exchange, J. W. Leach and E. R. Leach, eds. Cambridge: Cambridge University Press. Pp. 29–72.

Josephides, Lisette

1985 The Production of Inequality, Gender and Exchange Among the Kewa. Cambridge: University of Cambridge Press.

Krueger, General Walter

1953 From Down Under to Nippon. Washington, D.C.: Combat Forces Press.

Lauer, Peter

1971 Changing Patterns of Pottery Trade in the Trobriand Islands. World Archaeology 3:197–209.

Lawton, Ralph S.
1980 The Kiriwinan Classifiers. M.A. thesis, Australian National University.

Leach, Edmund R.
1957 The Epistemological Background to Malinowski's Empiricism. *In* Man and Culture, R. Firth, ed. Pp. 119–138. London: Routledge & Kegan Paul.
1958 Concerning Trobriand Clans and the Kinship Category *Tabu*. *In* The Developmental Cycle in Domestic Groups, Jack Goody, ed. Pp. 120–145. Cambridge: Cambridge University Press.
1966 Virgin Birth. Proceedings of the Royal Anthropological Institute, Pp. 39–50.
1967 Correspondence: Virgin Birth. Man 3:655–656.

Leach, Jerry W.
1978 The Kabisawali Movement in the Trobriand Islands. Ph.D. thesis, University of Cambridge.
1982 Socio-historical Conflict and the Kabisawali Movement in the Trobriand Islands. *In* Micronationalist Movements in Papua New Guinea, R. J. May, ed. Pp. 249–290. Canberra: Australian National University.
1983a Introduction. *In* The Kula: New Perspectives on Massim Exchange, J.W. Leach and E.R. Leach, eds. Pp. 1–28. Cambridge: Cambridge University Press
1983b Trobriand Territorial Categories and the Problem of Who Is Not in the Kula. *In* The Kula: New Perspectives on Massim Exchange, J. W. Leach and E. R. Leach, eds. Pp. 121–146. Cambridge: Cambridge University Press.

Leach, Jerry W., and Gary Kildea
1975 Trobriand Cricket: An Ingenious Response to Colonialism. Film produced by Office of Information, Papua New Guinea. Distributed by the University of California Extension Media Center.

Leach J. W., and E. R. Leach, eds.
1983 The Kula: New Perspectives on Massim Exchange. Cambridge: Cambridge University Press.

Lepowsky, Maria
1981 Fruit of the Motherland: Gender and Exchange on Vanatinai, Papua New Guinea. Ph.D. thesis, University of California, Berkeley.
1983 Sudest Island and the Lousiade Archipelago in Massim Exchange. *In* The Kula: New Perspective on Massim Exchange, J. W. Leach and E. R. Leach, eds. Pp. 467–502.

Lévi-Strauss, Claude
1944 The Social and Psychological Aspect of Chieftainship in a Primitive Tribe: The Nambikuara of Northwestern Mato Grosso. *In* Transactions of the New York Academy of Science 8:16–32.
1969 The Elementary Structures of Kinship. Boston: Beacon Press. Original publication in French, 1949.

Liep, John
1981 The Workshop of the Kula: Production and Trade of Shell Necklaces in the Lousiade Archipelago, Papua New Guinea. Folk 23: 297–310.

1983 Ranked Exchange in Yela (Rossel Island). *In* The Kula: New Perspectives on Massim Exchange, J. W. Leach and E. R. Leach, eds. Pp. 503–528. Cambridge: Cambridge University Press.

Lounsbury, F. G.

1965 Another View of the Trobriand Kinship Categories. *In* Formal Semantic Analysis, E. Hammel, ed. American Anthropologist Special Publication 67 (pt.2):142–185.

Macintyre, Martha

1983a Changing Paths: An Historical Ethnography of the Traders of Tubetube. Ph.D. thesis. Australian National University.

1983b The Kula. A bibliography. Cambridge: Cambridge University Press.

1983c Kune on Tubetube and in the Bwanabwana Region of the Southern Massim. *In* The Kula: New Perspectives on Massim Exchange, J. W. Leach and E. R. Leach, eds. Pp. 369–382. Cambridge: Cambridge University Press.

Malinowski, Bronislaw Kasper

1915 The Natives of Mailu: Preliminary Results of the Robert Mond Research Work in British New Guinea. Transactions and Proceedings of the Royal Society of South Australia 39:494–706.

1916 Baloma: The Spirits of the Dead in the Trobriand Islands. Journal of the Royal Anthropological Institute 45. *Reprinted in* Magic, Science and Religion and Other Essays. Pp. 149–254. New York: Doubleday.

1918 Fishing and Fishing Magic in the Trobriand Islands. Man 53:87–92.

1920 Kula: The Circulating Exchanges of Valuables in the Archipelagoes of Eastern New Guinea. Man 51.

1922 Argonauts of the Western Pacific. New York: E. P. Dutton.

1926a Crime and Custom in Savage Society. New York and London: International Library of Psychology, Philosophy, and Scientific Method. Patterson Littlefield, Adams.

1926b Myth in Primitive Psychology. Psyche Miniatures General Series 6. London. *Reprinted in* Magic, Science and Religion and Other Essays. Pp. 99–148. New York: Doubleday.

1929 The Sexual Life of Savages in North-Western Melanesia. London: Routledge & Kegan Paul. Reprinted 1987 by Beacon Press, Boston.

1931 Culture. Encyclopedia of the Social Sciences 4:621–646. New York: Macmillan.

1935 Coral Gardens and Their Magic: A Study of the Methods of Tilling the Soil and of Agricultural Rites in the Trobriand Islands, Vols. I and II. New York: American Book Co. Bloomington: Indiana University Press, 1965.

1944 A Scientific Theory of Culture. Chapel Hill: University of North Carolina.

1945 The Dynamics of Culture Change. An Inquiry Into Race Relations in Africa, Phyllis Kayberry, ed. New Haven: Yale University Press.

1954 Magic, Science and Religion and Other Essays. New York: Doubleday.

1967 A Diary in the Strict Sense of the Term. New York: Harcourt, Brace & World.

Malinowski, Bronislaw Kasper, and Julio de la Fuente
1982 Malinowski in Mexico. The Economics of a Mexican Market System. S. Drucker-Brown, ed. London: Routledge & Kegan Paul.

Mauss, Marcel
1954 The Gift: Forms and Functions of Exchange in Archaic Societies, Ian Cunnison, trans. London: Cohen & West. Original French publication in 1924.

May, R. J.
1982 The Trobriand Experience: The TK Reaction. *In* Micronationalist Movements in Papua New Guinea, R. J. May, ed. Pp. 291–300. Canberra: Australian National University.

Meggitt, Mervyn
1972 System and Subsystem: The *Te* Exchange Cycle Among the Mae-Enga. Human Ecology 1:111–123.

Mikloucho-Maclay, Nickolai
1975 New Guinea Diaries 1871–1883, C. L. Sentinella, trans. Madang, Papua New Guinea: Kristen Press.

Miller, John, Jr.
1959 Cartwheel: The Reduction of Rabaul. Washington D.C.: U.S. Government Printing Office.

Montague, Susan
1974 The Trobriand Society. Ph.D. thesis, University of Chicago.

Munn, Nancy
1977 The Spatiotemporal Transformation of Gawa Canoes. Journal de la Societé des Oceanistes 33:39–51.
1983 Gawan Kula: Spatiotemporal Control and the Symbolism of Influence. *In* The Kula, New Perspectives on Massim Exchange, J. W. Leach and E.R. Leach, eds. Pp. 277–308.
1986 The Fame of Gawa: A Symbolic Study of Value Transformation in a Massim Society. Cambridge: University of Cambridge Press.

Nadel, S. F.
1957 Malinowski on Magic and Religion. *In* Man and Culture: An Evaluation of the Work of Bronislaw Malinowski, R. Firth, ed. Pp. 189–208. London; Routledge & Kegan Paul.

Narayan, R. K.
1952 The Financial Expert. London: Meuthen & Co.

Needham, Rodney
1962 Structure and Sentiment: A Test Case in Social Anthropology. Chicago: University of Chicago Press.

Polanyi, K.
1958 The Economy as Instituted Process. *In* Trade and Markets in Early Empires, K. Polanyi, C. Arensberg, and H. W. Pearson, eds. Pp. 243–270. New York: Free Press.

Poole, F. J. P., and G. Herdt, eds.
1982 Sexual Antagonism, Gender and Social Change in Papua New Guinea. Social Analysis Special Issue Series No. 12.

Powell, Harry A.
1951 *Trobriand Islanders*. Film distributed by Royal Anthropological Institute Film Library. London.

1956 An Analysis of Present-day Social Structure in the Trobriand Islands. Ph.D. thesis. University of London.

1960 Competitive Leadership in Trobriand Political Organization. Journal of the Royal Anthropological Institute 90:118–148.

1969a Genealogy, Residence, and Kinship in Kiriwina. Man 4:117–202.

1969b Territory, Hierarchy, and Kinship in Kiriwina. Man 4:580–604.

Sahlins, Marshall

1972 Stone Age Economics. Chicago: Aldine.

Scoditti, Giancarlo M. G., with J. W. Leach

1983 Kula on Kitava. *In* The Kula: New Perspectives on Massim Exchange, J. W. Leach and E. R. Leach, eds. Pp. 249–276. Cambridge: Cambridge University Press.

Seligman, C. G.

1910 The Melanesians of British New Guinea. Cambridge: Cambridge University Press.

—— and W. M. Strong

1906 Anthropogeographical Investigators in British New Guinea. The Geographical Journal 27(3):225–242;347–369.

Senft, Gunter

1986 Kilivila: The Language of the Trobriand Islanders. Berlin: Mouton de Gruyter.

Service, Elman R.

1962 Primitive Social Organization: An Evolutionary Perspective. New York: Random House.

Spiro, M. E.

1968 Virgin Birth, Parthenogenesis, and Physiological Paternity: An Essay in Cultural Interpretation. Man 3:242–261.

1982 Oedipus in the Trobriands. Chicago: University of Chicago Press.

Strathern, A. J.

1971 The Rope of Moka: Big Men and Ceremonial Exchange in Mount Hagen. Cambridge: Cambridge University Press.

1982 Inequality in New Guinea Highlands Societies. Cambridge: Cambridge University Press.

1983 The Kula in Comparative Perspective. *In* The Kula: New Perspectives on Massim Exchange, J. W. Leach and E. R. Leach, eds. Pp. 73–102. Cambridge: Cambridge University Press.

Strathern, A. M.

1972 Women in Between, Female Roles in A Male World, Mount Hagen, New Guinea. London: Seminar Press.

Swift, Jonathan

1970 Gulliver's Travels, Robert A. Greenberg, ed. New York: W. W. Norton. Original publication 1726.

Tambiah, S. J.

1968 The Magical Power of Words. Man 3:175–206.

1973 Form and Meaning of Magical Acts: A Point of View. *In* Modes of Thought, R. Horton and R. Finnegan, eds. Pp. 199–229. London: Faber & Faber.

1983 On Flying Witches and Flying Canoes: The Coding of Male and Female Values. *In* The Kula: New Perspectives on Massim Exchange, J. W. Leach and E. R. Leach, eds. Pp. 171–200. Cambridge: Cambridge University Press.

Thune, Carl E.

1981 Death and Matrilineal Reincorporation on Normanby Island. Paper presented at the Second Kula Conference, University of Virginia.

1983 Kula Traders and Lineage Members: The Structure of Village and Kula Exchange on Normanby Island. *In* The Kula: New Perspectives on Massim Exchange, J. W. Leach and E. R. Leach, eds. Pp. 345–368. Cambridge: Cambridge University Press.

Uberoi, J. P. Singh

1962 Politics of the Kula Ring: An Analysis of the Findings of Bronislaw Malinowski. Manchester: Manchester University Press.

Valeri, Valerio

1985 Kingship and Sacrifice, Ritual and Society in Ancient Hawaii, Paul Wissing, trans. Chicago: University of Chicago Press.

Watson, Lepani

1956 Trobriand Island Clans and Chiefs. Man 56:164.

Weiner, Annette B.

1976 Women of Value, Men of Renown, New Perspectives in Trobriand Exchange. Austin: University of Texas Press.

1977 Review of *Trobriand Cricket*: An Ingenious Response to Colonialism. American Anthropologist 79:506–507.

1978a Epistemology and Ethnographic Reality: A Trobriand Island Case Study. American Anthropologist 80:752–757.

1978b Trobriand Kinship from Another View: The Reproductive Power of Women and Men. Man. 14:328–348.

1980 Stability in Banana Leaves: Colonialism, Economics and Trobriand Women. *In* Women and Colonization, Anthropological Perspectives, E. Leacock and M. Etienne, eds. Pp. 270–293. New York: J. F. Bergin.

1983a From Words to Objects to Magic: The Boundaries of Social Interaction. Man 18–690–709.

1983b "A World of Made Is Not a World of Born"—Doing Kula in Kiriwina. *In* The Kula: New Perspectives on Massim Exchange, J. W. Leach and E. R. Leach, eds. Pp. 147–170. Cambridge: Cambridge University Press.

1985 Oedipus and Ancestors. American Ethnologist 12:758–762.

1986 Inalienable Wealth. American Ethnologist 12(2):178–183.

Young, Michael W.

1971 Fighting with Food, Leadership, Values, and Social Control in a Massim Society. Cambridge: Cambridge University Press.

1983 Magicians of Manumanua, Living Myth in Kalauna. Berkeley: University of California Press.

1984 The Intensive Study of a Restricted Area, or, Why Did Malinowski Go to the Trobriand Islands? Oceania 55:1–26.

Films About the Trobriand Islands

Many films have been produced about the Trobrianders for special television series abroad, but only a few (marked with an asterisk) have been made in association with anthropologists. The major feature films produced by anthropologists and by filmmakers are annotated below, and the chapters in this volume related to the content of the films are noted under each listing.

* *Trobriand Islanders.* (66 min.) Harry A. Powell, 1951. Distributed by the Royal Anthropological Institute Film Library. 56 Queen Anne Street. London W1M 9LA England.

This film was produced and directed by the anthropologist Harry A. Powell during his fieldwork on Kiriwina Island in 1950–1951. Filmed primarily in Omarakana village, where Powell lived, *Trobriand Islanders* focuses on a range of harvest activities organized by the Tabalu chief, Mitakata, Chief Vanoi's predecessor. Of special interest are the gardening events that lead to the filling of the chief's yamhouse and the preparations for a *kula* voyage.

(Chapters 1, 6, 7, 9 and 10)

* *Trobriand Cricket: An Ingenious Response to Colonialism.* (60 min.) J. W. Leach & G. Kildea, 1974. Distributed by University of California Extension Media Center. 2223 Fulton Street, Berkeley, California 94720.

An award winning film, *Trobriand Cricket* documents the transformations of the staid, traditional British game of cricket, introduced by the missionaries at the turn of the century, into the politically powerful, sensuously aesthetic Trobriand version of today. The filmmaker, Gary Kildea, was assisted by Jerry. W. Leach, whose Trobriand fieldwork focused on the political events of the early 1970s. The cricket match around which the film centers was held expressly for the filmmakers by John Kasapwalova, who is in the film, and the members of his then-active political movement, as part of their strategy to gain attention beyond the shores of Kiriwina. The film is riveting, as it makes sense of Trobriand cricket playing the conveys the exuberance and pride that Trobrianders bring to any confrontation.

(Chapters 1, 4, 7, and 10)

Kula—Argonauts of the Western Pacific. (67 min.) Yascko Ichioka, 1971, for Nippon A-V. 6-27-27 Shinjuku, Shinjuku-ku, Tokyo 160, Japan.

The filmmaker and her crew followed a *kula* voyage in its entirety and produced a visually beautiful film made for Japanese prime-time television. The physical hardships of traveling in open outrigger canoes with pandanus sails are only the beginning of the dangers that confront the men as, once safely landed on the beach, they now must gain their partners' confidence and their *kula* valuables. The filmmakers use Malinowski's writings on *kula* to help them interpret the events.

(Chapter 9)

The Trobriand Experiment. (50 mins.) Alex Nisbett, 1974, for British Broadcasting Commission Horizon Series. London.

Produced for BBC television, this film was made with the help of John Kasaipwalova who, as the star of the film, tells Nisbett about his people, their culture and his then-successful political movement to make the Trobriand Islands economically self-sufficient. Unfortunately, the film was made from this one perspective; the opposition to John K's movement is not given a voice. The film does provide good footage on many Trobriand activities, including a brief segment on women's mortuary distributions.

(Chapter 1)

Trobriand Islands of Women. (50 min.) Yascko Ichioka, 1976, for Nippon A-V. 6-27-27 Shinjuku, Shinjuku-ku, Tokyo 160, Japan

This film was produced for Japanese television, and its focus on women includes a segment of a mortuary distribution where women are surrounded by huge piles of their wealth. But the main theme is less about the life of Trobriand women than it is about the events that took place during the harvests when the film was being made: for example, the rituals of bringing the yams into the village, young peoples' sexually provocative nightly harvest dancing, and also the violent moments that adultery precipitated. The film was shot over several harvest seasons and the segments are edited so that different events in time and place are condensed, resulting ethnographically in an emphasis on sexuality and violence.

(Chapters 5 and 8)

Index